Mind in Art

Cognitive Foundations in Art Education

Mind in Art

Cognitive Foundations in Art Education

Charles M. Dorn
Florida State University

LAWRENCE ERLBAUM ASSOCIATES, PUBLISHERS
1999   Mahwah, New Jersey   London

Cover credit: Copyright © 1998 Man Ray Trust /Artist Rights Society. NY/ADAGP Paris. Black and White. Man Ray, "Violin d'Ingres." Photograph courtesy of Andre Emmerich Gallery, New York, NY.

Lawrence Erlbaum Associates, Inc., Publishers
10 Industrial Avenue
Mahwah, NJ 07430

Cover design by Kathryn Houghtaling Lacey

Library of Congress Cataloging-in-Publication Data

Dorn, Charles M.
Mind in art : cognitive foundations in art education/ by Charles M. Dorn.
   p. cm.
  Includes bibliographical references and indexes.
ISBN 0-8058-3078-2 (cloth : alk. paper). — ISBN 0-8058-3079-0
  (pbk. : alk. paper).
1. Art—Study and teaching—Psychological aspects.   2. Cognition.
  I. Title.
N87.D67   1999
707—dc21   98-35913
                                      CIP

Books published by Lawrence Erlbaum Associates are printed on acid-free paper, and their bindings are chosen for strength and durability.

Printed in the United States of America
10 9 8 7 6 5 4 3 2 1

*To Masters Calder and Klee
and all their contemporaries, who will be among
the first to enter what hopefully will be the most
creative and authentic millenium in American
education, and in memory of the late
Dr. Glenn E. Barnett, my major professor*

Contents

Preface

This effort was prompted by the perceived frustrations of several former graduate students who studied the effects of art teaching on the development of student academic abilities and some afterthoughts about my earlier work *Thinking in Art* (1994). In their research, these graduates attempted empirical (quasiexperimental) studies on the effects of formal art study in art criticism, art history, and aesthetics on the development of students' cognitive abilities in art classrooms. These studies varied in the experiment's length of time and the media explored, which included drawing, painting, ceramics, and photography. These researchers all struggled with the null hypothesis that, at the close of their experiments, indicated that no statistically significant differences in art performances, art attitudes, and cognitive abilities were evident in the students who formally studied art and in those who were mostly engaged in studio activity. In contrast, the afterthoughts about my earlier work started with a call from a colleague who, while generally agreeing with what I said in *Thinking,* questioned what my claims mean practically for those who teach art in schools.

I certainly bear a certain burden of responsibility for encouraging these former students to pursue experimental studies and, therefore, share in their perceived disappointment that nothing really happened. Something, of course, did really happen—the discovery that, no matter how much they tried to enrich a studio environment in the elementary art classroom through interventions using traditional approaches to art history, art criticism, and critical activity, the students who received the benefits of such instruction did not end up making art better, liking art more, or becoming more intellectually competent than those who spent their time in what most would agree was simply good studio instruction. What disappointed these investigators most was that they were all good art teachers employing sound teaching strategies in their experiments and yet still failed to make art instruction in their so-called *experimental* sections better than that offered in the control group.

My colleague's comment, which questioned how the paradigms of Schema-Correction, Form-Gestalt, and Linguistic-Metaphor outlined in *Thinking in Art* (1994) related to classroom instruction, also reminded me that these former students, while aware of the paradigms, still failed to profit from them. I realized then that to merely claim that there are several frames of mind one can successfully use to teach art and that the production, history, and criticism of art when approached from the same philosophical viewpoint can yield important advantages in teaching art contents may not be sufficient. Therefore, the challenge is to go beyond just thinking in art to pose the question of what it also means to think in art intelligently.

This book will be especially appreciated by the reader who believes that thinking about and making art is intelligent behavior and that art as a subject in the K to 12 school curriculum should not be used as an alibi for other curricular objectives. Its objective is to examine and make explicit those cognitive behaviors normally associated with most higher order thinking and problem-solving activity, and to explain how they function in the act of creative forming. Ultimately, its goal is to find ways to use these behaviors in the construction of an intelligent art curriculum for K to 12 American schools.

An intelligent school art curriculum is, of course, not possible unless it is implemented by a core of intelligent art teachers who are knowledgeable about the true character of the artistic imagination and about the developing abilities of children and youth to use artistic activity as means for exploring the life of the mind. For these and other good reasons, *Mind in Art* is not a cookbook of recipes one can use to teach art, but is rather a serious attempt to explore several important philosophical, aesthetic, and psychological issues that need to be addressed if the art teacher hopes to understand the foundation of their own beliefs and the beliefs of the profession they serve.

Although the aims of artistic activity are individual and expressive, the teacher who provides that curriculum in a school is ultimately responsible to the students, the educational program and the education profession they are licensed to serve. For this reason, *Mind in Art* also focuses on the problems of art assessment to know how art programs in schools can be made authentically accountable to the children we educate and the public, which provides the where-with-all that makes American schooling possible.

To the teacher and student who use this work as an introductory text to the field of art education, I must caution that this text is aimed at inspiring a dialogue about the pressing problems art teachers face in providing accountable instruction in an ill-defined field that aims to free the consciousness and imagination of both teacher and student. In consideration of these constraints, no absolutes nor how-to's are forthcoming in this work, which seeks only to provide grist for developing the kind of ideas that fund a lifetime of contemplation and study. For these reasons and others, I urge the reader to examine the topic headings provided at the beginning of each chapter and the key terms and study questions provided at the end of the chapters. These should help define why these inquiries are necessary and how, through their discussion and resolution, it is possible to find grounding for the decisions teachers need to make in the teaching and evaluation of art learning.

Finally, to completely resolve the matter of art as intellect is, of course, not possible in a work of this limited scope. Hence, it is also appropriate to warn the reader that not all the questions raised about the problem of cognition in art are resolved in this work. What this effort does seek to do, however, is (a) show how we can go about understanding the role of cognition in creative forming, (b) suggest some strategies teachers can use in schools to demonstrate the feasibility of this approach, and (c) offer art education researchers ways to confirm that a unified conception of cognition in art does exist and that it can be used effectively to teach students how to think about and make art in schools.

To pursue this inquiry in an orderly and logical manner, this text is organized into eight chapters. Chapter 1 provides an introduction to and the plan for the text. Chapter 2 provides a brief overview of the functions of the mind as investigated by the fields comprising

General Psychology. Chapter 3 examines the history, organization, and research findings in the cognitive sciences according to the various disciplines that make up the field. Chapter 4 examines the mental processes used in artistic conception as described in the literature of aesthetics and in the research on child art. Chapter 5 explores the topic of cognition and concept formation from both the view of the cognitive sciences and the view of artists making art. Chapter 6 proposes a unified theory of cognition and concept formation and suggests implications for teaching art in schools. Chapter 7 discusses the learning environment and offers several suggested approaches to art assessment. Chapter 8 provides some of the major conclusions the author has reached in the pursuit of this work.

Finally, I would like to acknowledge the assistance of a number of people who helped make this book possible. First and foremost, I would like to thank Barbara Edwards, an artist in her own right, for the word processing of my hand-written scribbles and for really caring about how that effort was carried out. I am also indebted to Nancy Fudge, who designed a number of the tables used in the text, and to Emil Dickin, who made the line drawings. I am also indebted to Linda Dorn, Bonnie Bernau, Charles Owens, and Susan Slavik for pointing out several useful resources that were exceedingly helpful in developing some of the most important ideas in the text. I would also like to thank my editors and Lawrence Erlbaum, the publisher, for publishing this work, with special mention to Naomi Silverman, Senior Editor, who saw some promise in the prospectus and moved it through the review process, and of course to Eileen Engel and Clare Romeo, who carried out the hard work in the production process. Last but not least, I must also thank Karen Lee Carroll, Maryland Institute, College of Art and John A. Stinespring, Texas Tech University, who reviewed the entire manuscript and wrote some extremely supportive arguments as to why this work was needed by the field and, further, how it might be better organized to make it more useful.

1

Introduction

ART AS INTELLECT
Experimental Studies
New Goals in Schooling
Cognition and Art
Cognitive Research

PLAN OF THE BOOK
Asking Questions
Seeking Answers

ORGANIZATION OF THE BOOK

SUMMARY

Whether artistic forming is an act of intelligence is something rarely questioned by either aesthetitions or cognitive scientists. However, when one poses the question of whether the making of art is an act of intellect, both the aesthetition and cognitive scientist express serious doubts—the aesthetition because of the general belief that art cannot be a product of intellect and the cognitive scientist because as of yet, we have failed to make such a case experimentally. With a new century fast approaching, there will be even more stringent demands on school arts programs to show they are a positive force in improving academic performance, school attendance, and graduation rates in our nation's schools. Therefore, the question we now face is whether both the aesthetition and cognitive scientist are correct, which is to suggest that the arts will never achieve that goal, or whether we may have only failed to ask the right questions by looking to aesthetics and cognition rather than to art itself. This book seeks answers to these important questions.

ART AS INTELLECT

Experimental Studies

Up to this point in time, no nationally significant studies have experimentally confirmed that art study contributes to the overall intellectual development of students in schools. Even when we attempt such studies, they are rarely perfect in their science and, even if flawlessly done, still fail to positively prove anything. However, the studies that fail to make the case also suggest that we need to revisit the claims of those who believe that art study, in itself, can make students better citizens and learners or improve graduation rates and school attendance, as well as what means we are now using to verify such claims. The lack of empirical evidence to support art learning as affecting academic performance should be looked at as a challenge that requires a second look at both the claims and the means used to verify them.

Arts advocates who are critical of experimental studies that fail to support their point of view, claim that such studies are really not proof of anything, and that their failure to show that formal art study is a better way to effect cognitive abilities may really be due to the failure of existing test instruments to measure the behavioral gains achieved through such experiments. Although partially correct, the argument can also be made that the instruments used in these studies do have established national norms and are statistically reliable and valid, especially with regard to measuring general cognitive ability.

The truth of the matter, of course, lies somewhere in between the failure of instruments to measure what some want them to measure and what arts advocates want to prove about the effectiveness of current approaches to art study in improving general cognitive abilities. The problem with such claims begins with the fact, as Efland (1995) noted, that all learning requires strategies where different elements in the knowledge base are assembled to provide new perspectives on the same learning problem. In an ill-structured domain, like art, it requires retaining a network of concepts and principles that accurately represents key phenomena and their interrelationships to be engaged flexibly and, when pertinent, accomplish diverse and somewhat novel objectives. What this implies is that all higher order thinking skills or cognitive abilities are content-specific and, in art, require an in-depth understanding of art that may not be the same as the understandings required for learning math or physics, where concepts are based on laws, axioms, and theorems as applied to a variety of situations with predictability and consistency. Thus, we should be aware that the cognitive abilities needed in art may not be the same as the cognitive abilities needed in other fields; as a consequence, they may fail to transfer except under specific circumstances. The irony in all of this is that we have a pretty good idea about what cognitive abilities are evident in most domains except art. What we now need to know is what higher order thinking skills and abilities best characterize the phenomena of the artistic act and which ones show the most promise of transfer among domains both within and outside the field.

To begin thinking about such matters, we need to identify the skills and knowledges that may be domain specific and nontransferable as well as those that cross over the various domains included in art education instruction, finding out both what is and is not transferable. The main risk to face in pursuing such an investigation is that some of our current thinking may need to be reexamined and some of our current assumptions about art teaching might, as a consequence, be judged as questionable.

New Goals in Schooling

The pursuit of such goals places the discipline in danger of losing the leverage that our current niche provides in the "who gets what, when, and where" struggle to reinvent the nation's school curriculum. This is painfully evident in the *Goals 2000 Educate America Act* (1994), where art education, as a field, is already committed as players. Apparently, it is willing to pay the price of undergoing the standard setting and testing of art programs in terms of its success in improving children's general readiness to learn; high school graduation rates; and competency in such subjects as math, science, and reading; and ensuring safe, drug-free schools. This is in contrast to a few years ago when the arts were not even sure of being Goals 2000 players, much less being glad to be included in the game and anxious to please the other arts disciplines, which, as a political force, seek to shape current federal/state curriculum reforms. At this point in time, we have defined the so-called *art standards* (National Art Education Association, 1994), which focus on what students should know and be able to do in art in K to 12 educationally reformed schools. Unfortunately, these have not been widely discussed or debated by the rank and file in the field and are seen, at least by some in the field, as simply an effort to dissuade art teachers of the tired old notion that children learn best through making and doing in the arts.

The very notion of having national art education standards, which would have been an abhorrence to most art educators 10 years ago, is now considered by many as merely a matter of compliance and political correctness in the competition along with the other arts disciplines for a piece of the American public school curriculum pie. These standards are already viewed as relative to workplace know-how and improved SAT scores, without most practitioners being aware that such standards are, in management parlance, the main mechanisms used to measure the effectiveness of those who plan, lead, control, and evaluate systems. For example, the use of such standards in the corporate world is to set the acceptable range of performances or outputs that workers are capable of achieving mostly as a basis for determining whether management is achieving bottom line profitability.

However, corporate standards are also set at reasonable and achievable levels within the scope of what management realistically can hope to achieve, given the skill levels of the workers and the physical environment needed to accomplish the corporation's objectives. Such standards are not, then, for corporations solely a matter of economic greed nor are they necessarily a mechanism to make workers more productive in the interests of enhanced profitability. The standards imposed on the nation's art teachers also need to realistically state what art teachers can accomplish given the knowledge and skills they have in the teaching of art and the physical environment they are required to work in, which, in the last analysis, may not be that effective in using art to raise the school's graduation rate and improve student academic performance in other areas of the school curriculum. Such standards would not even be appropriate to pursue if the behaviors required in art forming are not germane, or are inappropriate to achieving other content-specific educational goals. If the true aim of school reform is genuinely to improve and test higher order thinking skills and cognitive ability, we need to know what these behaviors are in art and how they cohere or could be expected to affect student cognitive performance both within and outside the domain of art.

Cognition and Art

To investigate the relationships that exist among the arts, cognition, and basic skills is really not a new idea: Both Stan Madeja at CEMREL (Madeja, 1977) and David Perkins at Harvard's Project Zero (Perkins & Leondar, 1977) attempted this in the 1970s. Therefore, it would be difficult and unnecessary to compete and/or do better than the prominent scholars did with the same topic 20 or 30 years ago unless the approach used covers ground not addressed in these efforts and/or in a manner that may not have been possible 30 years ago.

My reservations about the Aspen and Project Zero Conference papers are not with their scholarship, but rather with their philosophy, which I believe was shaped by the goals of the federal art education bureaucracy of the 1960s. This particular philosophy was evident in the first federal conference at New York University (Art as Science; Conant, 1967), continued through the reign of Cathy Bloom over USOE's Division of Research, Arts, and Humanities Program, and continued later in Central Midwestern Regional Laboratory (CEMREL) and the United States Office of Education (USOE)-sponsored Regional Education Laboratory (Madeja, 1991). The Aspen conference's philosophy is clearly apparent in the lead paper by Anita Silver, then Professor of Philosophy at San Francisco State University. Silver, a positivist philosopher, noted that, although most consider the arts as being in the noncognitive domain, it can also be argued that art is really in the cognitive domain even where its products are not reiterative (i.e., not seeking to reproduce the same product). This is especially true, she believes, when one uses linguistic or analogic arguments to demonstrate that reiteration occurs in art study through denotation and exemplification. Through such a process, art becomes, in Silver's view, an effective mode of telling (Silver, 1977). Silver believes that art works provide educational models or exemplars that tell children something like how to make a bed, weed a garden, or learn to iron. Her admonition to arts practitioners is for them to reconsider art works as a mode of exemplification (example) rather than an object of denotation (effect).

Silver also wishes that science skeptics would see art works as conveying propositional truth rather than being merely accepting of ambiguous responses, which is akin to Henry Higgins (in the play *My Fair Lady*) wishing that Eliza Doolittle could only be "more like a man." Such wishful thinking really ignores what things are in order to make the case for things being what some think they should be. This kind of structuralist thinking also reflects a time shaped by the challenges of Sputnik, the new science and new math, and Jerome Bruner's dictum that to make a child a physicist, requires that you teach him or her as one would teach a physicist (Bruner, 1973). In the 1960s and 1970s, it was the character of the times to ask, "Why couldn't art be more like science?" (i.e., where laws, axioms, theorems, predictability, and consistency rule). This is an argument that, by the way, accommodates the logical positivist philosopher unwilling to note that no philosophy, including his or her own, can go beyond its assumptions in the search for truth.

However, these efforts by the positivists at Aspen and Project Zero in the 1970s are useful for revealing a point of view regarding art as a science and also what frames of mind have shaped current views of art cognition in the scientific community. These include the rather common notion that art is a representational system and a symbol for the communication of propositional truths through language to be interpreted through a public discourse.

Perkins and Leondar (1977) identified at least four points of view explored in the arts cognition efforts of Project Zero in the 1960s: (a) that all activity requires a knowledge base, (b) that cognition involves ways of knowing, (c) that cognition includes knowing how as well as that, and (d) that in knowing how we account for cognition as a form of action. The knowledge base approach assumes that we must have knowledge of the world as well as specialized knowledge of art history, genre, and style, which inform the apprehension of particular works. The ways of knowing approach suggests that, in addition to knowledge of things, one needs to know one's own emotional response to the acts of making and perceiving. The knowing how and knowing of that idea further suggests that knowing that we act on a world as well as apprehend it involves the matter of cognitive style and the perception as an action approach. This suggests that perceiving is essentially a work in progress that depends on a continuing update of our preconceptions.

Nelson Goodman of Project Zero, who influenced Silver's ideas discussed earlier, holds that something becomes art only when it becomes a symbol and only then can it be an act of intelligence (Goodman, 1977). In Goodman's view, all art works are symbols like speech, writing, maps, diagrams, cattle brands, and traffic lights, which communicate truth. Goodman resolved the problem of what art refers to by arguing that there are actually two kinds of art: one where representational pictures denote things in the world and another where symbols exemplify showing certain features, properties, or labels—similar to Silver's view that art provides a way to tell us something.

The idea that art is a symbol system is based on the assumption that the arts are a means for direct communication of thought between the artist and viewer. To understand what is being communicated, the viewer *reads* the art to detect the idea the artist intends to communicate. This approach to art as communication is not about the capacity of a work to evoke our responses to it, but rather about the artwork being more like a sign communicating a direction. Thus, one would not see a work of art as having alternative meanings for different people at different times, but rather as a form of direct communication.

The problem with the art as symbol explanation comes from both trying to decide whether a given work is a symbol and deciding what it intends to communicate—or, if used in teaching, whether everyone should expect to derive the same meaning from a work. Goodman added to the problem by also claiming that works may (a) represent something, (b) be expressive of something, or (c) exemplify or tell us something. He also argued that a work of art may not do all three things, but it must at least do one of them to be called a *work of art*. He further compounded this by noting that even if a work has one or more of these properties, it is only sometimes a work of art and that is when it functions as a work of art. For example, a Rembrandt painting used to block a cold wind in a broken window ceases, in his view, to be a work of art; a stone found in a driveway becomes a work of art when used as an object of contemplation in a gallery. This view of art as first becoming and then ceasing to be a work of art conjures up in the mind a museum curator's meeting to decide which works currently on display are not art on that particular day and/or whether one should remove, cover, or replace them with other works that, by chance, function on that particular day.

The form versus matter issue also has been a source of difficulty for the positivists analyzing the cognitive functions of art. This can be noted in the early work of Howard Gardner when he sought to distinguish between what he called the acts of figurative and operative cognition, especially in a non-Piagetian sense (Gardner, 1977). At that time, Gardner rejected Piaget's more holistic claim that scientific thinking entails actions, relations between actions, and actions on the structures derived from actions, and that thought was independent of language, thus becoming a symbolic tool reflecting, but not affecting thought. As a result, Gardner introduced the form-versus-matter issue through questioning how much figurative cognition (matter) or content is needed to balance with the operative cognition (form), which codes, classifies, and transforms the work into an art object.

Thus, Gardner rejected the idea of creative forming as integrating form and matter mostly because it got in the way of reducing evidence relevant to a taxonomic framework. Unfortunately, this inductive approach fails to account for the possibility of thought in action and form (what the painting expresses) being a part of matter (the means) through which it is expressed. However, the problem is not so much with his logic, but whether this form of inductive reasoning is the most effective way to identify the thought processes used in creative forming.

The form-versus-content argument also led Gardner to another conclusion, which was to think of artistic forming in the same way as one thinks about solving a scientific problem where, in fact, the artist may only be seeking a specific execution in a given art medium. As a consequence, he created an unnecessary dichotomy between the kinds of cognition used in science concept formation from that used in arts forming, ignoring the possibility that the creative act also converts perceptual data into concepts and therefore may not be all that different from other acts of intelligence. To argue that art is not a science and vice versa, even if it protects the interests of these subject matter domains, does little to constructively help us understand how the mind actually processes the perceptual data that are foundational to all concept formation.

Another problem that limits progress toward understanding cognitive ability in art comes from some child art developmentalists who assume that experiments with picture making in early childhood will lead to a greater understanding of both child and adult creative forming (Korzenik, 1977). Some problems that arise include assuming that pictures are really problems about the faithful rendering of appearances and that children failing to do so involve matters of will and self-concept rather than reflecting the differing cognitive styles of children—where some children pay more attention to some things than others. These assumptions have also led some researchers to believe that the schemata used by children are the same as the stylistic conventions of schema and correction used by mature artists, which is, in fact, contrary to what we know about the ways adults and children conceptualize and what we know about the nature of mature art, which is not always about the correction of historical schema.

Thus, efforts in the 1970s offer both threats to and opportunities for understanding the nature of cognition in art. The threats are that a structuralist view of the problem will still fail to entertain other perspectives and the opportunity being found in the enormous amounts of data directed to this matter, which, if correctly interpreted, would truly advance our understanding of the issues. For this investigation to be worth the effort, however, it must provide new perspectives on the problem as well as contribute to finding new curricular applications for practice. Further, these applications need to inform and empower the art teacher who is closest to both art and teaching to become the principal agent in the curriculum change process. Teacher responses to *Thinking in Art* confirm my original view that, not only do art teachers want to play a part in the curriculum decision-making process, but that they are also willing to think about that process philosophically and test what they intuitively know is good teaching in art with what others outside the field have discovered, especially as these discoveries cohere with the practices they know work well in school art classrooms.

Art teachers generally also resist being coerced into following the curricular fashions or fads of curricular reform movements, especially when the reformers think that all art programs should be concerned with only one kind of learning and that all teachers should teach art according to the same rules. Teachers also know that if they are to play a part in the curriculum reform process, they must be informed of the rationale and research claims these reformers cite as reasons for requiring curricular change. Art teachers also know that, to create an effective school art curriculum, they must play a proactive rather than reactive role in that process.

Thus, to become informed about the role of cognition in art, art teachers must embrace something more than the belief that cognition in art is not the same as cognition in science. Although most art teachers know the differences and know that art learning does not come about solely through the use of inductive or deductive logic, they also know that art learning requires the kind of intelligent thought needed in the overall development of all school learners. Therefore, art teachers want to know how higher order cognate learning relates to the systems of thought needed in art classrooms and also whether these cognate patterns of thought can appropriately be applied to thinking about and making art. This also comes with the realization that inductive and deductive modes of inquiry have, since the times of the Greeks, been recognized as the major systems for teaching cognitive skills, including higher order thinking skills in schooling, and that these modes are the ones considered by school administrators as the most valuable in school learning.

Cognitive Research

As to the scope of existing studies in cognition, more than 20 years ago Messer (1976) published a glossary of 19 cognitive style dimensions, each of which has become the object of empirical research efforts. Some have even inspired massive programs of research encompassing hundreds of empirical studies inspired by a variety of theoretical sources. These efforts were intended to explore individual differences in attention, perception, memory, conceptualization, thinking, informational processing, judgment, and decision making.

Individual differences in cognitive operations are treated under the rubric of cognitive style, which became an area for increased study following World War II and pointed to new studies of process dimensions linked to personality and developmental constructs. This area is conceptually promising in producing outcome measures generated in the psychometric intelligence tradition. In addition, the literature and range of research in the field of cognition covers numerous areas of study including cognition, cognitive abilities, cognitive style, mental test theory, and education for abilities.

Although a thorough review of all the research in cognition is not possible in this particular effort, at least an overview is necessary (i.e., if we are to understand the differences in what is known as *cognitive development* and how it relates to making and thinking in art). In addition to such a study, it is also necessary to understand how cognitive knowledges are organized in teaching, including how they are organized in an individual's knowledge and in the various domains of knowledge, and how the content of the art domain(s) are arranged for purposes of instruction.

In addition, we also need to know when children are ready to learn certain cognitive skills, what kinds of learning are possible or impossible to achieve without a knowledge base, and how prior cognitive learning improves on or inhibit later learning. All are important questions that need to be addressed. Answers to these and many other questions are thus necessary if we are to have any chance of knowing how cognitive abilities vary between and among domains of study and how expertise in one domain may not necessarily guarantee expertise in another. Of still greater importance may be the questions of whether knowledge acquired in one context will permit problems being solved in another, whether such advanced learnings are always possible, and/or whether the cognitive flexibility needed in art forming is also necessary and appropriate in all domains.

PLAN OF THE BOOK

In deciding what course to pursue in this effort, at least two primary considerations were involved. One was to avoid simply repeating or expanding on the ideas already presented in *Thinking in Art* (Dorn, 1994); the second was to pursue a functional metaphilosophical approach accepting of both the science and art used in studies of human cognition and in thinking about and making art. I briefly address these considerations to provide the reader with an understanding of both the focus and limitations of this effort.

In *Thinking in Art,* I made at least two major claims: (a) Thinking about and making art requires the same order of intelligent thought as is used in the study of the cognate disciplines of history, philosophy, religion, science, mathematics, language, and medicine; and

(b) aesthetic values, when organized as disciplinary paradigms, support philosophically consistent conceptualizations that cohere among the various ways we can think about and make art. I described these three paradigms in that work as schema-correction, form-Gestalt, and linguistic metaphorical.

In addition to addressing the ways art production, art history, art criticism, and aesthetics could be addressed as a unified concept, my intent in that work was also to demonstrate how various philosophies of art and the philosophical values of the art teacher could be effectively joined to provide alternative yet philosophically consistent ways for teachers to address the who, what, when, where, and how issues of school art curriculum construction. Because these have been identified and various arguments presented in *Thinking in Art,* I plan only infrequent reference to them, recommending to any reader not familiar with these arguments to consult that work.

My second consideration—that is, to pursue a metaphilosophical approach—was to avoid entanglement in what are the obvious dichotomies one can invent to biforcate thinking about cognitive research and testing from aesthetic experience and creative thought. I have already mentioned several good arguments that one might advance as to how these divergent fields of inquiry are incompatible. Still others occur to us—most especially the use and abuse of standardized tests that assess both cognitive and artistic development in school learning. Added to this are the frustrations felt by arts teachers who work in school environments that only seem to value the teaching of language and math and require them alone to define what their subject contributes to schooling.

It is doubly difficult for arts teachers to identify with advocates of school reform who ignore the broader question of what is the nature and function of intelligent thought and who justify the use of standardized tests that appear poorly related to the ways people succeed in life other than what is required for admission to higher education. Many feel that such values support only the educational needs of the future scientist, scholar, or theoretician and that they promote a privileged status for certain paths of learning, modes of understanding, and categories of knowledge.

When the scope of the school curriculum and the goals of schooling are restricted to what can be tested in the three Rs, it is easy for curriculum planners to assume that intelligent thought in the so-called *cognate domains* is not connected to thought in the expressive disciplines. This reductive approach to school curriculum construction also encourages schools to (a) separate the cognitive from the affective, (b) define *thought* as being either qualitative or quantitative, and (c) deny the important role of the senses in concept formation.

The reductionist approach also leads planners to reject possible connections between domains and pursue solutions that are more reflective of Ovid's Pygmalion—the mythological Greek sculptor who fashioned a statue of a woman after his own heart only to fall in love with the statue he made. To believe that we must, of necessity, divide cognate from expressive thought leads both to separating art instruction from the mainstream curriculum of the school and to reinventing it, in whole or in part, as a biforcated discipline. The so-called *disciplinary approach* to art education begun in the 1960s and, supported by forces both within and outside the art teaching profession, has conceptually divided art instruction into various learning domains, some of which are now being used to justify the cognitive dimensions of scientific thought and linguistic analysis in art study. Perkins' (1994) recent effort to define the cognitive operations used in art analysis and criticism is just one example of this.

Asking Questions

There are a number of problems attendant to using art analysis or art criticism as the principal basis for determining the nature of cognitive thought in the arts or, for that matter, in thinking that such an analysis may offer the most appropriate way to study aesthetic products. Although psychologists generally view thought as extended through language and some even see connections between manual skills and speech, there are also studies that question whether higher thinking is necessarily always dependent on language. Even if there are such connections, the use of discursive language as an analogue to describe the meanings or intents of aesthetic objects as propositional fact at least should be questioned.

Although objects created by artists could not exist without intent (i.e., even to make an object that is pleasing), art making may not necessarily be a wholly intentful process (i.e., insofar as an artist conceives of a meaning to be expressed and then inductively constructs a plan to make an object that is to be evaluated in light of preconceived intents). As Ernst Gombrich (1972) noted, the history of art is rather a history of right and wrong guesses in the pursuit of a satisfactory pictorial illusion, which is partly intent, partly unintentional, and proceeding more along the lines of Kant's purposeness without purpose. When students play "Twenty Questions" or Sherlock Holmes detective games in the pursuit of picture study, the end games pursued are more likely to become ones that either define aesthetic objects as being true or false or becomes in law parlance—a disputation involving defense and prosecution arguments to convince a jury not about some truth, but rather about coming to a guilty or not guilty decision without reasonable doubt.

In my view, and as I explain more fully later, the process of creating a work of art offers the most promise for revealing the true nature of artistic thought and the art product the most promise for revealing the true nature of artistic cognition. Because the process of artistic conception is neither linear nor clearly connected to specific means and ends, the critical analysis of an art work may in fact tell us more about the one who analyzes it than about the intentions or the right and wrong guesses of the maker. Most modernist criticism today is indeed more closely related to the intent of the critic than it is about the intent of the artist. According to some aesthetitions (Langer, 1953), criticism is not a science because its methods are not clear and, to some, more like a spectator sport where the viewer lives through the actions of those who play the game rather than being one who really decides an outcome. Although language and speech clearly has a place in artistic cognition, as is noted later, it may not offer the only or even the best approach to understanding artistic cognition.

Another path avoided here is the expansionist view of the social reconstructionists who hold that academic test requirements only promote individualistic achievement values and the social relationships most consistent with bureaucratic institutions. Those who hold this view can see reading and writing as thoroughly antisocial activities, their solitary nature leading to the idea that the use of intelligence is a purely individual and private matter (Emler & Heather, 1980). According to those who hold this view, literacy conspires to separate learning and discovery from an interpersonal context, thus becoming impersonal, universalized, disinterested, and socially detached. Some also believe that the central function of schools is to ensure social inequalities, causing many children from the working class to become failures and extol the virtues of White, middle-class life.

The expansionist view fails because its appeal is found in victimization. As a consequence, it emphasizes the delivery of educational products much as one might deliver health care. It also fails to recognize that schools are just *one* of the social institutions in the society, ignoring the responsibility of the home, church, and other cultural and social institutions in children's social development. Many of the things advocated by the expansionists are things the school is not best equipped to do and where it is reasonable for the school to focus on reading, writing, and math, which other social institutions are not likely to teach. As Eisner (1982) noted, there are even positive uses for tests that can be an efficient means for securing important information that, acquired through other means, would be too expensive and time-consuming. The problem with testing, he noted, is not that it sheds light on some aspects of human performance, but that it also neglect other aspects.

In addition to the reductionist and expansionist views, there are also those who believe that the failure of the cognate and expressive domain to cohere is due to the traditional way psychologists define *intelligence*. This influenced Gardner (1985) to recognize multiple forms of intelligence and include all the human problem-solving and product-fashioning skills, not just those that happen to lend themselves to testing via a standard format. Gardner named these seven kinds of intelligence as linguistic, musical, logical-mathematical, spatial, body-kinesthetic, personal intelligence, and sense of self and others.

Gardner's effort has had an important effect on revising the thinking of those in the field of cognitive psychology and has at least reintroduced the possibility of multiple intelligences, which is now part of the lexicon in current psychological thinking. However, Gardner admitted that there will never be a single irrefutable and universally accepted list of human intelligences and that, if such a list were developed, it might number into the hundreds. More important, Gardner viewed the artful choices he made to include some forms of intelligence when "enough demons holler" and, when not enough of them do so, to withhold approbation, regrettably, banishing some from consideration. Unfortunately, Gardner's demons banished the notion of a visual intelligence, substituting spatial intelligence to include only some aspects of spatial ability, including the task of matching one image with another and visualizing the rotation of such an image in space. Unfortunately, these operations alone will not guarantee the creation of aesthetic objects. To accomplish Gardner's loosely related abilities (including the ability to recognize the same element, transform or recognize a transformation of one element into another, conjure up mental imagery, and produce a graphic likeness, etc.), although necessary, are insufficient for the creation of a work of art. However, Gardner's work does contribute a good deal to the effort of redefining the concerns that have traditionally separated studies of cognitive intelligence and cognition in art. It should also be noted that, without some common conception linking the two, art learning will continue to play only a limited role in the total education of children and youth.

Seeking Answers

The path I have decided to follow is to: (a) pursue an understanding of the cognitive belief systems supported in the disciplines of both cognitive psychology and aesthetics, (b) determine what common conceptions these systems have, and (c) use these conceptions to begin the construction of a school art program model that can more effectively enhance both the cognitive and aesthetic development of children and youth. In this effort, approaches that push to conceive of art as science or science as art are not pursued and neither discipline is used to subvert the values of the other. My hunch is this: What divides conception and cognition in these disciplines relates more to the verification process rather than to conception itself. Therefore, this effort seeks to disentangle such conceptions from their disciplinary bias.

To accomplish the task of understanding the belief systems used in both art and science, it is necessary that we first mention some belief systems that reflect the current thinking of the times, including the importance placed in encouraging higher order and critical thinking skills in all art learning. Such learning strategies are now an important part of current educational thinking and are generally believed to be the means for achieving the integration of knowledge across all the disciplines in the school program. Both have been cited in a number of well-known art education texts as being the most appropriate way to make learning in art transfer and for art to become a part of basic school learning. This notion has particularly dominated the thinking of those who have advocated a disciplinary approach to art learning and has been a topic of investigation in a number of doctoral dissertations, the results of which, as noted earlier, neither confirm or deny that such skills do indeed transfer.

The standard higher order thinking strategies favored are those noted in Bloom's *Taxonomy of Educational Objectives* (Bloom, Englehart, Furst, & Krathwohl, 1956), which includes knowledge and information, comprehension, application, analysis, and synthesis. The critical thinking forms desired have been identified in Zechmeister and Johnson (1992) and are presented as (a) understanding people and events, and (b) solving problems, making decisions, and convincing others. Both strategies are based on the assumption that all school learning is based on remembering information, using inductive and deductive logic in problem solving, recognizing the laws of causality and probability, and using top–down sequential thinking processes and discursive argument. Because of the belief that using such skills in the art room will solidify art as a basic study, some recent approaches to art teaching have influenced only the deductive forms of logic used in the humanities, stressing only the study of historical and critical skills, with art production being considered only as a means to verify critical and historical argument. The fact that such approaches have not, as yet, demonstrated their effectiveness in schools may be due either to the possibility that expertise in the domain of art will not transfer to the other domains or that teachers of art are fairly ineffective in teaching language, science, and social studies in the art room.

In summary, the following chapters should answer four important questions: (a) Can the inductive and deductive systems of logic used in critical thinking in language science and social studies facilitate higher order thinking skills in art? (b) Can the knowledge base in these disciplines be organized in the same way for all learners? (c) Can they also be organized in the same way in the various art subdisciplines? and (d) How should the content of these disciplines be organized for the purposes of concept development?

Seeking answers to these questions as the means for determining the course of this investigation requires that the same investigatory means used in support of concept formation in inductive and deductive forms of thinking also be used to determine the kinds of thinking necessary for the creation and understanding of works of art. What follows is an effort to examine the knowledge contributed by both the cognitive sciences and the arts most especially as they illuminate the problem of defining conceptual learning behavior.

The chapters that follow also question whether the interpretations of most disciplinary investigations reflect a priori more about the logic of the disciplinary process being used than about what the data reveal in answering the questions being investigated. Should this prove to be the case, it may be reasonable to assume that the methods of both disciplines to be investigated tend to confirm their methods rather than serve the interests of truth. Therefore, the quest may be not so much about disciplinary methods as about how the methods bias the results of disciplinary experiments.

ORGANIZATION OF THE BOOK

Chapter 1 provides an introduction to and plan of the text; it also addresses the traditional understandings of the relationship between art forming and intellect. Included are discussions of the new Goals 2000 initiatives, experimental studies in art and cognition, and use of higher order and critical thinking skills in art.

Chapter 2, which provides a brief overview of the basic functions of the brain as revealed in the studies of the various subdisciplines in general psychology, offers basic data on what is already known about the various mental processes used in human perception, consciousness, memory, thought, language, concept development, reasoning, problem solving, decision making, creativity, and emotion. Discussed are the two basic systems used for interpreting scientific research described as the top–down (intellectual) model and bottom–up (Gestalt) model, which pose totally different conceptual organizations of the perceptual processes used in organizing and achieving a cognition of what the data mean. Discussed also are the various theories explaining the role of language in cognitive development, conditions of problem solving, various theories of intelligence, including multiple intelligences, and contrasting explanations of the role of emotions in cognitive development.

Chapter 3 examines the cognitive processes and learning from the viewpoint of the disparate fields making up the cognitive sciences. Included is the history, organization, and research findings and various philosophical arguments that fund the conceptions of the mind held by the competing paradigms in the field of cognitive science. Examined also are the influences of the competing analytical schools of thought on the role of language in cognition and the influences of the behaviorist, Gestaltist, developmentalists, psycholinguists, anthropologists, neuroscientists, artificial intelligence, and cognitive stylist perspectives.

Chapter 4 explores the topic of cognition in art through examining the literature in philosophy, aesthetics, and the psychology of art. Explored are the ideas of various aesthetitions and philosophers that form different theories of art, including the notions of art as idea, form, and language. Also discussed are the views of various scholars in aesthetics and the psychology of art on the issues of perception, consciousness, language, imagination, symbols, sensation, thought, thinking, intellect, feeling, and emotion. Both top–down and bottom–up approaches are presented and contrasted. The last part of the chapter introduces and summarizes the research findings on children's artistic growth and development. Section I describes the results of the studies undertaken from 1905 to 1962; Section II describes those studies conducted from 1962 to the present.

Chapter 5 discusses concept development from the objectivist viewpoint in an effort to frame the conceptual nature of artistic abstraction. Discussed are the art-forming behaviors of 10 American artists representing three different styles of art: abstract, realist, and pop. Presented are the artists' (a) methods for arriving at an image, (b) techniques and materials used, (c) assumptions made about pictorial form, (d) processes used in creating visual abstractions, and (e) decision-making processes that guide and determine when the work is complete.

Chapter 6 translates the conceptual processes identified in chapter 5 and provides a modest proposal for a conceptual approach to teaching art—laying out a model K to 12 art program based on a cognitive approach to art education. To construct this curriculum, the concept-formation process was examined according to these requirements: the students acquire visual data, the process relates to the age-specific development of learners, and the task of concept formation involves the integration of perceptual data and speech development. What is provided is a curriculum model based on the creative act, emphasizing both the focal knowledge students need to have and the procedural knowledge needed to do so. This curriculum offers a plan for the development of artistic conception or fusion according to both the K to 12 developmental stages addressed by Piaget and three stages of concept development, including the preconceptual, perceptual/conceptual, and conceptual. The curriculum model provided does not require that teachers add a lot of new material to their present curriculum, but rather to reorder what they already have to maximize the conceptual artistic development of their students.

Chapter 7 focuses on the classroom learning environment and authentic approaches to assessing art instruction, including the content of the art program, constructing an authentic assessment, and planning an assessment strategy. Included are examples of holistic, analytic, and classroom rubrics and how to plan an assessment strategy using numbers to report results, and making the assessment manageable through spreading the assessment among grade levels, teachers, various areas of expertise, and targeting grade levels.

Chapter 8 provides the author's conclusions, which attempt to answer the question of what influence the theories and concepts advanced in the text will have on the future of art education today and in the coming millennium. More specifically, it seeks to answer these questions: What will be the future role of the cognitive sciences in the shaping of art education theory and practice? What agenda needs to be set for the conduct of new research in the field? What new policies are needed to construct new and more authentic means of instructional assessment in art education?

SUMMARY

To require that the reader go in such a roundabout manner (i.e., through such a lengthy discussion of so many psychological, philosophical, and aesthetic values) may appear, at least to some readers, as being somewhat of an overkill, especially considering the modest reforms to be advocated. For those readers already familiar with the general literature in psychology and aesthetics, this may well be the case. For them I suggest skipping the early chapters and beginning with chapters 6 and 7, which get down to the specific problems of curriculum reform. For others less familiar with these writings and for those who over time may have forgotten what they learned in school, the decision to start at the beginning may well be worth the effort.

The review of the psychological and philosophical issues addressed in the earlier chapters will help most readers to get in touch with the foundation of their own thinking, ground what they do in their own personal philosophy, and convey to others the logic behind what they practice in their classrooms. Although the effort here should not be to preach to the choir, it should also be recognized that, over time, even the most experienced practitioners may lose at least some of the vision they once had about why what it is they do is important for the aesthetic growth of those whom they teach. In addition, some of the disinformation and the claims of wishful thinking that art advocates have diluted our journals and our schooling with are discussed; these dull our true sense of what it is we should be accomplishing in art classrooms and how others not in our field view what it is that we do there.

Finally, what this text is really about is how art educators and curriculum specialists can go about art learning as intelligent activity, how they can link that activity with other intelligent activities offered in K to 12 schooling, and how they can refocus the program so as to convince those responsible for providing quality schooling in our communities that the arts do make a difference. This will require much more, of course, than merely offering a book in support of that effort. In addition, it requires that we adopt policies in schools that make this kind of instruction possible, embrace practices that help carry it out in art classrooms, and provide the necessary research and evaluations effort to secure its continued success and recognition in American schooling.

REFERENCES

Bloom, B. S., Englehart, M. D., Furst, E. V. W. H., & Krathwohl, D. R. (1956). *Taxonomy of educational objectives handbook: I. Cognitive Domain*. New York: McKay.

Bruner, J. S. (1973). *Beyond the information given: Studies in the psychology of knowing*. New York: Norton.

Conant, H. (1967). *Seminar on elementary and secondary school education in the visual arts*. New York: New York University.

Dorn, C. (1994). *Thinking in art: A philosophical approach to art education*. Reston, VA: National Art Education Association.

Eisner, E. W. (1982). *Cognition and curriculum: A basis for deciding what to teach*. New York: Longman.

Emler, N. E., & Heather, N. (1980). Intelligence on ideological bias of conventional psychology. In P. Salmon (Ed.), *Coming to know* (pp. 135-151). London: Routledge & Kegan Paul.

Gardner, H. (1977). Senses symbols operations: An organization of artistry. In D. Perkins & B. Leondar (Eds.), *The arts and cognition*. Baltimore: Johns Hopkins University Press.

Gardner, H. (1985). *Frames of mind: The theory of multiple intelligences*. New York: Basic Books.

Goals 2000 Legislation (Public Law 103-227). (1994). Washington D. C. House Document Room, Ford House Office Building.

Gombrich, E. (1972). *Art and illusion*. Princeton, NJ: Princeton University Press.

Goodman, N. (1977). When is art. In D. Perkins & B. Leondar (Eds.), *The arts and cognition* (pp. 11-19). Baltimore: Johns Hopkins University Press.

Korzenik, D. (1977). Saying it with pictures. In D. Perkins & B. Leondar (Eds.), *The arts and cognition* (pp. 192-208). Baltimore: John Hopkins University Press.

Langer, S. (1953). *Feeling and form*. New York: Charles Scribner's Sons.

Madeja, S. (Ed.). (1977). *The arts cognition and basic skills*. St. Louis: CEMREL.

Madeja, S. (Ed). (1991). *Kathryn Bloom's innovation in art education*. DeKalb, IL: Northern Illinois University Press.

Messer, S. B. (1976). Reflection impulsivity: A review. *Psychological Bulletin, 83,* 1026-1052.

National Art Education Association. (1994). *A priority for reaching high standards.* Reston, VA: Author.

Perkins, D., & Leondar, B. (1977) A cognitive approach to the arts. In D. Perkins & B. Leondar (Eds.), *The arts and cognition* (pp. 1-4). Baltimore: Johns Hopkins University Press.

Perkins, D. N. (1994). *The intelligent eye: Learning to think by looking at art.* Santa Monica: Getty Center for Education in the Arts.

Silver, A. (1977). Show and tell: The arts cognition and basic ways of knowing. In S. Madeja (Ed.), *The arts cognition and basic skills* (pp. 31-51). St. Louis: CEMREL.

Zechmeister, E. B., & Johnson, J. E. (1992). *Critical thinking: A functional approach.* Pacific Grove, CA: Brooks Cole.

KEY TERMS

Cognition	Communications Theory
Denotation	Reiteration
Induction	Concept
Symbol	Exemplification
Deduction	Multiple Intelligences
Cognitive Style	

STUDY QUESTIONS

1. What is the Goals 2000 Educate America Act about and what effect will it have on students being educated in the arts? Are the Standards proposed closely aligned with the traditional aims of art teaching in schools or do they use art as an alibi for reaching other objectives?

2. Is art a form of communication like we use in the popular media, containing a symbol system that allows a direct communication between the artist and viewer? Do you think art instruction can be organized and taught as a form of communications theory?

3. What do we mean by the term *intelligence?* Is it the same as IQ, which has to do with predicting academic success? Is artistic intelligence the same as academic intelligence? Does having either one of these intelligences automatically ensure that one will have the other?

4. What is Gardner arguing in his claim that there are multiple intelligences? What are his so-called *seven forms of intelligence* and how do these intelligences relate to artistic forming and thinking?

2

Sensation, Vision, Perception, and Human Development

PSYCHOLOGICAL METHODS
  Fields of Study

COGNITION AND DEVELOPMENT
  Developmental Stages

MENTAL PROCESSES
  Sensation, Vision, and Perception
  Consciousness
  Memory Systems
  Thought and Language
  Concept Development
  Reasoning
  Problem Solving
  Decision Making

INTELLIGENCE THEORY
  Sternberg's Theory
  Gardner's Intelligences

CREATIVITY
  Guilford Theory
  Amabile Theory

EMOTION
  James-Lange Theory
  Canon-Bard Theory
  Schaehter-Singer Theory

SUMMARY

To begin thinking about how higher order and critical thinking skills can be achieved in schooling, it is necessary to think about what we already know about thinking behavior. The most fertile source of this kind of knowledge comes from the field of psychology, which is the scientific study of behavior and mental processes. As a science, it requires that it be based on information collected through the scientific method and that the information collected exist in the form of observations or measurements derived from such study. As a study of behavior, it is limited to any activity that can be observed, recorded, and measured; as a study of mental processes, it includes thoughts, memories, emotions, motivations, dreams, perceptions, and beliefs (Bernstein, Roy, Serull, & Wickens, 1981).

As a field of scientific study, psychology is also subject to other conditions, including those described by Kuhn (1982) in his *Structure of Scientific Revolutions*. In this book, he noted that the historian of science has two tasks: to determine by what person and at what point in time each contemporary scientific fact, law, or theory was invented and to describe the error, myth, and superstition that have inhibited the accumulation of the constituents of the modern science text (Kuhn, 1982). Unfortunately, Kuhn noted, historians have difficulties distinguishing between the scientific component of past observation and belief from what their predecessors already labeled *error* and *superstition*. The problem, he believed, is that past views of science are neither less scientific nor more the product of human idiosyncrasy than those current today.

What accounts for the differing scientific conclusions of both yesteryear and today, he believed, is firmly imbedded in the educational institution that prepares and licenses the science student for professional practice. This contributes to the various branches of science coming up with different conclusions based on the varied belief systems adopted by a particular field of scientific inquiry. Normal science, he noted, means research firmly based on one or more of the past achievements that a particular scientific community acknowledges, at least for a time, as supplying a foundation for further practice. Science, in his view, is thus made up of a number of competing paradigms, where members of that scientific community form with others who learned from the same models and therefore adopted similar practices about which its members rarely disagree.

PSYCHOLOGICAL METHODS

The existence of competing scientific paradigms suggests that a given specialty at a particular time will hold various theories in their conceptual, observational, and instrumental applications and that these are revealed in its textbooks, lectures, and laboratory exercises. The field of psychology, which is involved in the scientific study of behavior and mental processes, contains a number of divergent communities that support a number of differing scientific paradigms. Thus, psychologists with divergent scientific perspectives using the same data can arrive at different conclusions. The major psychological perspectives include: biopsychological, psychodynamic, behavioral, humanistic, and cognitive. Biopsychology combines study of the physiology of the brain with psychology, holding that, for every behavior, feeling, and thought, there is a corresponding physical event in the brain. Psychodynamic psychology is concerned with the unconscious, which grew out of the work of Sigmund Freud. Behavioral psychology is based on the study of only things that are observable—namely, behavior—and has its roots in the studies of Ivan Pavlov and

Edward Thorndike. Humanistic psychology emphasizes the importance of each person's subjective experience as is supported in the work of Abraham Maslow and Carl Rogers. The cognitive perspective, which is the main focus of chapter 3, studies the ways humans process or transform information about the world; it also looks at cognition, which includes the mental processes of thinking, knowing, perceiving, attending, remembering, and so on.

Because we are concerned here with higher mental processes, it is necessary to pay particular attention to the discipline of cognitive psychology, which specifically addresses the mental processes used in thinking, problem solving, and decision making. These mental processes are especially important to teachers who want to incorporate critical thinking in the classroom and develop questioning strategies that call for higher forms of thinking, especially those involved in analysis, synthesis, and evaluation.

This chapter addresses these concerns, especially as they are advanced in the field of general psychology to establish a basis for understanding the more advanced and specialized constructs and findings in the areas of cognition and cognitive abilities, which are presented and discussed in chapter 3. The discussion of these findings from general psychology borrows from a number of competing psychological perspectives and includes their differing points of view with regard to matters involving thought, memory, and perception. More specifically, it presents a brief overview of the literature in general and developmental psychology on the topics of cognition and cognitive development, with special emphasis on the findings of Piaget, the sensory system (especially with regard to vision, perception, and consciousness), memory, (especially as it is linked to thought, language, and consciousness), mental abilities, and emotions.

Fields of Study

This chapter also looks at the cognitive sciences as a psychological discipline, especially as it is manifested in the domain of *experimental psychology*—a term developed by Wundt, Edward Titchener, and Hermann Ebbinghaus to distinguish their laboratory work from the efforts of philosophers and others who thought and speculated about consciousness, memory, and other psychological matters but performed no experiments. These experimental methods are the foundation of every psychology subschool, including biological, personality, social, clinical, and counseling, developmental and quantitative. Experimental psychologists study the most basic components of behavior and mental processes—including perception, learning, and memory—in both animals and humans. Those who work specifically in the area of cognition are known as cognitive psychologists because they explore the mental activities involved in judgment, decision making, problem solving, imagination, and other aspects of complex thought or cognition.

COGNITION AND DEVELOPMENT

Developmentally, from conception through childhood, the human body and brain increases in size, complexity, and efficiency. These changes are related to advances in behavior and to cognitive development, which is the development of thinking, knowing, and remembering. Although scientists have not proved whether changes in the brain cause advances in thinking or vice versa, they have documented, analyzed, and tried to explain the changes in cognitive ability that occur from infancy to childhood.

The study of cognitive development learning theory grew out of Watson's behaviorism, which explains the development of children's thought in terms of the consequences of performing a particular behavior. However, the behavioral explanations did not take into account that learning is not always tied to the consequences of behavior and, as a theory, did not make predictions of how learning changes with age. As a result, cognitive psychologists now view Piaget's work and study of information processing as offering the most widely accepted approach to the development of a learning theory, which has value for understanding many different aspects of behavior.

Developmental Stages

Piaget proposed that children's cognitive development progresses through a series of distinct stages: sensorimotor (birth to 2 years), preoperational (2–7 years), concrete operational (7–11 years), and formal operational (over 11 years). He also proposed that infants' thinking is qualitatively different from children's thinking and that children's thinking is qualitatively different from adolescents'. Children's thinking, he noted, goes through all these stages, each building on the previous stage to reach a higher stage when its mental schemata are no longer able to process new information (Piaget, 1952).

According to Piaget, the development of schemata is guided by two processes: organization and adaption. *Organization* is the combination and integration of separate schemata into more complex patterns, and *adaption* is the modification of schemata that occurs with experience, which includes the processes of assimilation and accommodation. *Assimilation* involves testing new information about new objects through finding out whether they fit existing schema, and *accommodation* is the trying out of familiar schemata on new objects.

In the psychological literature, a schema is described as general knowledge acquired from experience about any object, event, person, or group. A person's schema creates an expectation of how one expects to respond in a situation. Schemata about roles or groups are called *stereotypes* and schemata about events are called *scripts*. Schemata are resistant to change, yet when we encounter information in the environment that is inconsistent with our schemata we might change. When we fit incongruent information into an existing schema, by shaping or distorting the information to agree with an existing schema we are said to have reached assimilation. However, when schemata do not change to fit incoming information, we deal with incongruent information through the process of accommodation, which occurs when schemata are revised completely or when they are simply developed further and made more complex.

During the first stage of sensorimotor development, children learn to form mental representations of objects and actions—a form of knowledge Piaget called *object permanence*. In the preoperational period, children begin to understand, create, and use symbols to represent things that are not present through drawing, pretending, and talking. Thinking at this stage, according to Piaget, is dominated by intuition or guess rather than by rational thought.

In the concrete operational thought stage, children can use simple logic, performing simple mental operations including the sorting of objects into classes or into sizes by systematic searching and ordering. Concrete operational children can perform these operations on only real concrete objects and not on abstract ideas, such as concepts of justice or freedom, which occurs in the formal operational period of adolescence.

Some psychologists today prefer to describe children's cognitive activities in terms of information processing, which examines how information is taken in, remembered, forgotten, or used. Information-processing research, while also focusing on what is going on in the child's head, also focuses on the gradual quantitative changes in children's mental capacities rather than on sudden qualitative advances or changes. Information research supports the notion that children get better with age in their ability to take in and remember information, although children do vary in the pace of their cognitive development due to heredity, experience, and the richness of their surroundings and experiences.

In Piaget's last stage, the formal operational period, adolescents begin to think and reason about abstract concepts and have the ability to engage in hypothetical thinking including the imagination of logical consequences. In addition, they can reflect on and analyze their own mental processes, focus on form and symbolism in art, and go beyond content to discover artistic or written intent.

MENTAL PROCESSES

The world is filled with objects and events that combine to create a kaleidoscope of potential information. Some of that information is vital for human beings' survival. So that they can use this information effectively, human beings are equipped with specialized machinery for capturing this information and translating it into a language that can be understood by the nervous system. This information is interpreted by the brain, culminating as perceptions of the world. These perceptions are what guides people's actions in the world around them.

Perception is the final link in a chain of related events that begins with the environment where we live and, to a great extent, determines what we perceive. The mental events that make up the chain begin with a stimuli caused by a physical energy. This is then converted in the nervous system into neural events through a process called *sensory transduction,* which includes the sensory receptors in the eye and ear. Once transduction has occurred, objects and events are represented solely as patterns of neural impulses within the various nerve fibers. From this point on, all further elaboration and editing of sensory information must be performed using this neural representation. According to the laws of psychophysics, perception represents the final product in that chain of events, beginning with the events in the physical world that have an effect on the perceiver. The translation of these events into patterns of activity within the perceiver's nervous system culminates in the perceiver's experiential and behavioral responses to these events.

Many researchers believe perception is the product of a biological process and can be explained at a biological level, where perceptual experiences can be related to corresponding neural events. However, there are also qualities of perception that can elude descriptions in neural terms and that entail complex patterns of neural activity, which are distributed over wide regions of the brain not yet verified in experiments. According to Sperry (1982), mental patterns and programs generated from neural events also have their own subjective qualities; they progress, operate, and interact by their own causal laws and principles, which differ from and cannot be reduced to neuropsychological explanations.

Mental phenomena, whether conscious or unconscious, visual or auditory, pains, itches, or thoughts are all part of our mental life and are caused by processes going on in the brain. Perception also depends heavily on a variety of biological processes, including the senses of seeing, hearing, taste, smell, and touch. Because more is known about vision than about the other senses and because this is a book about the visual arts, most of what is discussed here refers to vision rather than the other senses. Vision also represents the richest source of sensory information for humans, takes up the greatest part of the brain's functioning, and, when pitted against the other senses, probably dominates them. In addition, because our ability to communicate with one another depends so strongly on vision, it truly deserves our greatest attention.

Sensation, Vision, and Perception

The senses in each individual helps create his or her reality, which may or may not be in synchrony with that of others. Sense biologically comes through systems that translate information from outside the individual into neural activity, which in vision is the system through which the eyes convert light into neural activity. This informs the brain something about the source of the light or about the objects from which it is reflected. The messages from the senses are called *sensations,* which provide the link between the self and the world outside the brain. Psychologists distinguish between sensation, which has to do with the initial message from the senses, and perception, which is how this message is interpreted by the senses in light of previous experience.

According to psychologists, sensory systems process through four steps, which modifies the information received. These steps include accessory structures such as the lens of the eye, which modifies the stimulus, transduction, which converts incoming energy into neural activity, adaption, where repetitive responses are reduced, and, last, where the output of the receptors is transferred to the brain via sensory waves that are then processed into perception.

Perception biologically relates to how the brain codes the stimulus that translates physical properties into a pattern of neural activity that specifically identifies the physical properties of the object being seen (i.e., whether it is a cat or an ice cream cone). Specific neuron energies channel the response to the eye where the specific attributes of the object seen are coded in the language of neural activity. This can be coded simply through a neuron's rate of firing or in a complex way through several relay points in the brain.

Psychologists divide the process of perception into three processes: selection, organization, and interpretation. Selection is identified through the process called *attention,* by which we determine which sensations are perceived. Organization is how stimuli are organized in meaningful shapes and patterns, how we deal with depth perception, and how we deal with perceptual constancy. Interpretation is based on what one expects to see or a perceptual set.

The human body's visual sensory system is adapted to do many things, including combinations of great sensitivity and great sharpness enabling people to see objects near and far during day or night. Light is the form of energy that does not need a medium to pass through, and our sensations of light depend on two physical dimensions: intensity and wave length. Converting light energy into neural energy is a process called *visual transduction,* which takes place in the retina—a major structure in the eye that is sensed by its photoreceptors. Photoreceptors are specialized cells in the retina that convert light energy into neural activity and include photopigments that are chemicals that respond to light. The retina has two basic kinds of photoreceptors: rods and cones that differ in shape, composition, response to light, and location in the eye.

The eye actually sharpens visual images through the interactions among the cells of the retina. Physical sight is the result of the interactions of cells through the arrangement of convergence and lateral inhibition. Convergence increases the sensitivity of each bipolar cell; this in turn reduces acuity and lateral inhibitions, which are intercellular connections to excite or inhibit the response of a neighboring cell. Lateral interactions enhance the sensations of contrast, which makes it possible to distinguish certain features of objects (e.g., revealing an edge through a transition from light to dark and making a contrast that sharpens an edge and makes it more noticeable). One visual effect art students have experienced that involves lateral inhibition occurs in the Hermann and Ehrenstein grids (Fig. 2.1), which cause dark or white spots to occur at the intersections of black squares or crosses. The effect, which is seen as a virtual form, appears in the work of various pop artists.

Seeing color that is a major element in art physically results from the mixture of wave lengths striking the eye, producing the sensations of seeing hue, value, and intensity. This also includes mixing color as a subtractive process, where paints subtract wavelengths, thus creating black, or an additive color (light) where wavelengths of the colors are added together to stimulate more cones in the eye, thus producing white (light), which is a combination of all wavelengths.

Psychologists have also contributed to the work of artists through the development of color theory. These include the trichromatic theory of Thomas Young and later Hermann von Helmholtz, which said any color could be matched by mixing pure lights of just three wavelengths. Subsequent research suggested that we respond to color through three types of cones, the relationship of which indicates what color is sensed. In an effort to account for color afterimages, Ewald Hering also developed a color theory called the *opponent-process theory,* which holds that the visual elements sensitive to color are grouped in three pairs and that the members of each pair oppose or inhibit each other. When one part of an opponent pair is no longer stimulated, the other is automatically activated as an afterimage.

There are also visual pathways that process seeing in that part of the brain, which occupies the optic chiasm part of the bottom surface of the brain. This is organized in a region called the *lateral geniculate nucleus* (LGN), which is organized in layers of neurons; each layer contains a whole map of one side of the visual field. Neurons of different layers respond to particular aspects of visual stimuli, including form, color movement, and depth. These visual elements are handled separately by the first cortical they reach but later assembled to become an integrated conscious experience.

The retina's topographical map of the visual world is maintained all the way to the brain, with more than 10 complete visual maps existing in the primate's visual cortex, each point of which is made up of columns of cells that share a function, such as responding to a

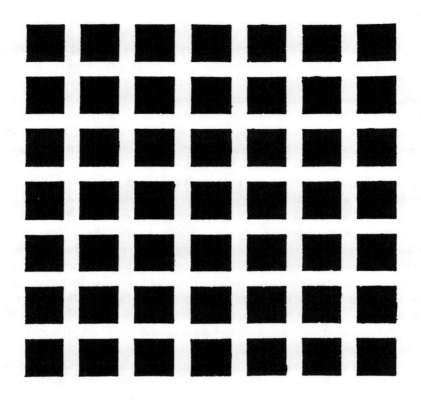

(a)

(b)

FIG. 2.1.　(a) Facsimile Hermann grid. Grey dots seem to appear at the intersections of the white strips. (b) Ehrenstein grid facsimile where diagonal contours appear connected by circles at the intersections of grid lines.

particular visual stimulus. Cells in the brain that respond to specific features of objects are called *feature detectors,* where cells have center surround receptive fields that might respond only to visual edges, moving objects, or objects with corners.

One theory of how the cortex puts together information as feature detectors is this: Any object seen is a compilation of features built up of more complex connections of simple feature protectors. It is thought that several center surround cells could feed into one cortical cell to make a line detector, with several of these feeding another cell to become a more complex shape detector. With reference to space stimuli, it is thought that the brain has a spatial frequency filter that analyzes patterns by examining gradual changes in brightness over broad areas rather than putting together separate information about lines, edges, and other features. This theory suggests that the brain analyzes the visual world into patterns of alternating light and dark frequencies, representing that pattern as a collection of sine waves.

The psychological literature also notes a division of labor in the brain: The right hemisphere receives information only from the left side of the body and the left hemisphere receives information from the right side. The left hemisphere almost always controls language and is involved with mathematical and analytical abilities. The right hemisphere is nonverbal, thinks in symbols not words, has excellent spatial abilities, and may be related to the ability to draw. The right hemisphere, which controls spatial skills, has frequently been treated as a second class citizen and is often referred to as the *minor hemisphere.* To a lesser degree, each hemisphere can perform some of the tasks for which the opposite hemisphere is specialized. Recent research suggests that the right hemisphere contributes the color to ordinary speech.

As previously noted, sensations in the brain provide the raw information about the environment but do not give cognitive meaning to the object or event seen. According to psychologists, perception is the process through which sensations are interpreted and where we use our knowledge and understanding of the world to make our experiences meaningful. Perception is not generally thought of as a passive process (i.e., simply decoding incoming sensations such as an "innocent eye" might literally record on the retina what the lens of the eye focuses on). Instead, our brains take these sensations and create a coherent world with individuals filling in the missing information and drawing from past experience to give meaning to what we see, hear, or touch.

Although the visual sensations caused by the outline of a square shape in a drawing (Fig. 2.2) tells the mind that four straight lines are contacting each other at 90-degree angles, what we actually see is the appearance of a square. Perception as a mental activity organizes our sense impressions of the world into an organized, recognizable place influencing our thoughts, feelings, and actions. Perceptions in both real and imaginary experience occur in the three stages of detecting stimuli, organizing them into a pattern, and recognizing that pattern.

Sensation as the thing sensed and perception as sense interpreted overlap because the sensory processes of the brain offer some preliminary interpretations, as in the retinal cells, which respond to the edges and light changes—thus physiologically an interpretation of a stimulus begins before the stimulus reaches the brain. Perception appears to add information based on prior knowledge of what comes from the sensory system. In psychological terms, perception is a primitive version of a knowledge-based process that helps us learn concepts, make judgments, and reach decisions.

FIG. 2.2.   A square composed of four straight lines contacting each other at 90° angles.

Perception involves six distinct features that make it: (a) knowledge based, (b) inferential as a system of right guesses, (c) categorical as seeking common features, (d) relational in making comparisons, (e) adaptive in suggesting proper action, and (f) automatic in that we do not have to be consciously aware of the activity. As to which of the six features is the most important, psychologists recognize two different approaches. The first one is by Rock (1983), who emphasized the constructionist position—that perception is knowledge-based and inferential, constructing an image of reality from fragments of sensory information much as a skeletal form is built up from its parts.

The second is the ecological approach, proposed by Gibson (1979) and others, which views incoming stimuli as providing most of the clues needed and that is registered directly from the senses. The constructionist view essentially explains how the mind fills in with right guesses to recognize an incomplete image, such as occurs in seeing a virtual or implied line in a gesture drawing. However, the ecological approach argues that when we perceive the sensation of depth, we do not first sense it as two dimensional and then reconstruct it three dimensionally. Rather, the stimuli interpreted in the brain automatically sees three dimensionality with no reasoning required.

Although both systems seem to rationally account for certain aspects of perception, the ecological system is viewed as not effectively explaining the cognition of objects that are partially obscured from view or, for example, account for form recognition in drawings and sculptures using virtual line or space. The constructionist view, which recognizes perception is knowledge-based and inferential, supports the notion of using right guesses based on stored schemata, whereas the ecological system recognizes a Gestalt or holistic view as forming a relational model where images are understood through relationships to environment or context.

Psychologists also view perception as being related to how we organize, recognize, and attend to our perceptual world. Organization is viewed through the principles of perceptual constancy, depth, motor perception, and perceptual illusion. The ability to recognize the perceptual world is psychologically explored through feature analysis, object recognition, and top–down and bottom–up processing.

Those trained in the arts are basically familiar with how Gestalt psychologists describe the principles of perceptual organization, which is primarily through both figure ground perception and grouping. *Figure ground* is looked at as the perceptual apparatus that automatically picks out certain objects as the object emphasized, and a *ground* as an object's background. Grouping explains how figure and ground come to be discovered through the way the inherent properties of stimuli lead us to group them together more or less automatically. These were identified by the German Gestalt psychologists through a number of principles or properties that lead our perceptual system to glue raw sensations together in particular ways and organize them into a world of shapes and patterns. Students of art are familiar with these principles through study of their art foundation texts. These principles are: proximity, similarity, continuity, and closure (Fig. 2.3). These are generally considered by psychologists as the ways we organize the world into identifiable shapes and patterns, which ultimately depend on still another factor—*perceptual constancy.*

Perceptual constancy is what makes the perception of objects become consistent in size, shape, and color despite changes in the image received by the retina. This includes the capacity of the brain to deal with size, shape, and brightness constancy even if perceived size is altered by distance and movement in location in an environment. Because of distance, human figures of the same size (reported as different size images on the retina) shapes, and value contrasts (altered by eye position in relation to the objects and conflicting value contexts) are, through the constancy of perception, perceived as coherently stabile objects. The mind uses visual stimulus clues much in the same way that artists employ visual devices in a drawing to establish relative size, height in a visual field, perspective, light, shade, and motion. One of the more amazing mental adjustments necessitated by the ways the eyes are built and positioned is the correction made for binocular disparity; this causes the two images produced by the eyes being processed into the impression of a single object with a correct depth, height, and width.

How we recognize what is actually being seen as contrasted with what we think is being seen in a perceptual illusion is explained in the psychological literature through two types of processing mechanisms. One is the so-called *top–down model,* which is guided by higher level cognitive processes and by the psychological factors of expectations and motivation (Lindsay & Norman, 1977). The other is a *bottom–up model* involving a stimulus that comes up to the brain from sensory receptors. In the top–down model, we know what things truly are because they are where we expect them to be; in the bottom–up stimulus, we discern meanings from abstract appearances and speech. Bottom–up processing is believed to produce the cognition of objects through a process called *feature analysis,* which triggers feature detectors in the brain to find a match between mental lists of features, categories, or mental schemata that mentally preserve the basic characteristics of an object. Top–down processing is used to explain how to handle the problems posed through seeing ambiguous objects or illusions and place them in one category or another. However, this model is criticized because it creates an expectancy or perceptual set that provides a

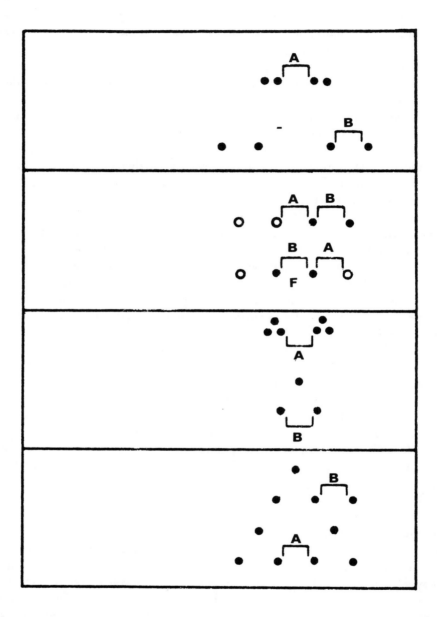

FIG. 2.3.   The effects of Gestalt grouping principles where distances between bracketed dots thought equal appear to be closer in B than in A where the principle operates. (From top to bottom: proximity, similarity, closure, continuation).

readiness or predisposition to perceive an object or event in a certain way. To meet this criticism, it is suggested that a more truthful vision will occur through combining the top–down and bottom–up processes with one filling in the blanks when the other process is impaired. Use of the two processes together presumes that the mind can fill in the gaps left because the world is redundant, offering multiple clues about what is going on.

Psychologist Julian Hockberg agreed, in part, with the notion that a more truthful vision is achieved through some combining of the top–down and bottom–up processes, which he viewed as representing both cognitive and noncognitive theories. The top–down theory he calls the classical psychological theory from Berkeley to Helmholtz, and the direct or noncognitive theory as characterizing Gestalt theory. His view is that both components exist and are important in understanding general education (Hockberg, 1978).

Helmholtz viewed cognitive theory as a form of perception that depends on mental structures and is involved in the creation of surrogates. He illustrated the production of cognitive kinds of surrogate as similar to creating an exterior view seen from a house by tracing the lines seen on a pane of the window through which the scene is observed. When that image is studied, he observed it shows how to represent depth and distance on a flat canvas as well as the basic clues of linear perspective, including relative size, familiar size interposition, texture-density gradient, and so on.

According to Hockberg, the fact that this surrogate image can act as a substitute for a scene, even if it represents only one of many other possible viewpoints from which that view could be constructed, means that our visual information about the scene or a representation of it must be ambiguous (i.e., a surrogate standing for a large number of different scenes where an infinite number of arrangements will produce the same image). This is, in his view, a cognitive theory that assumes we as perceivers fit our sensory patterns to the ideas we have about the world, which are the mental structures learned as art symbols or conventions.

Hockberg used the face and vase image (Fig. 2.4) to illustrate the Gestalt or direct perception theory, which argues that, no matter how faithfully the surrogate is produced, unless the pictured object is a figure it cannot be perceived and therefore cannot be represented.

Even when these processes are used singly or in tandem, psychologists recognize that there is no adequate way to deal with such truly ambiguous images as the well-known figures of the young woman and the mother-in-law (Fig. 2.4) or of the face and vase, which are intended to produce multiple interpretations. Which part of the surrogate is figure and which part is ground is therefore crucial to the making of a faithful surrogate representation. When the figure can be embedded in such a way as to conceal a familiar shape, we perceive that object or event that is the simplest among alternatives. Thus, the Gestalt approach is different from one that is obtained by adding clues together, thus arguing that the organization of the figure really determines the appearance of its parts.

According to Hockberg, the Gestalt theory, especially as it is argued by Gibson (1979), fails in part because it is noncognitive. Using the example of an anamorphic (distorted view) diagram, he believed the viewer cognitively corrects the distortion seen in the image to have a correct perception of the pictured object. This compensation process, which is a cognitive act, challenges the Gestalt surrogate theory of picture perception and argues in favor of the cognitive explanations of surrogates explained by the image drawn in the glass. Therefore, Hockberg concluded that a better theory is possible—especially one that recognizes that some features of picture perception are, for all intents and purposes, innate especially in regard to eye movements and canonical form.

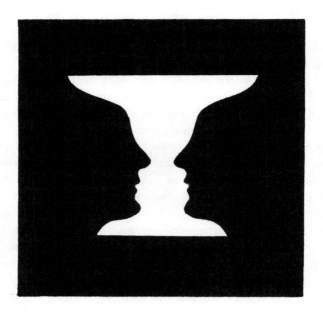

(a)

(b)

FIG. 2.4. (a) Reversible figure-ground pattern seen either as a goblet or a pair of silhouetted faces in profile. (b) Reversible figure-ground pattern seen either as a young woman or an old woman.

Using an Escherlike image of a rectangle that provides reverse depth configurations when viewed at different points in the image, he argued that the whole does not determine its parts, which he believed rules out a Gestalt theory of perception. Because we use only certain portions of eye-employing saccadic eye movements at the rate of four lines a second, Hockberg believed perception is a motivated, purposeful activity that involves taking successive glances that enable us to assemble a view of the world. As such, he viewed perception as being more like a motion picture than a static picture, where in normal seeing our peripheral vision is an undetailed but wide-angled view offering us a forecast of what we will see in more detailed fashion if we look at some particular spot and a reminder of what we saw there after we have moved on.

For Hockberg, visual perception is not like looking at a still picture, but rather like looking at a self-programmed montage, which we only attempt to do if we are not sure about something or we are interested in it. To perceive a picture or a scene, we test our expectations of what we will find. Put more formally, perception becomes the formulation and testing of sensory expectancies.

Psychologists generally believe that an illusion occurs when our perception of an object does not agree with the true physical characteristics of an object. Therefore, there are two kinds of illusions: those due to physical distortion of stimuli and those due to our misperception of stimuli. Psychologists are mostly concerned with illusions caused by distortions in perceptual processes. An illusion such as produced by the differences in the figure size perceived in an Ames room experiment is an illusion that occurs because we try to apply the standard perceptual process of size constancy in an extraordinary situation. Another example is the impossible figure, which occurs in an M. C. Escher drawing that is only revealed through the more lengthy process of scanning.

Psychologists view the perceptual illusions developed by Zollner, Wundt, Poggendorff, Ebbinghaus, and Ponzo as inaccurate or distorted views of reality—similar to the ones that come about through sleep, hypnosis, or drugs. The Hering and Wundt illusions of parallel lines, appearing nonparallel (Fig. 2.5); the Poggendorf illusion, which alters the direction of a diagonal line intersecting two parallel lines (Fig. 2.6); the Ebbinghaus illusion, which misjudges brightness (Fig. 2.7); and the Ponzo illusions (Fig. 2.8), which alters the length of two equal length lines between two converging lines are all offered as examples of such visual inaccuracies or perceptual distortions. Such distortions are believed to be violators of perceptual principles due to a response bias in detecting stimuli due to motivation, experience, and expectation.

Hockberg explained the ambiguity caused by the perceptual illusion in the so-called *Muller–Lyer illusion* (Fig. 2.9), where an arrowlike line intersects the middle of a straight line with arrowlike lines capping both ends. The appearance is that one section of the line is longer than the other where logically the intersection creates two equal halves. He explained that the segments appear unequal because the slanted lines are taken by the eye to be a depth clue of linear perspective, therefore one segment appears to be nearer and smaller. Because such events are less frequently encountered than real scenes, we have not had as much experience with them as we do with other surrogates, thus we tend to become confused.

In general, the psychological literature supports the idea that at least some building blocks of perception are present from birth, including cues as to depth perception through accommodation, convergence, binocular disparity, and relative motion. Also it is generally believed

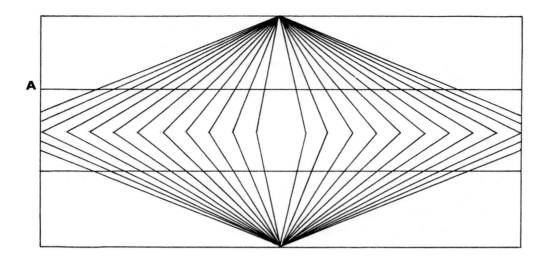

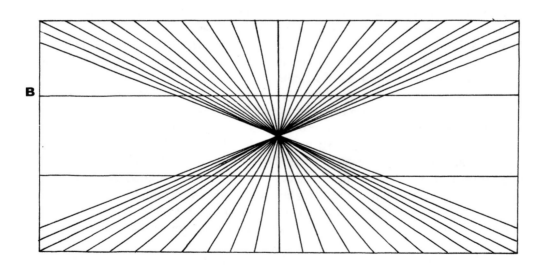

FIG. 2.5.   Artist's version of Wundt's illusion (a) and Hering's illusion (b) where parallel lines bond together in (A) and bow apart in (B).

that these clues are not sufficient but are rather augmented through learning such things as perspective, interpreting clues, recognizing and knowing objects that are near and far, and using depth and distance clues to move effectively through the world.

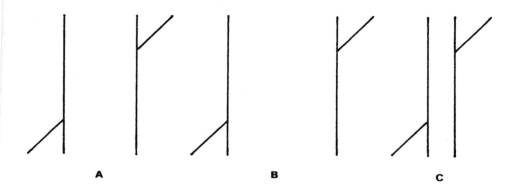

FIG. 2.6.   A rendering of the Poggendorf illusion where the colinear oblique lines in (A) are distorted in (B) and (C) through altering the distances between the parallel lines.

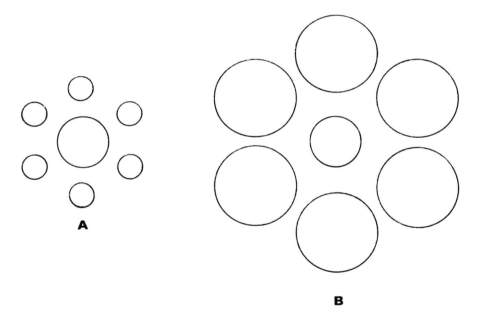

FIG. 2.7.   An interpretation of the Ebbinghaus illusion where the center circle in (A) appears larger due to the smaller surrounding circles.

Consciousness

Consciousness is defined as those mental processes that help make someone aware of their own thoughts, feelings, and perceptions. The study of consciousness focuses on perception, memory, cognition, and other aspects of mental life and is considered to be a property involving many mental processes rather than being a unique mental process.

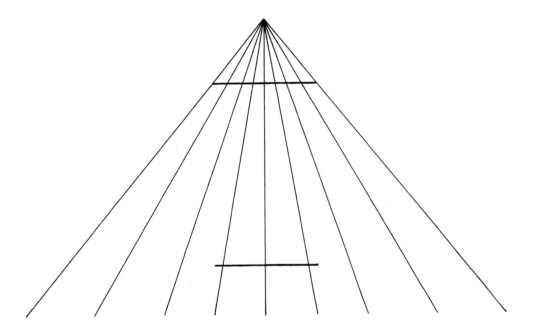

FIG. 2.8.   A version of the Ponzo illusion where the two horizontal lines appear to be unequal in length.

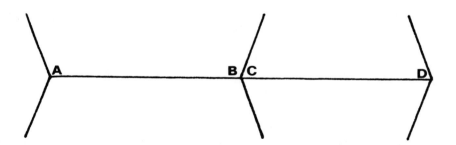

FIG. 2.9.   A representation of the Muller–Lyer illusion where distances A, B, and C, though equal, appear unequal.

The study of consciousness is a problem for psychologists because it is hard to directly observe someone else's conscious experiences. To study consciousness, psychologists have had to devise ways of externalizing what is, for all intents and purposes, an internal process. Studies have centered on such issues as time and memory, the cognitive unconsciousness or biofeedback, and the so-called *studies of consciousness,* including daydreaming, sleeping and dreaming, hypnosis, meditation, and the effects of psychoactive drugs.

Of special interest to those in art are the studies relating to consciousness and cognitive unconsciousness, which generally confirm that much mental activity occurs outside of consciousness, making some events incapable of being experienced consciously. Biofeedback is just one example of this: Someone connected to a measuring device can monitor unconscious events such as blood pressure and learn to control an unconscious process. Mental activities that are not conscious can be brought to consciousness or can influence conscious experience, thought, and action. These activities have been called the *cognitive unconscious* (Kihlstrom, 1987). Mental activity that is outside awareness but that can be easily brought into awareness is known as *preconscious,* which occurs in amounts far surpassing what is present at the conscious level.

According to researchers, mental activity is constantly changing; that which we are aware of thinking is usually referred to as the *state of consciousness,* with the most common state being what is called a *normal waking state.* When changes in the mental processes are extensive enough, people will function in a different manner that means to enter an altered state of consciousness. The altered states most frequently studied by psychologists are those induced by sleep, hypnosis, and drugs. The effects of such altered states induce cognitive processes to become shallow, careless, or uncritical; change self-perceptions and perceptions of the world; and weaken normal inhibitions or self-control. Consciousness as experienced in aesthetic response is not formally studied or researched by most scholars in general psychology.

The effects of hypnosis and drugs on human consciousness have been researched rather extensively by psychologists. Although such altered states are viewed generally as a relinquishment of control and as a diminishing of rational thought, some interesting notions about consciousness have been discovered. For example, hypnosis enhances the ability to fantasize and reorganize the ways in which behavior is controlled, creating a split in consciousness, where body movements normally under voluntary control take place on their own and involuntary processes such as reactions to sound and pain become voluntary. However, the altering of consciousness through hypnosis receives mixed reviews from psychologists who like its effect as a pain killer but are skeptical about the effects of posthypnotic suggestion, noting that several state courts disqualify testimony from people who have been hypnotized (Bernstein et al., 1981).

The effects of meditation have also been studied by psychologists. Meditators have been found to have significant reductions in stress-related problems, such as general anxiety, high blood pressure, and insomnia (Carington, 1986). More generally, meditators' scores on personality tests indicate increases in general mental health, self-esteem, and social openness (Shapiro & Gilber, 1978).

Psychoactive drugs act on the brain to create psychological effects. Although the effects of these drugs are sometimes found to be enjoyable and have some medically beneficial effects, they are also considered by psychologists to have insidious effects especially when drug use becomes drug abuse. The altered states experienced vary according to the drug being used. All drugs have the potential to create dependence and affect the parts of the brain that activate pleasant feelings or suppress distress. Drugs short circuit normal modes of activating the senses by directly stimulating the brain's pleasure center. Alcohol is noted as producing the states of happiness, sadness, adventurousness, lust, and anger. Sedatives cause deep sleep, tranquilizers relieve anxiety, stimulants provide a feeling of being wide awake, and crack causes a rapid rush followed by a depressed mood and so forth.

Memory Systems

Memory is what allows people to learn and survive; it is tied to many other aspects of psychology. Without memory we would not be able to communicate with each other because we would not remember what words or pictures mean, what we had just said, what we like or dislike, or who we are. However, memory is selective like perception, where we retain some information and lose some. What we remember also makes it possible to embellish or simplify what we report to others.

Memory is linked to thought and emotion and affects what you can think about and thus how you can solve problems and make decisions. According to psychologists, there are three basic types of memory that are named according to the kind of information handled. These include episodic, semantic, and procedural. The memory of a specific event, while present, is called *episodic*. Semantic memory is generalized knowledge of the world not linked to the memory of a specific event. Procedural or skill memory involves how to do things and often consists of a complicated sequence of movements that may not be adequately described in words. Many activities require all three types of memory.

According to psychologists, memory requires three fundamental processes: encoding, storage, and retrieval. Encoding is putting the information into the memory system in ways it can accept and use. Sensory information is encoded through memory codes including: (a) acoustic codes that represent information as sequences of sounds, (b) visceral codes that represent stimuli as pictures, and (c) semantic codes that represent an experience by its general meaning, which is to classify an object and tie it to a time and location. Storage simply means maintaining information over time, with retrieval occurring when you bring the stored information into consciousness.

In order to be retained in the brain, memory requires that it pass through three stages of processing: sensory memory, short-term memory, and long-term memory. Sensory memory is information from the senses, such as sight or sound. It is held in sensory registers for a fraction of a second. The information transmitted to the sensory registers is attended to, analyzed, and encoded as a meaningful pattern called perception. Short-term memory, which is the next stage, processes the memory and encodes it in the long-term memory where it may remain indefinitely. To recognize incoming stimuli, sensory memory must analyze and compare it to what is already stored in long-term memory; although it occurs over a short time, it must be held long enough to connect one impression to the next so that we can experience a smooth flow of information. The eye scans the image through a rapid jumping from one fixation to another, called *saccadic eye movement,* and there is a limit as to how much information a person can glean from a single fixation—with the limit being four or five items. Such a limit is called the *span of apprehension.*

Sensory memory can store an enormous amount of information (i.e., almost everything that we see and hear), but can only store this information for a brief period of time. The capacity for a visual memory in particular is large, but it is also very brief, which represents forgetting in sensory memory. Nevertheless, without visual sensory memory, we would experience a pause in the stream of visual information each time we blink. The transfer of information from sensory to long-term memory is governed by two control processes: pattern recognition and attention. Pattern recognition gives meaning to sensory memory, and attention involves the process of selecting what is passed onto short-term memory.

Short-term memory, or what is sometimes called *working memory,* lasts less than half a minute. For the most part, people live in short-term memory because it provides much of their consciousness. An example of short-term memory is the time between when one looks up a zip code in a directory and when one actually writes down the number. Short-term memory holds information so briefly it is not what people think about when they talk about memory. Mostly what they are thinking about is long-term memory.

Storage in short-term memory or duration is obtained through the repeating of information indefinitely; this is called *maintenance rehearsal*—a process of keeping information in short-term memory by repeating it. Constant rehearsal will maintain sensory memory in short-term memory indefinitely. Retrieval from short-term memory is achieved through scanning, which is a parallel search where all memory is examined simultaneously, or though a serial search, in which information is examined one chunk at a time.

The transfer from short- to long-term memory is governed by a control process called *elaborative rehearsal.* Maintenance rehearsal is the simple repetition of information; elaborative rehearsal involves analyzing the meaning of new information and relating it to information in long-term memory. Research in this suggests that the more we analyze the material for meaning, the better the recall. Some memory transfer also occurs through automatic processing, which is an effortless transfer not under conscious control.

Long-term memory requires the same actions as short-term memory—namely encoding, storage, and retrieval. Some memory is automatically encoded in long-term memory, especially when someone is engaged in tasks that are well practiced. Sometimes, however, encoding requires effort and conscious strategies, such as that required to rehearse lines for a play. Studies of long-term memory suggest that memory retention depends not so much on how the information is presented or how long one is exposed to it, but rather how one thinks about that information in relation to existing knowledge.

Meaning in long-term memory is encoded in two forms: semantic coding or imagery coding. *Semantic coding* is remembering the meaning of words and sentences; *imagery coding* is creating a mental image of an object or scene. Research in this area indicates that both semantic and imagery coding are used in long-term memory. Some experiments even suggest that imagery is a more effective memory system.

As previously noted, memory is an absolute necessity in our efforts to communicate with one another. According to researchers, our ability to remember objects and events is affected by factors such as the frequency of its use and the influence of other kinds of learning. For example, the decay theory suggests that if people do not use information stored in long-term memory, it gradually fades until it is lost. In contrast, interference theory holds that the forgetting of information in long-term memory is also affected by other learning being either retroactive, where new learning interferes with the recall of other information, or proactive, in which old information interferes with learning new information.

Psychological research also suggests that memory is affected by the environment and by the person's state of mind when attempting to recall objects and events. In general, people remember more when their efforts at recall take place in the same environment in which they learned it. A person's internal state or mood can also act as a retrieval cue, with positive incidents being easier to recognize when someone is in a positive mood and negative incidents when they are in a negative mood. The strongest responses come when an individual tries to recall their personally most meaningful episodes. Emotion in memory reflects a match of a person's emotional state at two different times, with positive emotions doing more than negative ones to facilitate memory and more intense emotional experiences producing memories that are the most vivid, detailed, and long lasting.

Memory in what gets encoded, stored, and retrieved is then shaped by factors such as what information is already retained, how people perceive and think about incoming information, or how they construct their memory. According to psychologists, what is stored in long-term memory is represented in the schematic representations of general categories of objects, events, or people. Schemata affect memory because they contain information that provides a basis for making inferences about incoming information; it also affects our ability to recall older information. Thus, human beings use their existing knowledge to organize new information as they receive it and to fill in gaps in the information they encode and retrieve.

Thought and Language

To solve problems, we must have the ability to think and make judgments. These are the higher mental processes needed to weigh the pros and cons of various kinds of actions and how to test and interpret them. Research into these mental processes is necessary if we are to know if our judgments and decisions are good and/or how our thoughts are transformed into actions. In the process of decision making, we perceive a complex pattern of incoming stimuli, evaluate that pattern, and make decisions about it. To understand what happens between the presentation of stimuli and the execution of responses, psychologists study people as if they actually were information-processing systems.

An information-processing system is a mechanism that takes in information, represents that information as symbols, and then manipulates these symbols. This requires a process involving four different stages, with the information being transformed at each stage. At Stage 1, information about the stimulus reaches the sensory receptors in the brain. At Stage 2, the information is perceived and processed. At Stage 3, the stimulus is recognized and some decision needs to be made as to what should be done with it. At Stage 4, an action is taken and a response or feedback occurs.

Language development is considered by many psychologists to be the most important index of higher order memory behaviors. The psychological study of language development, called *psycholinguistics,* traces how children pass from the early crying stages and babbling to the use of spoken words and meaningful sentences. Psycholinguistics involves the study of mental imagery, cognitive development, symbolizations, and speech. Although psychologists are aware that speech and language are related, they also recognize their differences (e.g., speech is the concrete physical act of forming and sequencing, oral language is the system of grammatical rules, and semantics makes speech more meaningful). There are at least three theories of language development including the reinforcement theory of B. F. Skinner, which views language acquisition as operant behavior; the social learning theory, which believes children acquire language by imitating adult speech; and the innate theory of Chomsky (1968).

Chomsky believed in the innate theory that the brain is programmed so that individuals can create and understand language. This system of programming is called the language acquisition device (LAD) and is thought to depend on mature cells in the cerebral cortex of the human brain. As the cortex matures in the child, it helps the child develop and understand words; this allows the brain to perform cognitive operations as sounds received, thus enabling infants to produce grammar and invent new sentences. Chomsky's theory supports language development as a genetic phenomenon that relates to the child's ability to analyze sentences, rather than just how sounds and words combine to form sentences.

The connections between language and thought in the psychology literature are represented in two ways: by psychologists who hold that language is the container of thought and by those who believe that thought takes place independently of language, making words only necessary for conveying one's thoughts to others. Thus, they believe some types of thought are contained in nonverbal visual images and feelings. Piaget thought that structured language presupposes the prior development of other forms of mental representation. He concluded that language plays only a limited role in the young child's mental activity because he or she forms mental images of objects and events based on mental reproduction or intuition, not on words. As such, language is the child's acquisition of words to map language into preexisting concepts. Other researchers support this notion, finding progress in mental representation as necessary for sentence production because children gain the ability to first represent activity as images. For example, mental images of objects are believed to be a conversion of auditory sound naming of the object into an implicit visual dictionary, thus becoming a semantic marker representing the qualities associated with that object. This supports the view that representation precedes language. At least in some respects, children's knowledge may be dependent on a prior mastery of concepts to which words can refer.

Language is also viewed by many psychologists as a determinant of thought, which means a knowledge of language shapes thought. This point of view is supported in the work of Vygotsky (1962). This perspective stresses the part that concepts play in separating stimuli into manageable units relevant to the learner's concerns. This occurs through the mental act of conceptualization, which groups perceptions into categories so the learner can identify and classify informational input. The use of categories allows the individual to (a) tune out or in certain stimuli, (b) view the same object as being the same on a changing stimulus display, and (c) treat two different or similar objects as equivalent. These concepts also allow individuals to go beyond immediate information to mentally manipulate concepts, imaginatively link them, form and use new concepts, and make additional inferences about the unobserved properties of objects and events.

Some social and behavioral scientists also claim that these manipulations can help facilitate thought, expedite memory storage and retrieval, and influence perception. However, critics also contend that language is neither the sole source for internal representation on which thought depends, nor the sole source for the representation of information in memory. Thus, at best, language has only a limited impact on perception.

Thinking in the psychological literature several decades ago mainly supported the behaviorist view that thought was a form of covert speech. In more recent times, experimental psychologists have made a convincing case that thought is more than speech. Thought is now considered to be that part of the information-processing model where cognitive processes transform and manipulate the information that has been encoded and stored in short- and long-term memory. Thus, thinking has more recently been defined as the manipulation of mental representations (schema). What human beings have in mind when they manipulate this information is unknown. Psychologists think that thought depends on the memory capabilities of short-term memory, where it takes attention and effort, and on information in the long-term memory, which it manipulates.

Studies in the language development of children suggest that, in the early years, language depends a good deal on vision. This is because we tend to image and organize our world in distinctly visual ways. This is due, in part, to the use of print media in reading, which disposes us to linear presentations of thought—another visual form of organization. This is especially true when we look at something closely and our eyes make a rapid scan of fixations over an object to construct a view of it. When we see something, it is easy to stop at a detail and explore it more slowly. Visually it is also easier to point out a detail to someone else or talk about it without being confused as to what is being talked about.

Further, when we analyze things visually, we organize things into smaller bits of information and put time aside to concentrate better on space and dimension. An image or picture of something tends not to go away and, in that way, remains both stable and available for further exploration. Thus, visual perception is believed to offer us the opportunity to play with things that remain in a position where we can attend to them not as a memory of something but rather as a thing in itself. Visual perception thus providies us with a perception of the world that is both static and stable.

Auditory perception lacks the moment-by-moment stability of vision. Some aspects of it must be brought to a perceived whole using short-term memory, which is not required in a continued visual experience. This is referred to by psychologists as the problem of perceptual availability. In early efforts to teach children to read, children experience difficulty in holding in mind and analyzing the bits of phonemes in the spoken word. This analysis and identification of parts presents a distinct problem both in kind and difficulty as compared with analyzing a visual experience.

As a result, linguists have good reasons for believing that experience with visual language or print in the early years may facilitate understanding the concept of *word*. This occurs because visual experience is the dominant mode used to talk or think about auditory experience. This suggests that perception is dominated by a visual and tactile world, where the thinglyness of things become evident even in sounds, feelings, and sensations. Thus, the principle of naming reflects our visual experience with things regardless of whether what we name has the character of being a thing.

In addition, language development has the added problem of requiring children to deal with symbols rather than things. Thus, spoken words represent reality in purely conventional ways sometimes unassociated with what they actually refer to. Written symbols then have an ambivalent relationship to their spoken counterparts. They are not only expressed linearly and spatially, but also as either representing spoken words or representing the same meanings as spoken language represents.

Normal visual experience depends on a time-spanning integration strategy that gives a picture of its integrity without our becoming aware of it. In the teaching of language, linguists have adopted visual forms of thinking by approaching language as one might perceive a picture (i.e., using a visual strategy to put many eye fixations together into a meaningful whole to develop a concept). Because children come to their first experience with the printed word already knowing how to speak, their approach to print in early childhood is to try to discover it as a manipulable object using visual strategies or discover how things of print operate. Hence, visual print makes language available. Doing so in a thingly way introduces children to phonetic principles via a visual strategy—thus, to name something is to grasp it. Undoubtedly, this has also influenced linguists to conclude that naming things also makes it possible to store concepts in short- and long-term memory.

Those who study the young child's development in language also recognize other phenomenological relationships between vision and language development. This is due, in part, to the fact that children's written symbols are a symbolic act that involves using a distinct form to refer to a separate experience. Symbolization is generally considered to involve a particular experience, a person constructing a symbol representing that experience, and an intended recipient. What the writer does is guided by intention or what the writer hopes to accomplish in the construction of a symbol.

Different symbol systems, including language, drawing, or symbolic play, are governed by different rules for rendering an experience into a symbol. Written language is what some reading specialists refer to as a second order symbol system making (e.g., the drawing of a house is a first-level system using a series of lines that directly denote a house). Thus, the written word *house* takes on a metalinguistic stance, which is to conceptualize a symbolic language to represent thought. Children use a variety of symbolic systems to convey meaning. Before learning to write, children engage in symbolic play and make drawings where children represent meaning by having the crayon assume the role of an agent in action. Children symbolize objects by eventually representing salient physical features—drawing simple objects that, by age 5 or 6, they can convert to graphic symbols (letters) to represent other symbols such as spoken words.

In this process, children are known to interchange the terms *draw* and *write,* sometimes using the term *write* when to adults the product is a drawing. Children not only use the term *write* both when they draw and write, but they also conceive of writings and pictures as gifts for others. What this suggests is that writing as a symbol system begins as a form of drawing that children talk about and later use as an orthographic representation, where the language surrounding the print takes form on the page.

Concept Development

To think about something involves the manipulation of concepts that are considered to be the categories of objects, events, or ideas with common properties. Concepts can be concrete and visual, such as square or blue, or they can be abstract, such as thought and beauty. To hold a concept about something requires that we recognize the properties or relationships shared by, and thus define, the members of a category. Concepts are vital to thought because we can both find something unique and yet also hold something to be in common with others in a known category. Thus, concepts make logical thought possible.

A concept can also be described as a way to categorize or classify the people, objects, and events in the environment. It is generally thought that concepts cannot be taught. It is even unlikely that fuzzy ones occur through discovering their critical defining features. Instead, it is believed that we identify prototypes that are the best examples of a concept. Prototypes are used to determine whether less obvious stimuli belong to a concept. According to research, so-called *fuzzy concepts* come from a strong intuitive sense about what is prototypical.

At least two kinds of concepts are possible: (a) artificial concepts, which can set by a certain set of rules or properties each member of the concept holds, such as all square forms have four equal sides and four right angles; and (b) natural concepts, which have no defining features but rather share a set of characteristic features such as can be noted in a bird or automobile. A member of a natural concept that possesses all or most of its characteristic features is said to be prototypical.

Thinking also involves relating concepts to one another, which are usually called *propositions*. A *proposition* is defined as the smallest amount of knowledge that can stand as a separate assertion. Propositions are usually presented as a sentence and may be judged to be either true or false. When clusters of propositions are organized to represent an understanding of how things work, they are called *mental models*. Thus, thought has been traditionally linked to propositions, which are in turn linked to language, thus making thought language based.

Furth's (1964) study of the cognitive abilities of deaf children suggests however that there also can be thought without language. As a result of his study of deaf children who communicate only through signing, Furth concluded that lack of language does not reduce thinking ability. His study verified that, at the very least, there can be thought without language. Although we may never know for sure what the precise relationship between thought and language is, psychologists do know that the importance of language in thought varies from person to person. Thinking sometimes requires language and sometimes is based on the manipulation of images.

Reasoning

According to psychologists, how people achieve the goals of thinking depends on how they manipulate the elements of thought. According to this line of thinking, the elements of thought are manipulated to reach a valid conclusion, which is said to be rational thought. Reasoning is the process by which individuals evaluate and generate arguments and reach conclusions. According to traditional thinking, reaching valid conclusions is achieved by rules of logic, where both knowledge of the world and understanding of what is logical provide prescriptions as to how people should think but not necessarily how people *actually* think. Thinking may also be intuitive, based on belief systems or mental heuristics.

Problem Solving

Problem solving in science involves at least four conditions: (a) deciding where you are now (the problem) is not where you want to be (solution), (b) the solution is not obvious,

(c) you need time to understand or diagnose the problem, and (d) to understand the problem you may need to consider several solutions (hypotheses) as to what is the correct solution and then test it. Problem solving involves understanding the problem (diagnosis), devising a solution, executing a plan, and evaluating the results. Four pitfalls in scientific problem solving are: (a) selecting the right hypotheses, (b) avoiding mental sets, (c) desiring to confirm rather than dispute, and (d) failing to note negative evidence.

Problem solving is thought to occur in three stages. First, people try to divide the problem into smaller, manageable segments. Second, they look for a rule or hypothesis that will solve the segment they are considering. Finally, they evaluate their hypothesis. Strategies used in problem solving include the sudden restructuring in perception or the use of algorithms and heuristics. An algorithm is a step-by-step process that considers all possible solutions, whereas heuristics are really rules of thumb or sets of knowledge that have helped solve problems in the past.

Decision Making

Once you diagnose a problem or analyze a situation, it is time to do something about it. Good decision making requires: (a) evaluating options, (b) deciding the questions of utility and value, and (c) avoiding the biases and flaws of decision making.

INTELLIGENCE THEORY

Much of the psychological research on mental abilities involves attempts to measure and predict those abilities through tests. As a result, psychologists believe the research has also helped to spur procedures for determining whether tests give consistent, unbiased results and measure what they are intended to measure. Boring (1923) defined *intelligence* as whatever an intelligence test measures. Other definitions range from the ability to think abstractly to the ability to deal effectively with the environment. More recently, Sternberg (1985) defined the three characteristics of intelligence as: the possession of knowledge, the ability to use information processing and reason about the world, and the ability to employ reasoning adaptively in different environments.

Sternberg's Theory

Since the early 1980s, psychologists have focused on the study of intelligence as information processing, which is to study intelligence as the process of intelligent behavior rather than to study its products as measured by answers to IQ test questions. This approach raises such questions as to what elements in performance depend on past learning and what elements depend on attention, short-term memory, and thought. Along these lines, Sternberg (1988) integrated information-processing research into a new and broader definition of intelligence, which he referred to as a *triarchical theory of intelligence*.

Sternberg believed that to have a complete theory of intelligence, it must address three aspects of intelligence: its internal components, the relation of these components to experience, and its external effects. The internal components consist of three processes used in thinking: performance components, knowledge acquisition components, and metacomponents. Performance components are the processes of perceiving stimuli, holding information in short-term memory, comparing values, retrieving material from long-term memory, and calculating sums and differences. Knowledge-acquisition components are processes used to gain and store new information; metacomponents are the processes that control performance and the knowledge-acquisition components that organize and set up the problem. According to Sternberg, metacomponents also determine the problem-solving strategies, the value of the problem, what performance components to use, what needs to be known, and how to evaluate the solution.

Sternberg's second aspect of intelligence—the relation of the internal components to experience and its external effects—involves the relationship between the internal components and the external world, which is the ability to profit from experience by altering how the components are applied. He sees intelligence as involving both the ability to deal with novelty and make some processes automatic (e.g., when a task is familiar, to carry it out without much conscious thought).

The third aspect of Sternberg's theory of intelligence is the process of adapting to or shaping environments, or selecting new environments. This is a form of adaptive behavior similar to what is thought of as *street smarts,* which suggests that intelligent behavior varies according to context. This makes the kind of knowledge and metacomponents needed to solve a math problem not being the same as needed to solve a visual problem.

Gardner's Intelligences

Sternberg's notion about the kind of intelligence needed to solve problems in different domains is also supported by Gardner's (1983) theory of multiple intelligence, which is based on evidence that many who have only average IQ scores show exceptional ability in one specific area. Gardner studied how people learn and use symbol systems such as those used in math, music, and language, asking whether all these systems require the same abilities and processes or the same level of intelligence.

Gardner believes all people possess a small number of intellectual potentials, or *intelligences,* each involving a set of skills that helps them solve problems. These intelligences are shaped by (a) biological forces, which provide the raw capacities unique to these intelligences; and (b) the culture, which provides the symbolic systems such as is found in language to tease out these capacities. He believes these capacities can both interact and function independently, with some individuals developing certain intelligences more than others. These intelligences include: (a) linguistic intelligence, (b) logical-mathematical intelligence, (c) spatial intelligence, (d) musical intelligence, (e) body-kinesthetic intelligence, and (f) person intelligence. Gardner's concern is that conventional IQ tests sample only the first three of these intelligences primarily because IQ tests predict academic success mostly on the basis of linguistic and logical-mathematical performances, which are the performances most valued in schools.

CREATIVITY

In each ability area identified by Gardner, psychologists also believe there are people who are also highly creative and can produce novel and successful solutions to problems. These have been measured through tests of divergent thinking, which is the ability to choose alternative approaches to problem solving and generate many different solutions to a problem (Guilford & Hoepfner, 1971). Amabile (1989) identified three prerequisites for reactive functioning: (a) expertise in a field, such as a painter who knows art processes and techniques; (b) creative skill, which is the ability to persist at problem solving and use divergent thinking; and (c) motivation, which is the desire to pursue production for intrinsic rather than extrinsic rewards. Studies by others in the field of psychology also suggest that (a) creativity is not simply inherited, (b) creative people are not all odd or strange, (c) they rely more on intuitive thinking, and (d) they also use divergent thinking appropriate to a situation or problem.

EMOTION

Psychologists have attempted to study human emotions through defining what they are, pinpointing the sources of sensory perception, and determining how humans communicate emotions to one another. They believe emotions are a multifaceted phenomenon whose qualities are not easily defined, but are rather reflected in the human feelings of joy, sorrow, anger, fear, anxiety, hate, and lust.

Generally speaking, psychologists view emotions as: transitory states, having valence, passions rather than actions, the result of a cognitive appraisal, projecting bodily response, and varying in intensity. As transitory states, they are viewed as experiences containing mixed and even contradictory signals. Having valence, they are considered feelings that can be either positive or negative and that can be reduced or enhanced, as passions, are emotions, not actions.

Emotions are considered by psychologists as being at least partly cognitive because they arise from a cognitive appraisal of a situation. Emotion from this point of view not only depends on what the situation is, but also on what one thinks about the situation and how one interprets its potential as threatening or rewarding. In general psychology, there is no such thing as an unfelt emotion or vague feelings, but rather it is an effort by a person to interpret their own emotions as they develop. Psychologically speaking, emotion is an experience that is triggered by the thinking self as experienced by and happening to the self. This comes philosophically close to the notion of a Kantian concept of self as both subject and object, being both controller of thoughts and recipient of passions. In summary, psychologists believe emotion to be a valence experience that is felt with some intensity and as happening to the self as a result of a cognitive appraisal of an event accompanied by both learned and reflexive physical responses.

Psychologists have identified at least three major theories of emotion: The James–Lange, the Canon–Bard, and the Schaehter–Singer theory. The James–Lange theory, inspired by psychologist/philosopher William James, holds that reflexive peripheral responses precede the experience of emotion with the consciousness of an emotion arising later. The Canon–Bard theory suggests that the brain sends signals to the autornic nervous system and the cerebral cortex where the emotion becomes conscious—a direct experience of emotion with or without feedback from peripheral responses. The Schaehter–Singer theory agrees with the James theory that the feeling of emotions arises from body feedback, but also accepts that a cognitive appraisal of what caused the emotions is a causal factor. This implies that cognitive interpretation comes into play twice: once when the individual perceives the situation through a body response and second when he or she identifies the feedback from those responses as a specific emotion. Another element of this theory claims that feedback can be labeled. In fact, it is believed that the act of labeling an undifferentiated pattern of physical response constitutes the core of the emotion. This is called *attribution,* which is the process of identifying the cause of an event.

Subsequent studies have both challenged and supported the Schaehter theory. Schaehter's theory, which suggests that if physical responses are reduced the emotion will be reduced, has received mixed reactions in the research. However, other findings are supported, including attributing arousal to an emotion intensifying the emotion and social clues in the environment playing a part in the labeling of emotional arousal.

As to how people express and recognize emotions, psychologists generally agree that movement and body positioning can convey a certain amount of emotional information. In humans, facial movement and expression play a major role in communicating emotions, where other human beings determine someone's emotional state mostly on facial expressions. Generally, although it is believed that such emotional expressions are innate, many other expressions of emotion are neither innate nor universal. For example, as children grow they learn to imitate facial expressions; as they grow older, they become more precise and somewhat more individualized. They also learn as they grow to participate in emotional culture, learning the rules that govern what emotional expressions are appropriately linked to certain circumstances and what emotions are allowed.

SUMMARY

The foregoing review of the psychological literature in general psychology and in human development suggest a number of issues about which these disciplines both agree and disagree. In general, practitioners in all these areas of study agree that the experimental study of human behavior through the scientific method is the most acceptable means for deciding what knowledge is needed to accurately structure effective learning environments. What they disagree about are what the findings of these experiments mean for practice.

Because of the commitment to experimental research, many who work in the psychological sciences remain skeptical of the existence of human behaviors that cannot be experimentally verified—or, if such behaviors exist, how they can be used to reveal any useful knowledge about psychological events. Although there are some notable exceptions to this rule, especially by psychologists who believe mental manipulations of thought in the preconscious or cognitive unconscious level is possible, many do not take such claims seriously enough to alter their general view that that which cannot be measured does exist. Because of this view, higher cognitive abilities are generally thought to be evidenced in language especially as it is applied in inductive and deductive problem solving. For these reasons, intuitive thinking as a means for ordering visual forms remains an area of investigation that is largely ignored in the field of psychology.

With respect to the issues raised in the introduction about higher order and critical thinking skills, the literature reported in this chapter does suggest that there is no one single agreed on process for acquiring knowledge, understanding, and comprehending. Also, problem solving is not always a product of the cold, logical, and conscious analysis of data and/or a rigidly sequential process of manipulating cognitive data through logically controlled systems yielding indisputable facts in the interests of pursuing truth. To the contrary, what is reported here with regard to human mental functions suggests that (a) there is no one way of ordering or analyzing data that can solve all problems, (b) whatever logical system is used is not always cold and unemotional nor devoid of human feeling, and (c) the process of solving problems is not always conscious or deliberate nor always resolved through the use of language.

Unfortunately, what we now know about these mental functions and about how learning takes place does not always guide what we do in schools. If Boring is correct in his claim that intelligence tests are whatever it is they measure and if these tests rule the decisions of school counselors and college admission officers as predictions of academic success in college, then the current view of what constitutes higher order and critical thinking is more influenced by the assumptions we make about academic schooling than by what we really know about how humans think. In fact, human beings do think differently at different levels in their development, intelligent behavior is linked to specific content so that learning in math or language is not the same as learning in other fields, and problem solving requires the ability to deal with novelty, carry out unfamiliar tasks, and reason and apply reason in differing environments.

As noted in the work of Piaget, the thinking of infants is qualitatively different from the thinking of children and the thinking of children is qualitatively different from adolescents. The notion that in cognition one size fits all is challenged by the fact that children progress through a series of distinct stages in the processing of information; as a result, there are gradual quantitative changes in children's mental capacities. Information research suggests children also get better over time in their ability to take in and remember information and that they vary in their pace of cognitive development due to heredity, experience, and the richness of their surroundings and experience.

The notion that higher order thinking is schooling in Bloom's taxonomy, where one first acquires information, second comprehends that information, and then, in rigid progression, applies, analyzes, synthesizes, and evaluates fails to look at concept development, which makes thought possible and is not always either orderly or complete. As noted in this chapter, concepts separate stimuli into relevant manageable units that put perceptions into categories to identify and classify information. Categories permit tuning out some stimuli and permit two things to become one thing. Concepts also permit the learning to go beyond information and to mentally link, form, and use new concepts and make inferences about, as yet, unobserved properties of objects and events.

Without the ability to manipulate concepts, one cannot think about categories of objects, events, and ideas that have common properties and relationships and define membership in categories. It is through the development of concepts that logical thought is possible, yet concepts are not things that can be taught. This further suggests that the teaching of higher order or critical thinking skills, without a context, is pointless. Concepts are not all alike. For example, some are artificial and made evident in the sense that all cubes have four equal sides. Others are natural or prototypical, where categories are about noticing things with common properties.

Logical systems that assume that concepts always involve the manipulation of language have also been questioned. Language is considered by many psychologists as the container of thought and not thought itself, which is independent of language. Types of thought also include nonverbal visual images and, as in the case of young children, representation most often precedes language. Thought is then more than speech, which is the cognitive process that transforms and manipulates information encoded in memory.

The notion that cognition is always rational, logical, and unimpassioned is also questioned by psychologists because emotions are a form of cognitive behavior not always seen in action. Cognition in emotion occurs both when we become conscious of an emotion and when we respond to that emotion. The fact that we can recall things best in the environment where we learn them, that positive events are best remembered when experienced in a positive environment, and that strong emotions are the most vivid, detailed, and long lasting suggest there is thought in emotions. Memory is also linked to thought and emotion and affects what we can think about and how we solve problems. Therefore, few cognitive acts are active in an anaesthetic atmosphere devoid of feeling and emotions.

That cognitive processes are always things we are conscious of and can know in advance of action is also challenged in this chapter. As noted, perception uses knowledge in such a way as to suggest that it seeks right guesses and common features, makes comparisons, and suggests actions that are at times processed by the brain automatically, most especially in the case of the skill functions contained in procedural memory. Interpretation generally depends on what one expects to see and where our brain creates coherency and individuals fill in the blanks. Psychologists note that the eye sharpens images according to visual maps contained in the brain, which help make sense of what we see. Different brain hemispheres also process perceptual data in different ways, with the right hemisphere thinking in symbols and adding color to speech. What all this suggests is that, in addition to the brain's built-up system of mental schema, there is also a system of direct perception where the brain organizes properties into a world of shapes and patterns that begin as early as birth. We do have mental actions that we are not directly conscious of having; when they become apparent in a conscious way, they influence cognition in a brain, where the preconscious is even greater than what we are conscious of.

Chapter 3 explores the ways humans process or transform information about the world as well as cognition, which includes the mental processes of thinking, knowing, perceiving, attending, remembering, problem solving, and decision making.

REFERENCES

Amabile, T. (1989). *Growing up creative.* New York: Random House.

Bernstein, D., Roy, E., Serull, T., & Wickens, C. (1981). *Psychology.* Champaign–Urbana: University of Illinois Press.

Boring, E. G. (1923). Intelligence as the tests test it. *New Republic, 35,* 35–57.

Carington, P. (1986). Meditation as an access to altered states of consciousness. In B. B. Wolman & M. Ullman (Eds.), *Handbook of states of consciousness.* New York: Reinhold.

Chomsky, N. (1968). *Language and mind.* New York: Harcourt Brace Jovanovich.

Furth, H. (1964). Research with the deaf: Implications for language and cognition. *Psychological Bulletin, 62,* 145–164.

Gardner, H. (1983). *Frames of mind: The theory of multiple intelligences.* New York: Basic Books.

Gibson, J. (1979). *The ecological approach to visual perception.* Boston: Houghton Mifflin.

Gombrich, E. H. (1973). *Art and illusion.* Princeton: Princeton University Press.

Guilford, J. P., & Hoepfner, R. (1971). *The analysis of intelligence.* New York: McGraw-Hill.

Kihlstrom, J. F. (1987). The cognitive unconscious. *Science, 237,* 1445–1452.

Kuhn, T. (1982). *The structure of scientific revolutions.* Chicago: University of Chicago Press.

Lindsay, P. H., & Norman, D. A. (1977). *Human information processing* (2nd ed.). New York: Academic Press.

Madeja, S. (Ed.). (1978). Visual arts and the structures of the mind. In J. M. Hockberg (Ed.), *The arts cognition and basic skills* (pp. 151–172). St. Louis: CEMREL.

Perkins, D. N. (1994). *The intelligent eye: Learning to think by looking at art.* Santa Monica, CA: The Getty Center for Education in the Arts.

Piaget, J. (1952). *The origins of intelligence in children.* New York: International Universities Press.

Rock, I. (1983). *The logic of perception.* Cambridge, MA: MIT Press.

Shapiro, D. H., & Gilber, D. (1978). Meditation and psychotherapeutic effects: Self regulation strategy and altered states of consciousness. *Archives of General Psychiatry, 35,* 294–302.

Sperry, R. W. (1982). Some effects of disconnecting the cerebral hemispheres. *Science, 217,* 1223–1226.

Sternberg, R. J. (1985). *Beyond I.Q.: A triarchic theory of human intelligence.* Cambridge, England: Cambridge University Press.

Sternberg, R. J. (1988). *The triarchic mind.* New York: Cambridge University Press.

Vygotsky, L. S. (1962). *Thought and language.* Cambridge, MA: MIT Press.

KEY TERMS

Schemata	Surrogate
Lateral inhibition	Illusions
Perception	Consciousness
Figure ground	Semantic codes
Grouping	Elaborative rehearsal
Gestalt	

STUDY QUESTIONS

1. What is the difference between seeing something and perceiving it? Describe the steps the sensory system goes through to modify the information received to perceive something.

2. Distinguish between the two main theories of how we perceive the world: the constructionist position and the ecological approach. Which theory comes closest to your own personal approach to seeing something and drawing it?

3. Compare and contrast the two most prominent types of mental processing mechanisms: the top–down and bottom–up model. Which system seems to make the most sense to you as an artist and why do you think that using both mechanisms is a good or bad idea?

4. What is a perceptual illusion and what is its significance in visual forming? What does it tell us about how we perceive things and how we should think about them as being either true or false as a form of visual intelligence?

5. What is consciousness and how does human consciousness differ from non-human animal behavior? What acts of perception are made possible by consciousness?

6. What are the three kinds of memory systems? How do they interrelate and how do they function? What kinds of memory codes are there and how do they represent stimuli, experience, and sounds?

7. Explain the two conceptions of language: one as the container of thought and the second as shaping thought. What is the function of language in visual learning according to these theories and what are the implications for teaching art?

8. How does Sternberg define *intelligence?* Explain his triarchial theory and compare his theory with that of Gardner. Which theory, in your view, comes closest to supporting the notion that there is such a thing as visual intelligence?

3

Cognition and Learning

PHILOSOPHICAL INFLUENCES
    Rationalism
    Empiricism
    Neo Idealism

PSYCHOLOGICAL INFLUENCES
    Behaviorism
    Gestalt Theory
    Child Development
    Psycholinguistics
    Anthropology
    Neuroscience
    Artificial Intelligence

LEARNING AND COGNITIVE STYLE
    Impulsive/Reflective Theory
    Independent/Dependent Theory
    The Pascual–Leone Model

SUMMARY

To provide the reader with a basic understanding of the psychological sciences' contributions to art learning, the previous chapter identified the various perspectives in the field of psychology and the contributions made to the body of knowledge in general psychology and human development. The discussion centered on the experimental findings in the areas of perception, consciousness, memory, thought, language, problem solving, intelligence, creativity, and emotion. Reported were the differing conclusions of experimenters from the various perspectives as characterized by the so-called *top–down* models, which emphasizes logical solutions using visual/mental schema, and by bottom–up systems, which are based on holistic and direct perceptions emphasizing innovation and creativity.

This chapter focuses on how humans transform information about the world as revealed by various philosophical, historical, and subdisciplinary influences in the cognitive science disciplines today. Included are the influences of the behaviorists, Gestaltists, developmentalists, psycholinguists, anthropologists, neuropsychologists, and cognitive stylists. Also discussed are several of the competing top–down and bottom–up interpretations, which exist both within and between the various perspectives representing the cognitive sciences today.

How cognitive scientists view the mental processes of thinking, knowing, perceiving, attending, remembering, problem solving, and decision making depends mostly on how they learned their trade. This includes whether they were educated to think behavioristically or in Gestalt terms or whether their teachers and the authors of the textbooks they studied in school were developmentalists, psycholinguists, neuropsychologists, or cognitive stylists. To understand what the field has discovered about such matters requires that we first understand how the cognitive sciences evolved and how they are structured, including (a) what philosophical assumptions about mind and body funded their research; (b) what behaviorist, Gestaltist, psycholinguist, or developmentalist bias influenced the results of their experiments; and (c) which of the various perspectives of neuroscience, artificial intelligence, or anthropology gave direction to their investigations.

PHILOSOPHICAL INFLUENCES

Any discipline seeking to address the key issues of mental life (i.e., thinking, problem solving, the nature of consciousness, language, and culture) must, of necessity, begin with a concept of mind capable of such thought. Psychology, like any other discipline, finds the basis for its methods in philosophy and, in particular, the philosophical assumptions that undergird its ontological and epistemological premises. The pursuit of knowledge and hopefully truth itself is shaped by the assumptions used to decide such matters as the nature of man, the mind–body relationship, the nature of knowledge, and systems for reasoning. All the various psychological perspectives depend on and are driven by these fundamental assumptions, but none is more dependent on the epistemological premise than the cognitive sciences, which, without a concept of mind, would literally have nothing to investigate. The cognitive sciences, which are said to have begun only in the late 1940s, were first organized to investigate how the nervous system controls behavior. It later adopted other areas of study, including feedback mechanisms in biological and social systems; problems in perception; and issues of observation, linguistics, artificial intelligence, and other areas of inquiry, which in time came to be considered the cognitive sciences of the mind.

Thought in science, like thought in any discipline, is shaped by the frames of mind used to study the nature of reality and knowledge. Like in art, the frameworks used to decide such matters depend on the philosophical systems that determine the methods a particular discipline uses to determine what it values, what is the logical character of its being, and how it decides what is true or false. Psychology, like other disciplines, also has been influenced by rationalist, empiricist, and Kantian philosophical thought.

Rationalism

Rationalism, specifically, the ideas of Rene Descartes (1596–1650), is considered by some cognitive psychologists as the prototypical philosophical antecedent of cognitive science. In particular, Descartes' concept of his own mind laid the conceptual groundwork for a cognitive science, where the mind stands apart from and operates independently of the human body rejecting, as it were, the behaviorist notion of a rational mind and a mechanical body. Descartes became, in effect, a physiologically oriented psychologist because he devised models of how mental states could exist in a world of sensory experience (Gardner, 1987). It is said that Descartes proposed a vivid and controversial image of the mind as a rational instrument, which even today cannot be simulated by any machine.

Descartes established four rules of method that he presented as valid for study of all the sciences, believing that objects were unimportant; what *was* important was the inquiring mind, which was everywhere the same. His first rule was intuition, which is the pure use of the mind as opposed to sense experience or imagination. The second rule, the rule of analysis, organizes complex problems into more simple ones. The third rule, the rule of synthesis, is reached by the first two rules. The fourth rule takes into account that deduction, unlike intuition, depends on memory. Deduction is thus given the character of intuition through the linking of first principles with their consequences.

Descartes, unlike Aristotle, rejected the validity of evidence provided by the senses making the only clear idea we can hold of objects being that they are extended in height, depth, and breadth, which is to say the idea of them can be expressed mathematically. Descartes reversed Aristotle's notion of thought; he moved from complex reality to unifying principles, proposing rather to go in the opposite direction from idea to the thing itself.

Descartes' method was to reject as false everything he could doubt in order to see if anything remained. He then used the arguments of the skeptics (i.e., criticism of the senses and criticism of reason) to conclude the skeptics were right in asserting that the mind is incapable of reaching any certainty. He then introduced this proposition: "I think therefore I am" (*Cogito ergo sum*), thus cutting out the ground from beneath the feet of skepticism by claiming that even doubting is thinking and therefore linked to existence.

For Descartes, the Cogito offered a clear conception of the fact that he exists. He believed that whatever else he perceives is equally true and he knows himself as a thinking being. Because he could then state that he knows himself independent of an outside world, mind is distinct and superior to matter. Along the same lines, Descartes argued that to know is a greater perfection than to doubt, which makes him as a doubter imperfect and allows him to create a conception of a perfect being as God. Throughout a succession of arguments, Descartes also created the conditions in which man is able to foresee and, in this way, help modern scientific experiment to become a possibility and the laws that govern the physical world to be discovered and used by man for his own ends.

Empiricism

Cognitive psychologists also recognize the importance of the empiricist philosophical arguments of John Locke (1632–1704), George Berkeley (1685–1753), and David Hume (1711–1776). Locke contributed by questioning whether one could accept knowledge introspectively, claiming sensory experience to be the only source of knowledge. Locke's epistemology, although poles apart from Descartes', made it possible for cognitive scientists to think of an organism as being capable of abstraction and generalization. Berkeley contributed through his faith in the primacy of the experiencing self and the perceiving mind, which made it possible to experience sensations and conceive of an idea. Hume's skepticism was also important because it challenged the idea of causality between one event influencing another, claiming that the most one can assume is that nature will perform in the future as it has in the past.

Neo-Idealism

Even the idealism of Kant played a part in shaping the thoughts of the cognitivists primarily because he said the mind is an active organ of understanding that shapes and organizes sensations and ideas, changing the disordered character of multiple experiences into ordered and unified thought. As the reader discovers later from the varied experimental results of the cognitive scientists, all three philosophical positions are evident especially in the way cognitivists interpret the results of their experiments. Although this may not be proof that the cognitive sciences are in fact only an eclectic philosophy, it may indicate that as a youthful science, it at least remains open to more than one perspective of science and presently is open to a variety of ways to interpret its experiments' findings. Gardner's (1987) analysis of philosophy's influence on cognitive psychology in *The Mind's New Science,* although perhaps more reflective of his own bias toward multiple intelligences, is particularly helpful to anyone interested in understanding the philosophical frames of mind that influence the interpretations of various cognitive scientists.

Most cognitive scientists, including Gardner, are generally accepting of Kant's Cartesian side, where the existence of self is a priori and something that does not need to be experientially verified because it exists in the mind. However, they are skeptical of Kant's scientific side, which also accepts what psychologists call the *top–down model,* with schemata as an a priori to mediate between raw sensory data, and which introduces imagination into interpretive experience. Because schemata are partly rules, and therefore linked to pure (Cartesian) understandings, and partly images, which are linked to empirical understandings, the cognitive scientists' criticism of Kant is that its duality mitigates against their being a science of psychology because the Kantian mind is ultimately affected by study of itself. The spatiality event is lacking for the conduct of experiments and there is no mathematical basis that is necessary for an investigation to become scientific.

The troublesome part of Kantian logic for them is not so much with Kant's duality (i.e., in being accepting of mind as a priori or that an external world shapes the mind), but rather with Kant's notion of self, which is both a subject that has unity through awareness of its own existence and as an object in the process of discovery. Thus, the individual in Kant's view becomes a self as a subject, which presupposes itself as an object. This provides a conception of self that is both aware of what it is and what it is becoming, which is at the same time both the subject and object. What makes the concept difficult experimentally is that objects and events in the external world are not then separated from the self, which undergoes them in experience. Although the paradox of self being both subject and object worked well for a philosopher like Dewey, who defined art (the object) as experience (self in experience), when examined experimentally, it has to examine a given event or object as existing internally rather than being something that can exist externally and therefore verified as separate from self. Psychological experiments in which subjects change into events are not stable; they place the results more in the mind of the one who is experimented on, also yielding results that are highly unlikely to be replicable in other human experiments or that can lead to predictions regarding future human cognitive behaviors.

The contributions of Locke, Berkeley, and Hume influenced the development of cognitive science from two viewpoints: analytical and linguistic. The analytical is an approach to science along the ideas of Descartes and Kant; the linguistic is along the ideas advanced by philosopher David Hume. The analytic school can be represented in the ideas of George Edward Moore (1873–1958) and Alfred North Whitehead (1861–1947), where cognitive knowledge is linked to the individual's perception of events. The linguistic school is represented by the ideas of Gottlob Frege (1848–1925), Rudolph Carnap (1891–1970), and Ludwig Wittgenstein (1899–1951), who supported Hume's view that matters of fact are derived from experience and are ideas expressed as factual propositions.

George Edward Moore, an important British empiricist, outlined his analytical approach in his *Principia Ethica* (1903), published by Cambridge University. Moore's analytical methods included four important steps: (a) establish clear concepts, (b) use unambiguous terms and definitions, (c) find discernible elements as descriptions, and (d) arrive at appropriate conclusions. For Moore, evidence exists in two forms: truth with regard to the action in question and causal ethical truth.

In *An Enquiry Concerning the Principles of Natural Knowledge,* Whitehead (1982) examined the problem of how space was rooted in human experience. His concern was not only to address the object as perceptual knowledge, but also the synthesis of what he called the *knower* and the *known.* Whitehead suggested that objects are known only through a full knowledge of their parts as situations of objects and the parts by a full knowledge of the whole. More important, he viewed human perception as relative and requiring verifiable interpretation. Whitehead and Cambridge colleague Bertrand Russell, both mathematically oriented logicians, sought to derive all of mathematics from the laws of logic. This led to much closer connections among empirical science, logic, and mathematics.

Russell and Whitehead's blend of scientific philosophy, which in some circles was found seriously deficient, also inspired the linguist influence argued by Wittgenstein, Carnap, and Frege, who in effect created a new metascience or science of science criticism. Carnap tried to pull together concepts in language, truth, and logic to translate into the language of sensory data, all sentences pertaining to the world. Wittgenstein attempted to demonstrate the logical structure implicit in language of sensory data all sentences pertaining to the world. He also attempted to demonstrate the logical structure implicit in language to provide a picture of the structure of facts, where the propositions of language become the perceptual expression of thoughts as logical pictures of facts. Both views are an outgrowth of Frege's philosophy of mathematical logic.

Frege's investigations led him to propose a philosophy of language based on mathematics, which he argued on three fundamental theses: (a) the mental images that a word arouses in the mind are irrelevant to its meaning, (b) only in the context of a sentence does a word have meaning, and (c) only proper names can be used to talk about an object. Wittgenstein went even further, noting that understanding a sentence can be compared to understanding a picture. When one sees a picture first one way and then another, it is comparable to the experience of first reading a sentence with and then without understanding. Carnap extended Wittgenstein's argument that mathematics was simply a system of logic by claiming that much of traditional metaphysics and ethical discourse is meaningless and that philosophy is really the logical analysis of science—an analysis whose function is to look at all knowledge, all assertions of science, and of everyday life to make clear the assertions and connections between them.

PSYCHOLOGICAL INFLUENCES

The historical development of modern cognitive sciences has occurred over the past 60 years, unlike the older field of psychology, which dates back to the work of experimental scientist Wilhelm Wundt in the late 1880s. Its history is linked to an effort to overcome the experimentalist model and be characterized by its efforts to assimilate a variety of disparate points of view including the various branches of psychology. As a result, the historical discussion that follows is not so much a history of cognitive science development, but rather a documentation of the several psychological perspectives that have shaped the field up to today. This provides a basis for understanding the catholicity of its findings, some of which show agreement and others of which do not.

Three conditions have played an important part in the historical shaping of the cognitive sciences in the last half of the 20th century: (a) the behaviorist paradigm, (b) the competing influences of the various psychological perspectives from both outside and inside the domain of cognitive sciences, and (c) the influences of the computer in shaping new discoveries. In the main, two philosophical perspectives dominate both the problems studied and the results of research. These include the Cartesian (top–down) model and the Gestalt (bottom–up) model. For reasons already identified, the neo-Kantian model does not seem to be a major influence. The top–down model, indicative of Bruner's work, was mainly supported by the science of the unambiguous computer, which assumed human beings to be rational and logical problem solvers, abstracting knowledge from everyday experience and employing Aristotelien laws of logic. The bottom–up model supports a basic structure built around a prototype such as imagery, definition, reasoning by analogy, and use of metaphors. This is reflected in the concepts of Gibson, where there is a dependency on the perceptual structure of the perceiver, the kind of activities one can engage in, and the physical structure of the environment. Thus, the Gestalt model depends on the brain to become invoked to understand what is happening using unconscious processes or ones that the individual receiving the input is unaware. In contrast, the Cartesian model suggests individuals adopt problem-solving and classifying behaviors that are carried out with some flexibility, explicitness, and awareness. In this model, for example, someone creating an image or transforming it conceivably could also be aware of creating a mental image that influences the resulting behavior.

Behaviorism

Wilhelm Wundt, an experimentalist, is credited with the establishment of psychology as a separate experimental discipline in the late 19th century. Wundt believed that psychology was the study of conscious experience that must be approached through internal observation of behavior and introspection. He recognized that, although individuals have such experiences, they are not reliable witnesses of that experience. Therefore, he advocated the method of introspection, where individuals describe the sensations felt and report them without reference to their meaning and context. Wundt also believed some human experiences could not be examined. He suggested that experiences subjected to introspection are social and communal and therefore ones for ethnic and folk psychologists to study. He also believed experience was composed of raw sensory content devoid of meaning and that all conscious thoughts were combinations of sensations and could be analyzed in terms of their quality, mode, duration, and intensity. Some have described Wundt's psychology as a form of mental chemistry focused on the pure elements of thought—an idea Wundt tried to promote for more than 50 years in the laboratories, handbooks, journals, and conferences of the field.

The actual founder of the behavioral approach to psychology was John B. Watson (1878–1958), who believed that patterns of reward and punishment form the basis for all human behavior. Watson urged psychologists to study only what they could observe directly so that psychologists could then begin to understand behavior, regardless of whether it occurs in adults, children, the mentally ill, or animals.

A key assumption of behavioral psychology is this: If psychology is to be a science, it must study observable behavior, leaving consciousness and other nonobservable phenomena to philosophers. This perspective also has its roots in the research of Ivan Pavlov (1849–1936). Pavlov's experiments with salivating dogs led to his identifying the phenomenon of conditioned reflex. Beginning in 1900, Pavlov studied conditioned reflexes. He continued to do so for the rest of his professional career, holding that he was investigating the structure and physiology of the brain by using these responses as a tool.

Another contribution to the behavioral perspective is found in the work of Edward Thorndike (1874–1949), a student of William James. In his study of cats, Thorndike found that when certain behaviors were rewarded with food the cats were more likely to repeat them later. Based on these experiments, he proposed the law of effect, which holds that when a behavior is followed by satisfaction it is stamped in and when not followed is stamped out. Thorndike's work dominated debate in the field of learning for at least the first half of the 20th century.

Watson felt that both of Pavlov's studies of conditioned reflex and Thorndike's studies of learning in cats by carefully controlling environmental stimuli had shown how behavior could be modified in predictable ways. As a result, behavioral psychologists conducted numerous studies on conditioning and learning. Some developed elaborate theories of learning, whereas others applied behavioral methods to problems in education, child development, social psychology, and mental illness.

Harvard psychologist B. F. Skinner was also a major contributor to the behavioral approach because of his belief, like Pavlov and Thorndike, that most behaviors and ways of thinking depend on the pattern of rewards and punishments that each person experiences. Thus, biological factors became the raw material on which rewards, punishments, and other experience mold each individual.

Today few behaviorists endorse Watson's original behavioral approach and now many include thoughts, beliefs, and other cognitive activity as being worthy of theoretical inquiry. However, they do suggest that most problematic behaviors can be changed by helping people unlearn old habits and develop new ones.

Gestalt Theory

In the 19th century, German physicist and physiologist Hermann von Helmholtz was one of several important figures who helped identify the importance of empirical investigations and laid the groundwork for the Gestalt approach to psychology. Helmholtz studied the transmission of nerve impulses, which led to the idea of an unconscious interference; this idea suggested that individuals draw on past knowledge to effect accurate interpretations. He believed that past perceptions were used to react to a stimulus, thus suggesting that the visual system made inferences based on an individual's retinal images.

Max Wertheimer is credited with actually introducing the concept of a Gestalt psychology in 1912, which began with his studies on motion. He found that perception of movement is not the sum or an association of different sensations, but is rather apprehended directly. The Gestaltists studied a number of qualities that could be explained in terms of analogous brain processes, including the laws of proximity, symmetry, and figure ground identified in chapter 1. According to Gestalt psychology, even the most primitive forms of learning can be explained in terms of mere repetition or piecemeal associations. The Gestaltists proposed a strategic approach to problem solving: (a) recognition of structural characteristics, (b) how structures are realized, (c) how gaps are sensed, and (d) what can be fitted to one another or rearranged to change an unclear relation into a clear, direct confrontation. Gestaltists believed that the best thinking was productive and a producer of novel rather than reproductive results.

No discussion of the Gestalt influence would be complete without mention being given to one of its greatest contributors, J. J. Gibson. Gibson believed that humans and the world in which they live is so constituted that they can readily gain the information they need to survive and prosper. He believed that the information available in the world needs only to be sensed, with no need to operate on it or process it nor to draw on prior mental models or visual schemata. Believing that the world is perceived directly, Gibson challenged past efforts of cognitive scientists to discuss and analyze the visual process in detail. He questioned how the human organism can obtain constant perceptions in everyday life despite continually changing sensations. His answer was that the problem of perception is one of recovering from sensory information as valid properties of the external environment. His analysis, called the *notion of affordances,* is that individuals throw things that are grabbable, devour things that are edible, and cuddle things that are lovable. Gibson further believed that the concept of affordances permitted the analysis of an organism's effectiveness within an environment without the need to invoke beliefs, attitudes, or mental effort. To him, objects are meaningful because they afford things that we can do with them or react to them.

Rudolph Arnheim also views Gestalt theory as being a theory of expression, where there is a direct correspondence between physical and psychical behavior and where expressive behavior reveals its meaning directly in perception (Arnheim, 1966). This approach is based on the principle of *isomorphism,* according to which processes that take place in different media may nevertheless be similar in their structural organization. Applied to body and mind, this means that if the forces that determine bodily behavior are structurally similar to certain corresponding mental states, psychical meaning can be read directly from a person's appearance and conduct.

Arnheim viewed the Gestalt experiments as suggesting that retinal stimulations are subjected to organizational processes in the brain. This means that the elements of visual patterns are grouped as an organized whole, in which some predominant structural features determine the overall shape and direction of the main axis, while others have subordinate functions. Further, perception appears as the means by which the organism obtains information about the friendly or hostile forces in the environment that it must react to. That reaction has what Arnheim called *physionomic qualities,* which are directly perceived and make expression the primary content of perception.

In a Gestalt theory of expression, past experience has little to do with perceptive expression and does not interfere with it except to modify its interpretation. The temporal context mostly influences the way a phenomenon is perceived, making an object appear larger or smaller based on whether it is seen spatially in the presence of smaller and larger objects. This is not proof of the lack of connection between perceptual patterns and the expression they convey, but rather that experiences must not be evaluated in isolation from their spatial and temporal whole context.

Child Development

Jean Piaget (1896–1980) had a key impact on the cognitive sciences through his developmental concerns. Although some of his ideas were already introduced and are examined in even greater detail later, his 60-year career requires that we give additional attention to his influence on the cognitive sciences. Piaget studied the nature of time, space, causality, number, and morality as categories to be constructed over the course of a child's development. His principle contribution to psychology was to identify the structure of thought used by children of different ages or stages of development and the mechanisms that enable a child to reach higher stages of development (i.e., his sensorimotor, preoperational, concrete operational, and formal operational stages). Piaget is credited with being the inventor of several important investigative paradigms, including studies on infant object location, objects from neutral perspectives, and liquids in vessels of different shapes.

Piaget is regarded as the leading authority in the field of cognitive developmental theory. He characterized himself as a genetic epistemologist who studied children. For him, the term *cognition* was synonymous with an intelligence derived from a biological process.

He believed intellectual development proceeds in an orderly sequence that is characterized by specific growth stages in a building process.

According to Piaget, the design for mental growth was based on the principles of organization and adaption. Organization is the ability to order and classify in the mind new experiences called *schemata*. Sensory stimuli in objects and events are just two examples of schematic organization, which he believed constituted the beginning of intellectual activity. Adaption, his second principle, cannot take place unless there is a schema. To be successful, adaption must give the individual a meaningful understanding of the surrounding environment, which depends on the mental processes Piaget labeled as *assimilation* and *accommodation*. In his view, the development of thinking relies on changes made in the mental structure of the child, which occurs when there is a balance between assimilation and accommodation, called *equilibration*, which is the ability to change old ways of thinking to solve new problems.

Psychologists generally credit Piaget with drawing attention to children's intellectual development. However, some also feel his stages imply longer periods of stability and abrupt change, which does not necessarily agree with other developmental findings that support that human cognitive development, has too many varied mechanisms, routes, and rates to be subsumed in an inflexible stage theory. Some also feel that Piaget underestimated the cognitive abilities of young children, which depend more on what kind of task is being performed. Despite such criticisms, developmental psychologists seem strongly committed to Piaget's stages of development.

Piaget's theory has also been criticized for being too self-evident, too factual, and too purely empirical in a search for a safe ground. He is also praised for unearthing new facts that he subjected to painstaking analysis and classification that opened new vistas and added to previous knowledge. His clinical method was considered to be an invaluable tool for studying the complex, structural whole of the child's thought in its evolutional transformation.

Doing more than just contributing to our knowledge of child development, Piaget also helped identify certain developmental levels of thought in a nonhierarchic way. This is apparent in his analysis of what he called children's directed, autistic, and syncretic thought. *Directed thought* is classified as conscious thought that is intelligent, adapted to reality, and communicated through language. *Autistic thought* is subconscious and pursues problems that are not present in consciousness; it is about satisfying individual desires and is incommunicable as such through language (Piaget, 1959). *Syncretism*, he concluded, is intermediate between logical thinking and the symbolisms used in dreams.

According to Piaget, directed thought is social and influenced by experience and logic. Autistic thought is individual and obeys a set of its own special laws. Between these two forms of thought are the thoughts of children, which seek to adapt to reality, but do not communicate what Piaget called *egocentric thought*. Piaget believed that egocentrism stands between autism and the logic of reason, both chronologically and functionally, noting that a child's thought is originally autistic and becomes realistic only under social pressure. According to Piaget, autistic thought, which is communicated through images, employs symbols, and involves feeling, does not devalue the intelligence of the child because logical activity is not all there is to intelligence. Therefore, imagination is important for finding solutions to problems but does not involve verification or proof. Developmentally, Piaget viewed autism as the original earliest form of thought. Logical thought appears relatively late, with egocentric thought becoming the genetic link between them.

Piaget's stages of autistic and logical thought development have also been challenged by some cognitive scientists; some have come to doubt that the autistic function is really primitive and is of a higher order than the simplest forms of the reality function. It has been noted that only lower animals function with a total reality function, and no human being would have an autistic function alone. Therefore, some researchers suggest that, at some point in the development of human intelligence, the two forms of thought come together to form the autistic and reality function, which then evolve together over time.

Current thinking about the autistic and reality functions suggests that, as thinking becomes more complex and differentiated, it becomes better adjusted to external reality and less dependent on effects. However, past emotional events become more influential and multiple possibilities occur in the merger of these thought processes. Some researchers have also challenged Piaget's idea that autistic or egocentric thinking is actually divorced from reality and that there may actually be different kinds of autistic thinking, including one where an alert human being using some variant of autistic thinking does also forge strong connections with reality and firmly established concepts. However, the concept that Piaget developed about egocentric speech remains the cornerstone of his theory of language.

Today, developmental psychologists are directing more attention toward the study of what is called *inner mental activity*. They are finding, for instance, that mental schemes sometimes called *scripts* or *frames* that function selectively do influence what information people attend to, how they structure it, how much importance they attach to it, and what they do with it. Psychologists are also finding that learning involves something more than connecting two events because humans do not simply act on external events, but rather evaluate them individually and determine their reactions accordingly. Such notions signal the abandonment of classic behavioral theory and direct reinforcement for more social models, where learners can avoid tedious trial and error by watching other people solve problems through observational learning, social learning, and modeling.

Cognitive learning theorists today are also looking at the use of symbols in language and imagery to represent events, analyze conscious experience, communicate with others, and plan, create, imagine, and engage in foresightful action. Symbols are viewed as the foundations of reflective thought enabling individuals to solve problems without having to enact all possible solutions. It is believed that external stimuli and reinforcement have little impact on us unless we first develop mental representations and engage in self-regulatory processes.

Researchers have found that infants possess a set of search skills that are more sophisticated than what Piaget observed. Errors that children make in searching are not caused by a lack of basic concepts of objects and space, but can be attributed more to the lack of coordination of movement—as even a child of 5 months may know an object exists when its view is blocked. Also challenged is Piaget's view of infants' lack of object permanence, attributing the failure to represent objects out of sight as being more a case of children's perceptions of objects in three-dimensional space when they do not realize that two objects can be in the same place if one is put on top of the other.

Psycholinguistics

The field of psycholinguistics has also held an extremely important position in the shaping of the cognitive sciences, both as a means for language development and supporting more holistic or Gestalt views of direct perception. The philosophical grounding of the psycholinguistic approach in cognitive science can be found in the writings of empiricist Thomas Hobbes (1586–1679), who claimed that words acquire meanings through representing thoughts. Historians of philosophy generally believe that empiricism began to be taken seriously only after it began to align itself with Hobbes' comprehensive theory of language. With a philosophical concept of language, it was then possible to determine what can and cannot be said. This challenged the Cartesians in what was believed to be their weakest spot. Hobbes sought a theory that could tell how words acquired meaning to demonstrate that certain metaphilosophical doctrines are, in effect, meaningless.

Hobbes is said to have provided a genetic account of the origin of meaning, where words have meaning through representing thoughts and where the origins of thought are believed to be in sense experience. He believed that the meaning of any statement to be discovered must be traced back to the observable conditions that inspire it, thus revealing the thought contained in the sentence. He further argued that sensory knowledge gives us a knowledge of particulars, where words (names) express other thoughts with reference to particulars.

John Locke (1632–1704), influenced by Hobbes, also advanced that words acquire meaning through representing thoughts and that all communication depends on the common significance of words. Locke is credited with developing a theory of ideas where words acquire meaning by standing for ideas and where ideas only enter the mind through experience. Locke's most important contribution to the cognitive sciences and to the field of psycholinguistics was his theory that all communication depends on the common significance of words, which refer to the experience being explained.

In the 20th century, the growth of psycholinguistic thought was encouraged by the logical positivists, most especially through the writings of Russell, Moore, Whitehead, Frege, Carnap, and Wittgenstein. The logical positivists viewed mathematics as a logical system that could contribute to the advancement of psycholinguistic thought. In particular, Carnap furthered the connections between language and thought by claiming that most traditional metaphysics and ethical discourse is meaningless and that philosophy is really the logical analysis of science and all knowledge and assertions of science in relation to everyday life. His method of verification was directed either to perception or indirectly through propositions reduced from original assertions. Any assertion that could not be deduced from other verified propositions would therefore be no assertion at all. In addition to his language as picture theory already described, Wittgenstein also believed that, for language to achieve status as a propositional truth, it must be both an accurate description and understood in the context within which the description is used.

The linguist who has contributed most to bringing psycholinguistics into the cognitive sciences is Noam Chomsky (1967). In his early work, Chomsky was able to draw attention to certain properties of sentences that all speakers and hearers know intuitively. He also went beyond his predecessors to set out rules that allow a writer to generate all correct sentences, know that they are correct and what they mean, and decide what sentences violate rules and, while ungrammatical, are not necessarily devoid of meaning.

Chomsky's linguistic goals went beyond the data of language, insisting that principles would never emerge from a study of language alone, but that one must first figure out the kind of language system being used and state one's conclusions in terms of a formal system. He believed this would result in the development of a set of rules that can account for any sentence and at the same time not generate an incorrect or ungrammatical sentence. In setting up this system, Chomsky's goals were founded on two important assumptions: (a) that the syntax of language could be examined independently, and (b) that the discipline of linguistics could proceed independently of the cognitive sciences, which meant that linguistics would be tied to other areas of human cognition.

Chomsky's ideas with regard to his theory of syntactic structures were considered by some to be the first serious attempt by a linguist to construct a theory of language—one that linguists could understand as a chemical or biological theory is understood by scientists in those fields. In doing so, Chomsky showed how linguists should work and what cognitive science was about. He clarified that he was interested in language in a particular sense, not as a general means of communication or a blanket word used in all symbol systems. He was interested in its capacity to structure verbal symbols to create an infinite number of grammatically acceptable sentences, where verbal symbols are manipulated without reference to their meanings or sounds. Therefore, he considered language as an abstraction that can merely be seen as an impure form in an individual's utterances.

Unlike the logical positivist linguists, Chomsky believed that our interpretations of the environment are based on representational systems in the mind that do not reflect the external world. He also questioned the necessity of experiments to confirm every conclusion. He thought that there were a number of integrative processes involved in syntactic structure and argued for the need to look more to intuitive thought (e.g., that youngsters are born with a strong desire to learn language and, despite the lack of language in their environment, are still able to learn it rather rapidly and relatively error free). Therefore, Chomsky was committed to the existence of abstract mental structures in the mind and to the belief that much knowledge is universal and inborn.

Ferdinand De Saussure, a modern linguist, also added some additional thoughts to Chomsky's theories of language and mental activity. He contributed to the Gestaltists who were also interested in establishing the interrelationships of visual perceptual elements. He was interested in the investigation of language in contemporary life through synchronic linguistics, which is the study of language at the single moment in time. For Saussure, language resembled a chess game, where the size and shape of the pieces were irrelevant and where any piece could stand for a bishop as any sound could stand for the concept of any object. This inferred that no entity by itself had meaning because meaning occurs only in the relationships held with all other elements in the environment.

Saussure viewed language as a mental cognitive system. Unlike many of today's linguists, he thought much knowledge is universal and inborn. Saussure also believed the elements of language were built up from the simplest to the most complex elements. Today scholars believe it is wrong to consider the subject matter of any discipline (e.g., language as the subject matter of linguistics) without connecting it to the range of related fields that can be investigated. From Chomsky's viewpoint, language does not belong to a discipline, but is instead a part of cognitive science—or, as he thought, a language through which distinct cognitive structures can be identified.

A language approach, which led to a different set of conclusions, is found in the work of Harvard psychologist Jerome Bruner, who is credited with the start of the so-called *disciplinary approach* to school studies in the 1960s. The book, developed by Bruner and his colleagues Jacqueline Goodnow and George Austin, called *A Study in Thinking* (1956), grew out of Harvard's Cognition Project on concept formation. Bruner and his colleagues examined abstract forms of categorization and classification. In their study, they analyzed the information of long sentences through acts called *strategies,* which involved the subcategories of successive scanning and conservative focusing. *Scanning* is the strategy used to simplify the search, and *focusing* is the means to limit the burden on memory and allows for a steady progress toward a solution.

Bruner's work also showed a strong Piagetian influence especially with respect to his stages of cognitive development. However, it disagreed over Bruner's view that the foundations of any subject may be taught to anybody at any age in some form. In contrast, Piaget felt that knowledge of a subject could be gained only when all the components of that knowledge are present and properly developed. Bruner also believed that cognitive development was related to favored modes of representing objects and events. In what Piaget viewed as the sensorimotor period, Bruner believed that children represented the world through their motor acts of ikonic representation, where mental images and pictures are closely related to perception. In the middle school years, Bruner believed the emphasis shifts to symbolic representation, where children use arbitrary and socially standardized representations of things to internally manipulate symbols characteristic of abstract and logical thought. Therefore, according to Bruner, we know something by doing it—through a picture or image of it (ikonic) or through some symbolic means such as language. The use of these three means increases children's ability to acquire and use knowledge.

No review of the literature in psycholinguistics would be complete without at least a mention of the work of Russian philologist/psycholinguist Lev S. Vygotsky (1896–1934). His theories first came to the attention of American psychologists in 1962 with the publication of his monograph, *Thought and Language* (Vygotsky, 1988). He was a student of psychology in the heyday of Wundt, James, Pavlov, Watson, Wertheimer, Kohler, Koffka, and Lewin and therefore was fully aware of their discoveries.

Vygotsky's greatest contributions to the cognitive sciences were his experiments, which focused on process (methods), rather than traditional experimental work, which focused on performance. One of his most important discoveries challenged the tradition separating the study of tool use and speech, where the development of speech and other sign-using activity were treated as independent of the organization of the child's practical activity, unlike traditional psychologists who studied sign use as evidence of pure intellect and separated it from practical intelligence.

Vygotsky believed the most important stage of intellectual development was when speech and practical activity, once thought to be completely independent lines of development, converge. He believed that the child, before mastering his or her own behavior, masters his or her surroundings with the help of speech, which produces new relations with the environment and with the organization of behavior. He also believed these uniquely human forms of behavior later produce what he called *intellect,* which became the basis for productive work through the use of tools. He explained this process in three developmental stages: (a) when children are unable to solve problems and use speech to acquire the assistance of an adult, (b) when such socialized speech is turned inward to guide them in problem solving, and (c) when children mature and use words to describe the problem encountered.

Vygotsky viewed Stage 2 (internal speech) as the socialization of children's practical intellect. Unlike earlier forms of speech, which accompany the child's actions, it is speech that precedes action. One example is that young children name their drawings after they see them because they need to see them to decide what they are. Later, as children get older, they can name their pictures in advance because they know what they are going to draw. Developmentally, speech is then moved to the starting point of the activity, where speech dominates the course of action (Vygotsky, 1978).

Another of Vygotsky's discoveries was the relationship between speech and perception. His observations of children led him to believe that, although independent elements in visual perception are simultaneously perceived and speech requires sequential processing or analysis, they are both linked in the child's early stages of development. One specific feature of human perception at an early stage that fascinated him was the child's ability to perceive real objects not simply as color or shape, but rather with a clear parts-to-whole meaning, suggesting that all human perception consists of categorized rather than isolated perceptions.

According to Vygotsky, language is an aid to perception where the child moves through progressive stages. At first the child labels things to choose a specific object for attention, which means children begin to perceive the world both through their eyes and speech. Later speech acquires a synthesizing function, which brings speech and language together. At a still later time, children perceive real objects, which indicates that they perceive the world as having meaning and suggests that human perception consists of categorized rather than isolated perceptions.

The structure of the child's decision-making process differs radically from that of an adult. Unlike adults, who make a preliminary decision and act on it directly, a child's choice resembles a somewhat delayed selection from his or her own movements. According to Vygotsky, the child does not choose a stimulus as the starting point for a movement, but rather selects the appropriate movement. When children progress to recognize some signs about what movement to take, they make a more structured response and abandon groping movements. At this point, children give up impulsive problem solving and begin to solve through an internally established connection between stimulus and the sign. At such a time, the child masters its movements and reconstructs the choice process. Using such strageties, attention becomes detached from the perceptual field, a reconstruction of memory function occurs, and intentions and representations can be pursued as purposeful action.

Vygotsky's work also addressed the problems of memory and thinking development. One of his more significant observations was the differences in these functions between the younger and older child. For the young child, to think is to remember or to recall; for the adolescent, to recall means to think, which is to establish and find logical relations where all ideas and concepts cease to be organized by family types and become organized as abstract concepts.

Anthropology

Another important area of research in the cognitive sciences that sprang from the empirical philosophers and, in particular, the logical positivists is found in the field of anthropology, which involves both the study of social structures and the uses of language in society.
Its impact on the cognitive sciences is mostly through its structuralism—a newer,
20th-century method founded on the ideas of Claude Levi-Strauss, Roland Barthes, and
Noam Chomsky. Levi-Strauss' view of structuralism adumbrated in his structural anthropology supports that unconscious mental processes remain fixed in all cultures, primitive
and literate alike. According to Levi-Strauss, all customs fill specific functions and act as
supplementary language. Levi-Strauss' ideas in anthropology came from several sources
including communication theory, Hegelian dialectics, and structural linguistics
(Levi-Strauss, 1976).

Before Levi-Strauss, a number of other important thinkers were also involved in the
development of anthropology as a cognitive science. These included Lucien Levy-Bruhl,
Edward Tylor, and Frank Boas. In his study of the thinking processes of primitive peoples
over a century ago, Levy-Bruhl discovered that primitive people do not reason badly, but
rather reason differently; this notion proposed that the primitive mind follows a prelogic
system best understood on its own terms rather than on contemporary views of logic. Edward Tylor is credited with actually launching the discipline of anthropology, which integrates the scientific study of society and culture. Tylor, influenced by Darwinian ideas,
declared that human capacities were not simply a matter of birthright, but were rather derived from being a member of a group and could be changed if someone were reared in a
different group or the group altered its practices or values. Unlike Tylor, the German
physicist Frank Boas felt that culture was best studied in terms of its own most important
practices, needs, and pressures rather than in comparison with other cultures with a more
or less advanced organization. Boas emphasized the importance of language and linguistics
in anthropological study and its relation to a primitive mentality where primitives developed in a crude and unreflective manner, rather than in more recent literate populations,
which have systemized knowledge more akin to the rational sciences.

Levi-Strauss' contribution to the anthropological science is found mainly in his demonstration that the key aspects of culture are linguistic and best approached through the
methods of the structural linguist. As applied to his early writings on kinship, Levi-Strauss
classified the nature of dual organizations, which mask the forces of women and reflect the
actual social relations of village life.

His most important contribution to the cognitive sciences was his discovery of how the
human mind classifies objects and constructs and understands myths. His method is
viewed as Cartesian, being largely intuitive and relying on the scientist's own mind rather
than on the validation of the scientific method. In his classification studies, Levi-Strauss
found that the principle features of all minds is to classify, with primitive people doing this
in much the same way as modern people do. In his view, the primitive mind classifies objects and experiences in terms of their overt perceptual and sensory qualities, which do
not lead to the same categories or classifications used in the Western scientific approach.

Levi-Strauss' method is to use the empirical properties that are evident in myths, such
as sound, smell, light, darkness, rawness, and so on, as conceptual tools for understanding

abstract constructs such as social conflicts, which can be formulated as logical propositions. Each myth changes the one that went before it and cannot be fully understood except in relation to other myths.

Neuroscience

Because cognitive scientists want to present something more than a mystical accounting of human behavior, they have long been interested in how certain processes and information are represented in the brain. Once the brain has been selected as that region of the body most logically connected to thought and for discussions of the neural basis of thoughts and actions, the brain becomes the logical site for such investigations. In the 19th century, it was generally assumed that the brain is divided to carry out many discrete functions. This resulted in the belief that the brain is composed of as many independent organs as there are powers in the mind. Subsequent studies pointed to the contrary—that cerebral regions function as a whole and that, although there is some specificity in the nervous system, all parts of the system join together to contribute to a common activity.

Today neuropsychologists think localizers were correct about certain organisms, certain behaviors, and certain portions of the life cycle, whereas holists were correct for other organisms and other behaviors for other periods of life. Some even believe the two systems work in tandem; such is the case with visual perceptions. These are built up gradually over time through cell assemblies, which later become phase sequences. These develop alternative pathways and later become capable of performing the most complex behaviors.

Karl Lashley, an American neuropsychologist in the early 20th century, was one of the first to question the significance of specific neural zones or connections. Lashley's ideas were a sharp challenge to the neuroscientific community, whose interests in the field were founded on the presumption that the specific neural basis of particular behavior could be found. Having concluded that particular behavioral patterns cannot be assigned to specific cortical regions, Lashley spent the rest of his scholarly life pursuing the view of Gestalt psychologists, which states that a direct perception only later becomes sensitive to other realities.

Lashley's views also challenged the conceptions of the brain as a digital computer, which was inspired by the fact that the neuron, like a switch or valve, does or does not complete a circuit. Unfortunately, the switch in a digital computer is constant in its effect, related to the total output of the machine and with the number of neurons involved in any action being in the millions, reducing the influence of any single neuron as negligible. Therefore, Lashley believed the brain machine is more analogical than digital.

Artificial Intelligence

John McCarthy of Dartmouth, founder and first director of the artificial intelligence labs at both the Massachusetts Institute of Technology and Stanford University, is credited with coining the term *artificial intelligence* (AI) and being the organizer of a 1956 AI conference at Dartmouth. The purpose of that conference was to discuss the possibilities of producing computer programs that could think or behave intelligently. Those who attended were interested in devising the machines and programs to process symbols rather than numbers to define the role of computers in listing scientific theories. Artificial intelligence seeks to produce in a computer a pattern of input that would compare favorably with the patterns exhibited by human beings. Some researchers view AI as simply a means for testing theories of human cognitive operations; others feel the computer is a mind that understands and exhibits cognitive states.

AI began by using the assumptions of Boolean logic to express logical propositions as symbols that could be used to form new expressions or conceptions amounting to a mental algebra. This was coupled later with John von Neumann's computer programming models and Newell and Simon's experiments into AI computer programs, which demonstrated that computers could engage in intelligent humanlike behaviors and steps akin to human problem solving.

Although today AI remains a relatively controversial topic among cognitive scientists, it has improved a good deal since the 1960s. Newer work in perception now permits programs to analyze an entire graphic scene contriving a three-dimensional description of objects in a drawn scene recognizing two different pictures as representations of the same scene. When programmers label the elements that are used to make up a picture, for example, they compile a list of a few thousand ways that edges in a picture can be formed, a match between two pictures can be established, and even ambiguity in figures can be resolved. Despite problems, AI can be used as an aid in conceptualizing and testing theories of human intelligence. However, it is still criticized because it has used superficial models unlike human thought processes. Some argue it has yet to reach the standing of being a genuine scientific endeavor.

Recent efforts in the MIT COG project suggest some radically different approaches to intelligent machines inspired by biology and sociology. These efforts, under the direction of Rodney Brooks, are attempting to construct humanoid robots that can learn to think by building on bodily experiences. This requires designing robots that will acquire a sense of space and learn concepts such as up, down, near, and far through sensors that experience the real world. In the development of their latest robot, called *COG,* it is hoped that the robot may sit across the table from human beings passing toys back and forth. Although this project may not succeed in the robot's learning how to learn, it is at least a radical departure from other so-called *brains in a box* approaches, which provide a ready-made database filled with commonsense facts ready for use.

LEARNING AND COGNITIVE STYLE

Although *cognitive style* research weighs heavily on how cognitive researchers look at learning and cognitive development, it is neither a subdiscipline of cognitive science nor necessarily a major research influence. What is known is that humans dealing with various aspects of the environment employ differing cognitive styles in organizing and categorizing their perception.

Reflection/Impulsivity Theory

According to one theory, children differ in their approach to problem solving in two ways: impulsively or reflectively (Kagan, 1965a, 1965b). Reflective children tend to perform better than impulsive children in reading tasks, recognition memory tests, reasoning tests, and on creative products. In contrast, impulsive children excel at intellectual tasks. Reflective children favor a direct and assertive approach to a reasoning task, whereas impulsive children prefer a more yielding and passive approach.

Independent/Dependent Theory

A second theory of cognitive style is found in the independent/dependence theory (Witkin & Goodenough, 1981). This theory supports that some people tend to be splitters while others are lumpers. Such skills are identified through visual tests; although some individuals progress from field dependent to field independent at each age, differences remain.

Field-dependent people tend to analyze the elements of a scene and categorize it as a whole, while overlooking the individual elements that compose it. Field-independent people are characterized as having an impersonal orientation toward others, whereas field dependents tend to behave more interpersonally. People who are field independent are also described as being cold, manipulative, and distant, whereas field dependents are thought to be warm, considerate, and accommodating. Some research suggests field independents in college are attracted to math, the natural sciences, and engineering, whereas field dependents are attracted to the humanities, social sciences, and education.

Different views relating to the perspectives of cognitive style and cognitive development have created a number of problems for the cognitive sciences, in part, because there has been only limited research connecting the developmental and individual differences approaches. Supporters of the cognitive style approach believe that those who support Piaget's approaches seek developmental approaches as universals and treat individual variations as irrelevant—or mere differences in developmental rate along the same developmental path. According to cognitive style advocates, such views are based on a unidimensional approach to development, where individual differences are considered mere deviations from the one ideal dimension of development.

At least four important questions with respect to cognitive style remain unanswered today: (a) whether cognitive style is a useful theoretical construct, (b) whether cognitive style is a unitary or multifaceted construct, (c) whether style is a preference in the ways humans process information or a different way to describe people's abilities, and (d) what is the nature of the relationship between cognitive style and cognitive development.

Cognitive style can be broadly defined as an individual's preferred approach to problem solving; it characterizes an individual's behavior across a variety of situations and content domains but is independent of intellectual competence (Waber, 1989). However, there is a lack of consensus as to essential determinants of cognitive style. Some researchers focus on control processes (impulsivity), whereas others focus on the processing requirements of tasks, which is an analytical-gestalt approach. Others take a neuropsychological approach, which views styles as an interplay between control and analytical-gestalt aspects of tasks. Researchers supporting the neuropsychological approach believe that individual differences in cognitive styles reflect a variation in the efficiency of cognitive processes associated with the frontal brain system and have a physiological basis in the function of these systems.

The most researched dimension of cognitive style is found in the field-dependent/field-independent studies of Herman Witkin and his colleagues (Witkin et al., 1962). According to Witkin, psychological systems become progressively differentiated with development; these differentiations exist across domains and can be measured empirically by performance on a variety of perceptual tasks.

The two tests most frequently used as measures of perceptual differentiation are the Embedded Figures Test (EFT; Figs. 3.1 and 3.2) and the Rod and Frame Test (RFT). Both tests require disembedding items found in an organized perceptual context. In both cases, test takers encounter conflicting visual clues and must resist the tendency to respond to the more salient one to achieve a correct solution.

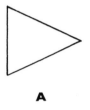

A

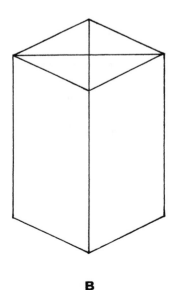

B

FIG. 3.1.   The student is asked to find a simple form hidden in a larger form. The student is given the form "A". The task is to find form "A" hidden in form "B" below.

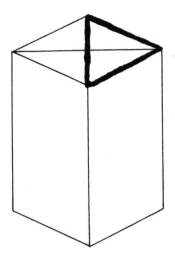

FIG. 3.2.   The solution is traced over the form. This is a typical item in the group Embedded Figures Test (EFT), with the correct answer being to draw the form "A" shape in the correct orientation on form "B."

The Reflection–Impulsivity Theory.   A second construct of cognitive style is the reflection–impulsivity model of Kagan, Rosman, Day, Albert, and Phillips (1964). Reflection–impulsivity is described as the tendency to validate a problem, where several alternatives are possible with some uncertainty about which is the most appropriate course of action (Fig. 3.3). This is also evaluated in a perceptual task called the Matching Familiar Figures Test (MFFT; Fig. 3.4), where children make choices that exactly match the standard. The test involves detailed line drawing that differentiates between reflective and impulsive children through calculating the eye movements used in performing the MFFT. These differences are interpreted as revealing children's basic attentional processes.

In looking at the various empirical treatments of the two style constructs, it can be noted that the style determination of individuals is based exclusively on a finite set of perceptual tasks, all of which depend on the allocation of attention between conflicting sensory clues. Theoretically, these perceptual tasks are also independent of intellectual level, yet correlate well with at least some measures of general intelligence.

One model used to illustrate student cognitive style is the comparison of two secondary students: One is good in math; is logical, reflective, and analytical; has a high IQ; and is a formal operational thinker. The other is an average student; has difficulties in math and science; is not logical, a good artist, rich in intuitive thinking, sensitive, or perceptive; but has an average IQ and probably should consider becoming a nursery school or art teacher (Globerson, 1989). According to Globerson, such descriptions are quite prototypical of stylistic children.

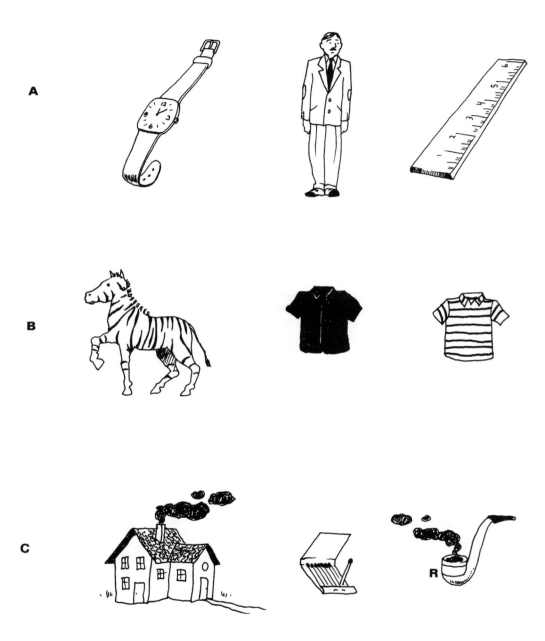

FIG. 3.3.   A facsimile reflection-impulsivity test item to examine the modes of cognitive style in children ages 6 and 11. The children are asked to determine which two figures are alike or in some way related. (The superordinate style student would supposedly pair the two shirts in "B" rather than pair the stripped shirt and the zebra. An analytic style student would pair the watch and the ruler because both are used for measurement). Children ages 4 to 6 would choose the functional relational style, that is, the match lights the pipe and the man wears the watch.

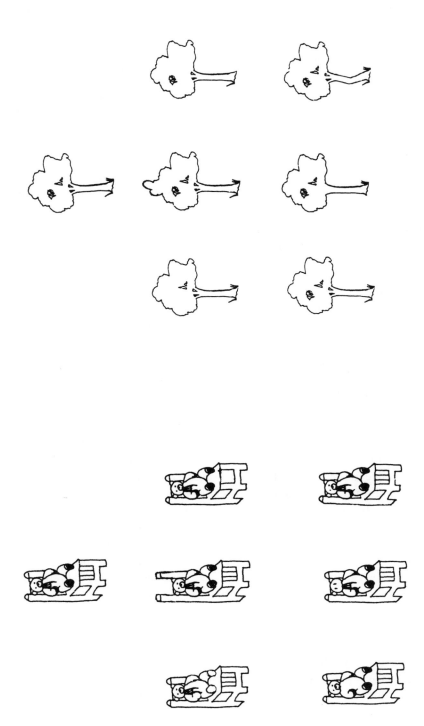

FIG. 3.4.   A facsimile test item from a Matching Familiar Figures Test (MFT) to measure impulsiveness-reflectivity. The student is asked to select from the lower six items which one is identical to the figure at the top.

In general, researchers claim that field-independent and reflective children, in comparison with field-dependent and impulsive children, have been found to have superior performance on a wide range of cognitive/academic tasks, including developmental and intelligence tasks. There are two explanations offered for such findings: ordinal description and differential description. Ordinal descriptions rank people according to their cognitive abilities, which accords high rankings for being field independent and reflective. Differential descriptions assess capabilities without ranking these abilities with each other. Ordinal explanations link style, intelligence, and developmental tasks performance and stylistic differences with development differences. Differential descriptions accept that people are essentially different in their competencies in ways that cannot be measured statistically and without regard to an achievement performance score. In general, the research has explored at least three possibilities to account for the differences between the styles: field-dependent people are less developed cognitively, less mobilized in their use of mental capacity to the task situation or attending to different clues, and less able to organize information and use different problem-solving strategies.

Some researchers, however, reject that the differences are due to less developed cognition or the mobilization of mental capacity explanations. They support that different style children perform differently on the same task because they attend to different cues and use different information-processing strategies. These researchers also suggest that when children who are strong in visual processing are coached on their strengths and made aware of their cognitive style (i.e., *metacognitive processing* and *reflective abstraction*), by being taught such strategies, they achieve as high a level of performance on cognitive tasks as their field-independent stage peers. Still other research seems to support that field-dependent children perform as well as field-independent children on interpersonal perceptions; on length estimation, the former performing even better. However, such performances are often discounted as not being cognitively demanding.

Questions remain regarding cognitive style and its relation to performance on intelligence tests and its apparent relationship to development. However, because field-dependent students can learn to perform equally as well as field-independent students on cognitive measures, we also need to consider how we can best engage different learners in learning processes that will realize their cognitive potential. In other words, the challenge may be to find out what kind of learning activities or environments need to be constructed to enable learning to occur in the best possible way. Some researchers feel that such an environment should: (a) be multifaceted, through presenting many different symbol systems (e.g., pictorial, verbal, symbolic, formal, etc.); (b) be style appropriate, capitalizing on the capabilities of the learner; and (c) integrate multiple representations, which utilize knowledge in a variety of problem-solving solutions.

Some researchers also feel that the Piagetian model addresses only formal thinking analogous to logical thought and ignores so-called *realizing* types of thinking. Formalized thinking uses developmental schema to solve certain problems, whereas realized thinking is interrelated thinking establishing immediate links between stimuli and responses. *Realization* is defined as a process that allows the individual to quickly adapt to different situations and is somewhat analogous to Gestalt thinking which also characterizes field-dependent subjects. As a consequence, field-dependent thinkers see visual size (when pictured as heavy appearing objects) to be an index of actual weight and volume, and therefore tend to be more sensitive to an illusion of weight rather than to actual weight and volume calculations.

The Pascual–Leone Model

The Pascual–Leone model, or theory of constructive operators (TCO), models the psychosocial organism as being composed of two interlocked systems: the subjective system of schemes and the silent systems of operators (Ribaupierre, 1989). Cognitive schemes are processed according to their function in processing information and according to the relationship between elements, whereas silent systems distinguish between the logical and infralogical as generic structures composed of concepts, relations, and propositions. Silent systems tend to act only on these schemes and not on the sensory input.

Studies of these systems lead some researchers to conclude that cognitive styles are multidimensional and cannot be expected to correlate across tasks. In addition, they believe we need to consider cognitive development and cognitive style as two different constructs yet applying to all subjects as empirically measurable general development patterns of performance across types of subjects and tasks.

When researchers examine that different individuals have different dispositions toward analytical and holistic processing, they raise a number of questions. Is it because of a preferred skill in processing information in a particular way? Is it a lack of ability to process information otherwise? Or is it that one disposition or the other is rarely activated? The answers to such questions mostly relate to whether the researcher accepts that there is such a thing as cognitive ability, where children have unequal cognitive capacities, or whether they accept the notion of cognitive commitment, which suggests children differ in the actual mental energy, effort, or resources they physically commit to problem-solving tasks.

The development literature tends to see these points of view as being actually parallel, where holistic processing is the preferred mode of younger children but is not necessarily characterized as childlike cognition. Performance is believed to improve with age in dozens of memory, reasoning, conceptual, and problem-solving tasks, but not all such processes can be described as analytical. In general, the developmental literature accepts that young children are likely to be holistic processors. However, compared with older children, they are less able, less active, less strategic, or less likely to function at a metacognitve level.

In addition, cognitive researchers are now beginning to believe that holistic thinking, compared with analytic processing, is a less resource-intensive fallback mode of cognition, especially associated with nondeliberative strategic learning approaches. Analytical cognition is believed to occur through controlled, effortful rule seeking or a hypotheses mode of cognition. Experimental studies with adults now suggest that where learning occurs in incidental conditions, where acquisition strategies are unintentional and nonstrategic, individuals tend to process holistically; where controlled conditions are true, they learn intentionally.

Although it is highly unlikely that we can immediately resolve the relationships that exist between holistic thinking and the analytical process, its entanglement in the use of perceptual measures as determinants may yield further interesting insight into the character of visual forming. For example, researchers tend to agree that problem solving involves processes at both the perceptual and conceptual levels and that the tasks used to measure the two cognitive styles are principally perceptual tasks. The dimensions are attention and organization, which reveal both how information is attended to and how it is organized.

Attention includes two aspects: Selective attention is that which receives attention, and attention control is the ability to focus on and pay attention to stimuli relevant for attaining a solution. Stimulus organization refers mainly to transformations of the stimulus input on the spatial configuration of the stimulus, which affect various aspects of spatial information processing, including spatial relations or mental notation, spatial orientation or perspective, and visualization as in hidden figures. One type of transformation involves movement such as rotation. The others involve construction or synthesis, which are ways of reorganizing stimulus events. These three dimensions—selective attention, attention control, and stimulus organization—are critical in visual perception because psychologists believe they determine the nature of the stimulus input that is accessible for further processing.

How we account for the differences in field-dependent and field-independent children (i.e., as to whether it is a matter of style or ability) remains a controversy among cognitive stylists. What we do know is that both cognitive styles show a developmental trend, with reflectivity and field independence increasing with age (i.e., older field dependents perform like younger field independents and older impulsives perform like younger reflectives). However, because cognitive style measures are linked to visual processing and the manner in which attention-perceptional problems are solved, perceptive processes can be viewed as styles in problem solving. What is not clear is whether problem-solving deficiencies should be viewed as differences in style or differences in ability.

Researchers also see the processing characteristics of traditional cognitive styles and individual differences as related to and influencing ability because they determine the quality of the stimulus information accessible for additional problem solving. Focusing attention on a whole visual stimulus, for example, yields information from a wide angle and low resolution, is data-limited, and is carried out on a degraded stimulus input. However, choosing such a strategy for visual processing depends both on the individual's predisposition as well as task demands, and it affords alternative optional solutions to the problems. Researchers also find that problems unmatched with the learner's preferred style and the only alternatives for solution lead to failures in problem solving. When subjects perform two versions of the same problem, the version that best fits the preferred processing mode of the individual leads to the greatest success. Therefore, different individuals and different tasks require different combinations of attention and organizational dimensions for successful performance. Expected performances are determined by the success of the match between an individual's profile and the task demands that bear on the problem (Zelniker, 1987).

SUMMARY

The literature in this chapter suggests that cognitive scientists, unlike general psychologists, may have a greater acceptance for the general notion of the mental manipulation of thought and images and the possibility that evidence of such images is not always experimentally verifiable. Although psychologists in both groups are committed to the same burden of scientific proof, cognitive science as a field is also equally committed to the study of mental processes, which remains open to creative and intuitive thought as being a higher form of cognitive behavior. As in general psychology, the results of cognitive science's experiments also reveal both top–down and bottom–up perspectives, which again frequently suggest disagreements about the meaning of their experiments. As a discipline, however, cognitivists are also firmly committed to looking at both cognitive development and cognitive style. This suggests that the way one approaches learners with differing cognitive styles depends mostly on whether the researcher seeks to rank them according to their style or whether they view style as something relative to task performance. This questions whether the same or different styles are needed to solve problems in different disciplines and whether styles of learning are an index of differing capacities or an index of individual choice and the nature of the environment paid attention to.

As noted in this chapter's review of the literature, although cognitive scientists hold many of the same views as the generalists, especially with regard to the necessity of experimental verification, they also differ with respect to the influence of inner mental activity in the life of the mind, the role of language in cognition, the contextual influences in cognition, and the effects of individual differences. Because cognitivists are philosophically committed to a separate mind–body concept, they are more accepting of the following notions: (a) that there can be separate life of the mind that is influenced by mental structures we do not fully understand, (b) that there are differing environments requiring different mental functions to attend them, and (c) that individuals have differing strategies for solving problems and do not always pay attention to the same things.

The Gestalt notion of direct perception, Piaget's idea that knowledge of a subject is gained only when all its components are present and properly developed, and the linguistic argument of Vygotsky and others connecting inner speech to practical activity have dramatically affected the views of the cognitivists toward conceptions of human intelligence and learning. It is because of such notions that cognitivists today recognize there is such a thing as inner mental activity, where mental schemes or scripts influence what information people attend to, how they structure it, how much importance they attach to it, and what they do with it. As a result, it is being discovered that learning requires something more than connecting two events together because humans do not simply act on external events, but rather evaluate them individually and determine their reactions accordingly.

Efforts by cognitivists to study the methods people use to solve problems rather than the products of their performance have also radically changed how cognitive scientists view the role of language in cognition. Rather than being seen as something separate from practical activity, language is now seen as a tool for measuring new relations with the environment and with the organization of behavior. Speech is now seen as being linked to visual perception, and, while independent and simultaneously perceived, still requires sequential processing and analysis, especially in the early stages of the child's development.

Even more dramatic than the acceptance of a separate life of the mind and the changing role of language is the cognitive stylists' discovery that learning abilities are linked both to the different ways humans process knowledge and the differing learning requirements of alternative ways of knowing. In particular, studies by the cognitive stylists have questioned whether differences in human performance are due to the way learners attend to different clues, what different information and processing strategies are required to learn different tasks, and what learning processes help learners with differing learning styles learn best.

In raising such questions, cognitive investigations have shifted to inquiring more into the abilities of people to perform certain tasks than about who can or cannot perform them, to learn more about who can learn what, how best they can learn it, and what strategies are needed to learn to do specific tasks. These efforts have also shifted attention away from stereotyping learners as either bumpers or splitters or successful or unsuccessful and toward looking at different human capabilities, how to mobilize human mental capacities to attend different clues, how to organize information in different ways, how to achieve different problem-solving strategies, and what learning processes best help realize learners' cognitive potential.

Most of all, what such inquiries suggest is that what we learn from our environment and whether that learning in humans is manifested in scientific, aesthetic, or humanistic products may be less important than helping learners learn to learn. Furthermore, we acknowledge these different forms of cognition of the world as having equal value and recognize them as potential forms of intelligent activity necessary for achieving a full understanding of the mind.

The next chapter discusses how these cognitive processes are interpreted in artistic thinking. It examines various art perspectives offered in the literature of aesthetics, philosophy, the psychology of art, and in the research on child artistic development. These include the mental processes used in artistic perception, consciousness, imagination, expression, emotion, thought, intellect, and language, especially as they relate to thinking about and making art.

REFERENCES

Arnheim, R. (1966). *Toward a psychology or art.* Berkeley, CA: University of California Press.

Bruner, J. S., Goodnow, J. J., & Austin, G. A. (1956). *A study in thinking.* New York: Wiley.

Chomsky, N. (1957). *Syntactic structures.* The Hague: Mouton.

Gardner, H. (1987). *The mind's new science.* New York: Basic Books.

Globerson, T. (1989). What is the relationship between cognitive style and cognitive development? In G. Tamar & Z. Tamar (Eds.), *Cognitive style and cognitive development* (pp. 71–86). Norwood, NJ: Ablex.

Kagan, J. (1965a). Impulsive and reflective children: Significance of conceptual tempo. In J. Krumboltz (Ed.), *Learning and the educatonal process* (pp. 133–161). Chicago: Rand McNally.

Kagan, J. (1965b). Reflection-impulsivity and reading ability in primary grade children. *Child Development, 36,* 609–628.

Kagan, J., Rosman, B. L., Day, D., Albert, J., & Phillips, W. (1964). Information processing in the child. *Psychological Monograph, 78* (1, Whole No. 578).

Levi-Strauss, C. (1976). *Structural anthropology* (Vol. 2). New York: Basic Books.

Ribaupierre, Anik de. (1989). Cognitive style and operational development: A review of French literature and neo-Paigetian reinterpretation. In T. Globerson & T. Zelniker (Eds.), *Cognitive Style and Cognitive Development* (pp. 86–115). Norwood, NJ: Ablex.

Piaget, J. (1959). *The language and thought of the child.* London: Routledge.

Vygotsky, L. S. (1978). *Mind in society.* Cambridge, MA: MIT Press.

Vygotsky, L. S. (1988). *Thought and language.* Cambridge, MA: Harvard University Press.

Waber, D. (1989). The biological boundaries of cognitive styles: A neuropsychological analysis. In T. Globerson & T. Zelniker (Eds.), *Cognitive Style and Cognitive Development* (pp. 11–35). Norwood, NJ: Ablex.

Whitehead, A. N. (1982). *An enquiry concerning the principles of natural knowledge.* New York: Dover.

Witkin, H. A., Dyk, R. B., Faterson, G. E., Goodenough, O. R., & Karp, S. A. (1962). *Psychological differentiation.* New York: Wiley.

Witkin, H. A., & Goodenough, D. R. (1981). *Cognitive styles: Essence and origins.* New York: International Universities Press.

Witkin, H. A., Oltman, P. K., Raskin, E., & Karp, S. (1971). *Group embedded figures test.* Palo Alto, CA: Consulting Psychologists Press.

Zelniker, T. (1987). Cognitive style and dimensions of information processing. In T. Globerson & T. Zelniker (Eds.), *Cognitive Style and Cognitive Development* (pp. 172–191). Norwood, NJ: Ablex.

KEY TERMS

Rationalism	Field dependent
Empiricism	Field independent
Behaviorism	Holistic processing
Linguistics	Attention
Artificial Intelligence	Stimulus organization
Cognitive style	

STUDY QUESTIONS

1. Why should one study philosophy to understand the differing perspectives of the psychological sciences? In your answer, consider what may be the issues and problems associated with having many differing points of view rather than only one basis for decision making.

2. Describe the three differing philosophical positions of rationalism, empiricism, and idealism. What are the differing epistemological assumptions that these systems use to know how we know? Which system seems to come closest to your beliefs and your assumptions about the world and the origins of the universe?

3. Compare and contrast one or more of the various psychological perspectives with respect to their agreement or disagreement with the so-called top–down and bottom–up theories held by cognitive scientists. Which theory do you feel comes the closest to how you believe humans solve problems?

4. How do cognitive scientists associated with the Gestalt and behaviorist paradigms differ in their understanding of human behavior? How do they differ in the way they gather behavioral evidence and how they interpret behavioral outcomes?

5. Explain the different viewpoints held by psycholinguists in the functions of language in the mental development of humans. How do these viewpoints differ with respect to the issue of language and perception? Which point of view do you believe most closely matches your own observations?

6. What do you believe are some of the strengths and weaknesses in the artificial intelligence community in using the computer as a model for studying

the functions of the human brain? Using your own experience with the computer, frame up several arguments you would make in support of or in disagreement with the computer as mental model.

7. Distinguish between the so-called control processes (impulsivity) and the analytic-Gestalt approach to interpreting a student's cognitive style. What a priori assumptions do these systems make with regard to learning behavior and problem solving? Compare and contrast how an art learning environment would differ when using these two divergent systems.

8. What are the differences between individuals who use analytical or holistic processing systems? How do individuals using these different approaches differ in the way they process information? What differing conclusions do scientists come to on their cognitive abilities?

4

Cognition in Art

PHILOSOPHICAL DEFINITIONS OF ART
Art as Idea
Art as Form
Art as Language

PSYCHOLOGICAL EXPLANATIONS OF ART
The Top–Down Aesthetic Model
The Collingwood View
The Gombrichian View
The Bottom–Up Aesthetic Model
The Langerian View
The Rudolph Arnheim View

CHILDREN'S ARTISTIC DEVELOPMENT 1905–1962
Children's General and Drawing Development
Draw-a-Man Test

DEVELOPMENTAL RESEARCH STUDIES AFTER 1962
General Development
Drawing, Memory, and Language
Skill Development
Perceptual Training
Copying
Media and Tools

SUMMARY

The previous chapter focused on the philosophical, historical, and subdisciplinary influences comprising the cognitive science disciplines today. Discussed were the influences of the behaviorists, Gestaltists, developmentalists, psycholinguists, anthropologists, neuropsychologists, and cognitive stylists. Also identified were several of the same competing top–down and bottom–up interpretations existing both within and between the various perspectives representing the cognitive sciences today.

This chapter examines the philosophical, aesthetic, psychological, expressive, and developmental literature in the visual arts as they illuminate the mental processes used in artistic conception. Contributions from various art perspectives are discussed as they relate to the various higher order mental processes used in art, including perception, consciousness, imagination, expression, emotion, thought, intellect, and language, especially as they influence the processes of thinking about and making art. Discussed are contributions from the fields of philosophy, aesthetics, psychology of art, and children's artistic development as they relate to cognition and conception in both art objects and events and in the general cognitive and artistic growth of young learners.

PHILOSOPHICAL DEFINITIONS OF ART

As in the cognitive sciences, the rationalist philosophers Descartes, Spinosa, and Liebnitz provided the conceptual thinking necessary for conceiving of the arts as existing in the life of the mind. Descartes supported the notion that art could exist as a mental idea, Spinosa conceived that direct perception of art was possible, and Leibnitz viewed art objects and events as existing in a particular time and place. To grasp what mental processes are involved in the arts, we first need to understand how these three frames of mind define the self and its relation to works of art. I define these frames as (a) art as idea, (b) art as form, and (c) art as language.

Art as Idea

Descartes' methods, which began with thinking, made it possible for us to (a) think of objects and events as mental concepts to be experienced and manipulated as mental schema, (b) achieve cognition through intuitive reasoning, and (c) recognize the function of personal and self-knowledge in expressive thought and action. Descartes' separation of mental from physical life opened up the possibility that a life of the mind existed separately from the sensory system of sight, touch, sound, and smell.

Descartes' mathematical method of verification (i.e., to deduce that, in knowing two angles of an equilateral triangle, one can know the third) provided a foundation for arguing that reasoned thought could, as reasoning in mathematics, provide proofs where disciplinary context sets the conditions for cognition. Art could then be interpreted as fact through a self-verifying system where proof, as in mathematics, is determined through its own methods.

Art as an idea or mental concept, rather than as a physical thing, is used by a number of aesthetitions to lay out a definition of art, which relies mostly on the artist's thoughts, which are mentally manipulated in the process of planning and executing a work. Art as a mental thing makes it not a material thing but rather an idea, which, while expressed in a product, still remains either as standing for a general concept or an expressive idea, which is mental and not physically present in the art work. In general, artists who hold such views believe artistic thought to be an extended concept, where art objects over time are sort of freeze-dried impermanent versions of the thoughts held at the time the work was created. Artists who hold this belief view their older paintings and drawings as passe, holding little real meaning in terms of the artists' present expressive efforts.

Art as an idea is also a concept that challenges Plato's dictum of art being an imitation of an imitation, or craft. The notion of art as not being craft is thoroughly developed in Collingwood's (1975) *Principles of Art.* In this work, Collingwood argued the reasons for art not being a craft and also what distinguishes the art object as a work of art rather than craft. The main distinction between art and craft, according to Collingwood, is that a craft, unlike art, can be known in advance of its making. Thus, art is a that which cannot be known in advance of its making and exists as an expressive form shaped by the artist's imagination and consciousness. Collingwood helped art to become Plato's idea of the bed itself rather than the real bed, which he called an imitation of an idea, or the drawing of bed, which is an imitation of the imitation of an idea. What is important to know in understanding Collingwood is that his concept of craft refers only to work, where ends and means are related and not to the use of a medium such as clay, yarn, glass, reed, cloth, and so on.

In Collingwood's view, Art is not about means and ends, but is rather the expression of an idea. According to Collingwood, there are several kinds of craft (i.e., works where emotion is aroused for its own sake, those for sensual pleasure, works that arouse feelings of loyalty such as in a flag at a football game, works that educate, those that are a visual puzzle, or that instruct us about something). In his view, what makes art is not the same thing as what makes it useful, noting that an aesthetic experience is an autonomous activity that arises from within and is not a reaction to an external stimulus.

Collingwood supported that art is schemata; he stated that a work of art is imitative by virtue of its relation to another work of art, which affords it a model of artistic excellence. However, works of art are not copies of other art works or necessarily unlike them; originality is something more than unlikeness to other works of art. Representation, he believed, is possible in art, but what makes it a representation is one thing and what makes it a work of art is another. The true definition of *representative art* is not that it resembles the original, but that the feeling evoked by it resembles the feelings evoked by the original.

Although Collingwood did not use the term *schema* or mention mental images, his view on representation clearly suggests that art comes at least in part from art—both as a model for judging its form and as a means for linking common content (idea) in works reflecting similar themes. In his view, art proper is a product of consciousness, where sensation becomes an awareness of feeling and emotion acted on by the imagination and through intuition is resolved in expressive activity. Although not all of Collingwood's beliefs about these mental processes can be verified scientifically, his conceptions, like those of Descartes in philosophy, are foundational for understanding the nature of this view of expressive activity. More of his conceptions are discussed later on in this chapter in the section dealing with his top–down view of artistic perception.

Works of art that are considered mental things or as ideas existing in the mind can be either figurative or abstract works, but are usually works where the artist's way of working is to discover the idea of the work at the time the work is finished. This is what the American abstract artist Richard Diebenkorn probably meant when he said, "When I arrive at the idea the picture is done. There seems something immoral about touching up an idea" (cited in Nordland, 1967, p. 169). Works of art as mental things use mental schema or visual motifs usually appropriated from other art works or adapt religious or classical themes, visual motifs, or patterns from figurative, abstract, and primitive work, such as seen in a Roy Lichtenstein ben-day patterned Braque or Picasso, a Peter Saul painting adopting images from a de Kooning (Fig. 4.1), or a Richard Diebenkorn abstract expressionist Matisse interior.

Works of art using mental or pictorially inspired schema span the history of art from medieval times to the present. Although visually recognizable by their appropriative appearance, they are nonetheless objects whose final appearance is probably not known to the artist until the work is complete. Works of this order, while owing something to older styles, are essentially re-created works in the form of metastyle or style about a style. As such they may openly reveal or point out appropriated devices used in the work to acknowledge that the work is a variation on a theme or motif that any knowledgeable viewer should be acquainted with. Because most painters paint for other painters, the work may also go to some length to reveal the evolution of the work technically as revealed in the artist's right and wrong guesses revealing errors and corrections. Artists who work in this manner may even use these errors to reveal to other artists their working signature and to provide evidence that the work was a direct consequence of the trial-and-error process used to bring the painting into being.

An artist's style of working may also evolve in such a way that the artist repeats an earlier schema—using it over and over again, such as seen in Motherwell's "Elegy" series, which repeats the image as a motif altered over time (Fig. 4.2). Such practice has only been recently revived by the older New York School abstract expressionist and pop artists who create works that may seem to be incomplete, but where one might find some completion in some future work.

Art as Form

The rationalist philosopher Spinosa extended Descartes' "I think" notion to a more objective stance—where objects are self-verifying through the ideas we hold about them. In Spinosa's view, substance is that which is in itself and conceived through itself and does not depend on the conception of another thing from which it is from. Thus, Spinosa's claim made it possible for ideas to exist in things and conceptually made it possible for things to be perceived directly as in Gestalt psychology.

Direct perception, although not mentioned as such in his writings, is reflected in Spinosa's two levels of mind: (a) sense perception or imagination, and (b) reasoned reflection leading to principle and the highest level of thought—intuition. Spinosa's notion of ideas as existing in things made it conceptually possible for 20th-century aesthetitions to advance the notion of the objectification of form, where feelings can exist in objects that are nonfeeling. The objectification of form notion argues that objects, like ideas, conceived intuitively become fact through the reasoning process used to bring them into being. Art objects as form (Gestalt) are articulated feelings attached to things that, when perceived, inspire the viewer to have or experience similar feelings but as interpreted in

FIG. 4.1.   Peter Saul deKooning's *Woman with Bicycle*. Acrylic on canvas, 101 x 751½ in. (256.5 x 191.8 cm.) Collection of the Whitney Museum of American Art purchased with funds from the Sara Roby Foundation 84.49.

FIG. 4.2. MOTHERWELL, Robert. *Elegy to the Spanish Republic, 108*. (1965-1967) Oil on canvas, 6'10" x 11'6 1/4" (208.2 x 351.1 cm). The Museum of Modern Art, New York. Charles Mergentime Fund. Photograph (c) 1998 by The Museum of Modern Art, New York. (c) Dedalus Foundation/Licensed by VAGA, New York, NY.

the mind of the viewer. The Gestalt view of such encounters is that the way the visual elements of a work are displayed causes a kinesthetic response as a kind of body language interpretation of the elements in relation (i.e., as a response to open or closed, compressed or expanded forms, spatial orientations, etc.).

The 20th-century philosopher and aesthetition who is best known for supporting this view is Suzanne Langer. In *Feeling and Form,* Langer (1953) argued that art works contain feelings but do not feel them and that the viewer reacts to an apperception of these feelings with pleasure or displeasure, which are the viewer's own feelings held at the time the object is viewed. Visual symbols, she believed, were capable of articulating ideas about something we want to think about and are different from language or discourse, which involves discursive meaning. Using Clive Bell's notion of significant form, Langer viewed art as significant form, which by its structure can express vital experience through feeling, life, and emotion, which language is unfit to convey.

Langer supported the notion of direct perception by noting that it is useless to dwell on one's state of mind in the presence of a work because it does not further one's understanding of the work or of its value. She viewed activity such as observation, analysis, and verification of art as operations more consistent with the natural sciences, such as is seen in the fields of psychology and sociology. Such operations, in her view, are inadequate as aesthetic values, which must be treated either as direct satisfaction (i.e., pleasurable), as having instrumental value, or as fulfilling biological needs. We might do better, she thought, if we look at the art object as something in its own right separated from our prepared reactions—making art the autonomous and essential factor that it is in every human culture.

For Langer, art is also a form of abstraction, where content is pure appearance made more apparent by abstracting it from real circumstance. Her view is that art presents itself purely to our vision, which is a semblance or other reality, and that it is virtual and therefore a nondiscursive concept of feeling. Art is also a symbol that cannot be said to refer to anything but itself—an idea discussed more fully in the section on consciousness and thought.

Thus, art as form involves the direct use of shape, color, line, and so on to create a pure appearance. Normally the work is abstract or nonobjective, compared with representative work, which contains subject matter lending itself to associational response. This kind of work springs from the minimalist notions that less is more and the more abstract the greater the content. Abstraction is viewed as the result of what occurs on the picture plane, which generally makes no reference to anything outside itself. However, this would not prevent an artist from finding abstract forms in nature as an inspiration for the organization of work. Creation is not the product of visioned fact.

Some examples of form abstract painters include such artists as Albers, Mondrian, Lewis, Kelly (Fig. 4.3), Riley, Stella, Hoffman, and Rothko. Although some of these artists' works reflect other orientations, over time most have been primarily abstract painters. For these artists, lines, colors, shapes, and so on function because of their relationship to the picture plane and edge. Like Kandinsky (1979) noted, these artists' works depend mostly on different possible configurations of the point, line, and plane, where inanimate form is thought to be capable of expressing feelings such as looseness, compression, heaviness, and so on.

FIG. 4.3.   KELLY, Ellsworth. *Colors for a Large Wall*. 1951. Oil on canvas, mounted on sixty-four wood panels; overall, 7'10 1/4" x 7'10 1/2" (239.3 x 239.9cm). The Museum of Modern Art, New York. Gift of the artist. Photograph (c) 1998 by The Museum of Modern Art, New York.

Some formalists view art as form as being perceived as a mental, physical involvement (i.e., the imaginative projection of one's own consciousness into another being or thing). Therefore, the artist's task is to intuit and sense formal or partial relations or tensions and discover the psychological and plastic qualities of form and color.

The art medium is used as both the form and content of the work, giving it a life of its own through which creative impulses are visualized. Thus, art as form is considered a creative interpretation of nature, where the artist's feelings are translated or interpreted through a medium (i.e., stone, clay, paint, etc.). To explore the nature of the medium is considered parallel to exploring nature itself and is therefore believed to be part of the creation.

Abstract painting generally is thought to observe two fundamental laws: (a) the two-dimensional character of the picture plane, and (b) the requirement that the picture achieve a three-dimensional effect but not by illusion. Thus, the act of creation involves the effects that the marks, dots, shapes, lines, and so on achieve as they agitate the picture plane. This is considered to be nature, rather than a naturalistic imitation of nature. Hence, the aim of abstract (form) painting rests mostly on the use of the large shape, the reassertion of the picture plane, and flat form.

Art as Language

Rationalist Leibnitz and the empiricist David Hume formulated the philosophical argument that art objects are analogical and related to factors outside of art. Leibnitz believed everything that was true could be expressed as language and that ideas about objects could not depend on other objects, but by the objects' relationship to some event in time and space. In his view, no created substance acts on any other substance, but that it is possible to infer from the state of one substance to a corresponding state in any other substance, which is known as *psychophysical parallelism.* Psychophysical parallelism is the view that mental (psychical) and bodily (physical) events occur in separate but parallel sequences, where psychical events cause other psychical events and physical events cause other physical events, but in mind and body relationships, the physical does not directly relate to the mental.

According to Leibnitz, every substance must have a complete concept and is a law-governed whole where it is possible from any one state to infer the others. From this viewpoint, substance strives for an end. This is supported in Leibnitz's law—if one thing is identical to another then anything that is true of one must be true of another. Leibnitz's view of the separation of mind from body also challenges the possibility that physical events can cause mental events (i.e., that feeling an emotion can make the heart beat faster or that a response to an aesthetic object could cause a poignant memory).

The mind–body problem has become, in the literature of philosophy, a substitute for the philosophy of the mind. This is sometimes referred to as the *philosophy of psychology,* which is the study of the specific mental concepts of consciousness, emotion, imagination, introspection, intention, thinking, and the will. Descartes separated the mind from the body through the cogito, Spinoza argued that the physical and the mental are simply two aspects of the same underlying reality, and Leibnitz believed that they were related in noncausal but harmonious ways. However, it was empiricist philosopher David Hume who first conceived of an empirical psychology, which made it possible to view mental operations definable in terms of the association of ideas.

Hume believed we cannot base any knowledge of the external world only on our sensory experience because we can only examine the psychology of our beliefs about the world. Through his system of value, which was radically naturalistic and noted for containing his dictum *to feel,* Hume provided a psychological description rather than an analytical one. Hume defined *virtue* as any mental action or quality that gives the spectator the pleasing sentiment of approbation. Hume challenged the a priori of Descartes, which he believed could cause anything to appear to produce anything. Instead, he observed that both the concepts of causation and natural law cannot be drawn from observations of the environment, but are rather derived from the felt force of our habitual associations of perceptions of the mind. From this, Hume developed his account of argument from experience, which others later labeled as *induction.*

To dwell a bit more on Hume at this juncture may seem to the reader to be a bit of a stretch if the topic is visual conception. However, it is worth doing so if only because his ideas are, as empirical thought, a radical departure from his colleagues, Locke and Barkeley. He is also important because of his conceptions and influence on what is called *art as language,* which is reflected in the modern movement of structuralism and conceptual art.

Hume believed that an idea could be represented as a mental picture and that it was composed of copies of actual impressions of senses or feeling. He believed that the analysis of an idea consisted of two stages: (a) breaking the idea into simpler elements, and (b) identifying the single impressions of which the simple ideas are copies. This idea or mental picture contains features that are obscure and, therefore, as introspection of the idea alone, can fail to reveal its true character. Therefore, it is necessary to have a word for the idea as context rather than content and then construct an experiment that links the idea to an actual experience. Through the actual experience, we find the missing part to be a feeling in the mind that gives a clearer view than simple use of the natural faculties.

For Hume, verification was achieved through a look to the future rather than the past. To think concretely about the concept of cause reflects on what we actually do and say and the conditions under which we do it when we decide that a particular thing is the cause of a problem. In effect, Hume becomes the imaginary skeptic who refuses to believe in the regularity of nature and is compelled to reject not only his unremembered past and the not as yet observed future, but also evidence of his sense, memory, testimony, and significant speech. As a predeconstructionist, Hume believed that every successive act of reasoning carries its own risk of error and cumulatively diminishes the probability of the original conclusion, which is reduced to nothing—the consequence of which is thinking too much or too logically.

Hume also believed people to be substances: Minds are modes with which to talk about beliefs and feelings, and the states of mind, such as joy, belief, and so on, are public meanings without which one could not communicate. Finally, he thought states of mind must be analyzed in behavior. Through these conceptions, Hume lay out both the structuralist's and poststructuralist's conceptions of: (a) criticism of art becoming the substance of art, (b) deconstruction of art as an antidote to logical reasoning, (c) public talk about art as the means for the construct of value, and (d) the necessity of art events as means to verify the idea or concept contained in the art experience.

Philosophically, the art as language point of view is best reflected in the writings of Ludwig Wittgenstein (1889–1951) and Morris Weitz. Throughout his career, Wittgenstein was preoccupied with the scope and limits of language and, in particular, with how the user is bound by its limits. For Wittgenstein, language was the primary means for conveying how things are in the world and what must be true about the world and language to make such representations possible. He is most famous for his belief in the picture theory of atomic fact, where there is a one-to-one correspondence of elements between the picture and the thing pictured. In his view, all propositions consist of pictures that can account for the versatility of language; once its conventions are established, one can construct and understand an indefinite range of propositions.

Wittgenstein later changed his picture analogy for a tool and game analogy. For anyone to understand and assess a language, they must know what game is being played and what its rules and objectives are. A linguistic move, thus like any move in a game, needs to be understood as being more or less weak in a particular game. For Wittgenstein, such language use is essentially social, where there cannot be such a thing as a private language outside of ordinary public language that had no rules for being used correctly. Private language, which uses such terms as *truth, beauty,* or *art,* are, in his view, nonsense and cannot be understood in a propositional sense. Thus, a person judging the arts cannot use terms such as *how marvelous* because they convey that the person does not know what he or she is talking about. The same applies to someone calling someone else *musical* because he or she says "ah" when a piece of music is played.

The aesthetition Morris Weitz expanded on Wittgenstein's ideas. He claimed that art could not be a logical concept because it has no set of necessary and sufficient properties—hence, no theory of it is logically possibly (Weitz, 1959). Utilizing Wittgenstein's game theory, Weitz described the problem of discovering the nature of art as being in a game where we look at what we call art and find no common properties (propositions) consistent with a common game.

For Weitz, art is what he called an *open concept* that is always changing and novel. It is not sought through a theory, but rather through a concept that is both an accurate description of the work or event used and an evaluation of that event. He believes that all art events result in the use of clear speech, which is articulated and debated as criteria for public evaluation and as recommendations to attend in certain ways and to certain features of a work of art. Thus, reasoned debate is related to the falseness of all theories about art and their usefulness or inadequacy in providing an agreed on evaluation of a given work by a given audience at a particular time. In Weitz's theory, art is essentially reduced to talk about art, or *metatalk,* which is talk about the way you can talk about it.

The end game of the art as language theory is found in the method of structuralism, which is an extension of Hume's basic skepticism of reason, meaning as a product of language analysis, and verification through experience. Structuralism was developed by anthropologist Levi-Strauss, who referred to the human subject as the spoiled brat of philosophy. He believed that the goal of the human sciences was not to constitute man but to dissolve him (Sarup, 1989). Levi-Strauss' ideas were interpreted by the structuralists as a way to conceive the self as self-synonymous with consciousness, which it decenters con-

sciousness and provides a critique of historicism that challenges the notion of history having any overall pattern.

Structuralism actually evolved from the linguistic theories of Saussure, who emphasized the distinction between the signifier and the signified (i.e., where the word used to
describe an object is the *signifier* and a concept of the object is the *signified*). The structural
relationship between the signifier and signified constitutes a linguistic sign within a language made up of such signs. In structuralism, the linguistic sign is arbitrary, which means
it has semantic value by virtue of its position within the structure of language. Thus, the
sign (e.g., parts of speech, phrases) as an element of language depends on the balance between what the object is called (signifier) and what is its concept (the signified) while still
existing in a one-to-one relationship between propositional claims in language and what is
reality. Hence, language about art depends on the structure of all the possible signs for the
separate and distinct relations between the words used to discuss art and their conceptual
meaning. Thus, what can be said about art is limited to the various language texts developed and is not a matter of direct observation or individual impressions of an aesthetic object or event.

One example of analogical approaches as form adapting the linguistic theories of
Saussure occur in what is referred to as *conceptual art* (Fig. 4.4). According to Burnham,
conceptual art's ideal medium is telepathy, where the closest analogy would be a form of
computer communication through a verbal or neural relay (Burnham, 1974). Conceptualism in art was thought to have evolved as a reaction to the planning of gallery and museum exhibits, which were organized not on existing work but on the basis of submitted
proposals considered more intellectual than gestural and therefore redundant.
Bertalanffy's (1968) system analysis is also viewed as an influence because it looks at the
symbolic world of culture as unnatural and as a means for negating biological nature,
which drives usefulness and adaption. Thus, conceptualism is more concerned with the
nature of ideas, how they are transformed and disseminated, and how we free ourselves
from the confusions that exist between ideas and physical reality (Fig. 4.5).

Examples of conceptual work include objects such as one sheet of plywood secured to a
floor or wall, one standard dye marker thrown into the sea, common steel nails driven into
the floor at points designated at the time of an installation, or paint poured directly on the
floor and allowed to dry. Under conceptual guidelines, such works can be either a thing
constructed or a statement of intent to construct. Once the piece is stated (as language)
publically, it can be said to exist.

Other examples of conceptual works include those that are conceptions of conceptions, such as occur in actual studio installations. There, the exhibited work is made public
in the form of an interview, where the artist indicates that the piece consists of the ideas
people get from reading the interview—noting that the actual work cannot be shown because it is unknowable (i.e., existing only in the minds of many people). Burnham (1974)
felt such responses are in the form of logical regressions, which as a series of propositions
have no beginning and thus provoke circularity.

Conceptual works can also be works that cannot be discussed because they are ongoing
(i.e., things not having a physical presence, but rather the power to generate concepts),
works not made because their forming would be considered irrelevant, or as information
theory on the topics of predictability, improbability, complexity, message structure, dis-

FIG. 4.4.   KOSUTH, Joseph. *One and Three Chairs*. (1965). Wooden folding chair, photographic copy of a chair, and photographic enlargement of a dictionary definition of a chair; chair, 32 3/8 x 14 7/8 x 20 7/8" (82 x 37.8 x 53 cm); photo panel, 36x24 1/8" (91.5 x 61.1 cm); text panel, 24 x 24 1/8" (61 x 61.3 cm). The Museum of Modern Art, New York. Larry Aldrich Foundation Fund. Photograph (c) 1998 by The Museum of Modern Art, New York.

FIG. 4.5.   DUCHAMP, Marcel. *Fresh Widow*. New York, 1920. Miniature French window, painted wood frame, and eight panes of glass covered with black leather, 30 1/2 x 17 5/8" (88.5 x 44.8 cm), on wood sill 3/4 x 21 x 4" (1.9 x 53.4 x 10.2 cm). The Museum of Modern Art, New York. Katherine S. Dreier Bequest. Photograph (c) 1998 by The Museum of Modern Art, New York.

semination, delay, and distortion. As a result, conceptualism has been described as a communication with the unverifiable consistency of a rumor.

PSYCHOLOGICAL EXPLANATIONS OF ART

Although both aesthetitions and philosophers can effectively tell us about the frames of mind we use to know how we can think about the self and the art object, they rarely deal with the science of the cognitive operations carried on in visual perception, consciousness, imagination, emotion, thought, and intellect. Also, although a number of aesthetitions and scholars in the psychology of art have dealt with such issues, they rarely do so in as comprehensive a manner as do the cognitive scientists.

As already noted, most aesthetitions harbor suspicions about their even being such a thing as a psychology of art. Rather, they feel that if such a field exists, it has to be like the field of sociology—one of the weakest of the sciences. In general, they question the notion of aesthetic experience being linked to intellect or as having any purely causal relationship to human behavior. For them, art is an idea in the mind or in an object, a metaphor, or a symbol—things not easily verified through human psychological experiment.

Nevertheless, art historians like Ernst Gombrich and aesthetitions like Robin Collingwood have an extensive knowledge of the psychological literature. Psychologists like Rudolph Arnheim are also well acquainted with thinking about and making art. Some visual artists are also knowledgeable about the mental processes involved in creative thinking and forming. However, these ideas are scattered about in the history, philosophy, and psychology of art literature. As such, they have had only a limited impact on the cognitive scientists and practitioners seeking an understanding of how certain mental processes affect thinking about and forming creative objects.

To bring all these far-ranging and disparate resources together as they impact on the artistic cognitive functions of perception, consciousness, emotion, and thought would be more confusing than helpful to the reader seeking to find some coherence between how artists think about such matters aesthetically and how cognitive scientists think about such functions psychologically. Therefore, to make these connections possible, I have chosen to synthesize the psychology of art literature into two exemplary categories that correspond to the top–down and bottom–up models that psychologists use to interpret their own experiments. These categories represent a distillation of thought on such matters and represent only the key ideas of a few individuals, which is, admittedly, accepting of the risk of being reductive. The alternative is to either confuse the reader with too many views or, worse still, provide no aesthetic link of scientific cognitive behaviors to art.

The Top–Down Aesthetic Model

How aesthetitions describe the act of perception or as really seeing something varies according to the same top–down and bottom–up models psychologists use for interpreting the results of their experiments. These are the top–down notion of sensations as elements in structuring ideas or mental schema and the bottom up view of direct perception, as in Gestalt psychology. The top–down model that follows is based on the ideas of the aesthetition Robin Collingwood and the art historian Ernst Gombrich.

The Collingwood View

E. G. Collingwood's view of perception begins with what he called *sensa* or *sensum,* which he distinguished as having either real or imaginary properties. Collingwood argued that an illusory sensum can be an imaginary one mistaken for a real one, such as occurs in seeing the forms of objects or animals in cloud formations. He believed this is an error in that it converts imaginary sensa into illusory sensa. Likewise, real sensa can be ruled as an error when viewed as imaginary, as in the case of a child or primitive viewing an image in a mirror as indicating a space existing behind the mirror. Thus, for him, any sensum is illusory insofar as there are no errors in interpreting it. All that can be said of sensum is that it is presented to us as an act of sensation (Collingwood, 1975).

For Collingwood, to see something is to make a distinction between appearances and images. He illustrated this through comparing the actual sight of a railroad track converging on the horizon with a three-point perspective drawing of the same scene. The essence of the relationship between the real event and drawing is that, while both present the same perspective of the scene to us, the drawing is called an *image* because it obeys like the event seen. Thus, he challenges that sensa viewed as actual space and as a faithful drawing of that space are the same. Hence, art is something to be viewed apart from actual seeing.

For Collingwood, imagination is that part of perception that permits us to know that a box seen from three sides has a fourth side and an inside space that can be imagined as being pretty much as is actually there. If one could only see but not imagine, one could not know of a world with solid bodies and interior spaces. Thus, to imagine is to perceive a thing as being real—not because it is fully revealed in appearance, but because the conditions or clues present allow one to construct a thing as if it actually were totally present to vision. The same holds true of a dream, where the person dreaming holds certain events later in imagination and we inquire whether the things dreamed are real because of the affect on the dreamer. Using this analysis, Collingwood argued that there are really three kinds of sensum: a real sensum correctly interpreted, an illusory sensum such as one falsely interpreted, and an imaginary sensum, which has not been interpreted.

To explain his theory, Collingwood constructed a model in which imagination (a sensum not interpreted) forms a link between sensation (a thing actually perceived) and intellect. Sensation is something like a sound or color that is present but held in what psychologists term *sensory memory,* which does not remain fixed in short- or long-term memory as a schema to be manipulated. Later, when a sense impression moves from being pure sensation to something retained before the mind (as in short- or long-term memory), it can be anticipated, recalled, and manipulated even after the sensory object that inspired it is no longer present. This act of manipulation is what Collingwood called *imagination.*

For Collingwood, thought is that which detects relations between sensa, which is, in a sense, an effort to perceive through contrasting the thing sensed with a mental concept or schema; this allows the sensation to be interpreted. He called this act the *act of attending.* To attend to the sensation in relation to the schema held in the mind allows sense to be made out the object or event which he believed is to think. Thinking becomes the attentive act of matching sensa with mental or visual schema held in short- or long-term memory. Therefore, thinking is an intellectual activity involving attention, which constitutes consciousness of thought.

According to Collingwood, consciousness occurs in a mind shaped by sentience using senses that are too intimate, in his view, to be knowledge. Consciousness indicates the togetherness of the two things—the sensation and sensum—both of which are present in conscious thought. Thus, the difference between seeing and looking is that the person looking is aware of his own seeing as well as the thing seen—a close approximation to what cognitive psychologists call *metacognition*. In his view, consciousness is a rational process that dominates feeling and is the sole source of attention. Attention to feelings made conscious through attention does not constitute successive attention to all other possible states of consciousness because this would be making a choice as to what feeling to attend to—which is, in Collingwood's view, intellect itself.

Accordingly, consciousness is also a consciousness of self, which is not yet to fully know who one is, but rather that I am something to which a feeling belongs and not something belonging to a feeling. Thus, the conscious self is not dominated by its feelings and can select and isolate any one element contained in their placing that element in the focus of attention, thus changing impression into an idea.

Collingwood believed consciousness is also a mental function that converts impression into idea (i.e., crude sensation into consciousness and imagination). It is thought, but not necessarily intellect, that apprehends and constructs relations. Consciousness is the activity of thought that belongs to thought itself and cannot err as intellect by referring things to wrong concepts. As Collingwood noted, true consciousness is the confession to ourselves of our feelings; a false consciousness would be disowning them, as in thinking that a particular feeling is not our own.

Thought/Thinking/Intellect. According to Collingwood, thought is mainly concerned with feeling, where feeling is its sole and universal subject matter. To think a thought and express it in words such as *I am tired* is to think about feelings. The same appears true when we make a statement like "This is my hat," except that feelings in this case, while not explicit, are implied because of the knowledge and feelings about one's hat that makes such a statement possible. With respect to a declaration such as "That this or that thing is mine," he believed that it takes all kinds of sensa and relations between them and that errors are possible. Therefore, statements or propositions that involve complex sets of thoughts, feelings, and judgements are thus empirical.

For Collingwood, thought is one of two kinds: (a) thought about feelings themselves, and (b) thoughts about our thoughts to determine the relation between feelings, which are propositions affirming one act of thinking with another. However, Collingwood did not accept that propositional (scientific) thought is superior to thoughts about feelings because, in both cases, knowledge is derived from experience and in either case we must verify any claims made in light of that experience. To verify this, Collingwood challenged both the argument of Kant (Scruton, 1981) that we can verify things independently from experience and the linguist argument regarding the equivalence of words. With regard to verification through experience, he argued that to believe otherwise (i.e., that thought is not an experience and is of a second order) is to reject the notion that all knowledge is derived from experience, where a thought, no less than a sensation, is implied by experience.

According to Collingwood, thought or intellect is not related to expressive activity in the same way as thinking about one's feelings is related. Thought, which involves comparing two simultaneous sensa and considering the relation between them, always occupies a period of time where the sensa have passed from the mind. Thus, sensa removed from thinking over time moves feelings in direct response to color, sounds, and scents to the level of language about such things, which are substitutes for what is actually felt. Borrowing from Hume, Collingwood separated the notion of ideas (imagination) and made them distinct from impressions (intellect).

Feeling/Emotion.   According to Collingwood, feeling can be described by two different kinds of experience: one in which we talk about the feeling, color, or sound that is a sensation, and the other in which feeling pleasure or pain is an emotion. The difference between the two is mainly a matter of duration, where feeling as a sensation is fairly short-lived and feeling as an emotion is something separate and apart from direct sensory activity.

To point out the differences between feeling and thinking, Collingwood argued that thinking is concerned with things that last, even if not forever, and is therefore a factor in experience. Sensation and emotion both exist in our experience, but sensation takes precedence of the emotion not as its cause, but rather as a distinct and autonomous element in the experience. In his view, sensa provides the emotional charge on the corresponding sensation. The separation of the two, while not evident experimentally, is evident at least socially, where individuals as a part of their conscious life distinguish between the thing observed and the subsequent feelings and emotions that respond to the thing. Therefore, feeling is something independent of all thinking and functions below the level of thought and is unaffected by it.

Language.   In Collingwood's view, art is a language if only because its characteristics are expressive and imaginative. It is an act of consciousness (attending) and rules out the possibility of it being a product of sensations or emotions (the physical) or as intellect, which has to do with concepts. Art lies within humans, whose nature is to become a thinking being. Therefore, he believes it is an imaginative activity and, as in the activity of speech, stands in relation to emotion, where in one way it expresses an emotion and through the process of expressing it discovers feeling as independent from expressions of it. Thus, speech or art expresses an emotion that the artist/speaker only feels because he or she expresses it and it is found in the emotion of consciousness.

Collingwood believed that, as a language, art is not a ready-made language, but rather creates language as it goes along—a language that does not tolerate cliches and, as a genuine expression, is an original one. In his view, art is not the utilization of language (communication) as a ready-made language (i.e., a repertory of cliches to produce states of mind with persons on whom these cliches are used). To make another person think or act in some way is to induce someone to do something that is an emotion and not art. When an artist seeks to advance his or her political views through expressive activity, it may help to discover what these views are and convert others to that view; this does not advance art, but rather stifles it.

For Collingwood, language is also imaginative because it describes what it is and is expressive because it describes what it does. Its function is to express emotions. For example, the emotions of love, hatred, anger, and shame are emotions of consciousness and not at the psychical (physical) level of experience. In his view, intellectual language, is the same thing intellectualized or modified to express thought. When language is used as intellect, it must be formally or linguistically expressed not only materially or psychologically expressed. In Collingwood's view, body actions are also a form of language because it is bodily expression of emotion dominated by thought in a primitive form of consciousness.

Speech, like body language, is also a system of gestures where speech as a gesture produces characteristic sounds that can be perceived both through the eye and ear. Painting is also related to the expressiveness of the gestures made by the hand in drawing and is likewise evident in the gestures of the stage musician and dancer. Early in the life of a child, speech is not addressed to any audience (inner speech) and is initially a function of self-consciousness, where the child is conscious of the speech being used and is thus becoming a listener. Therefore, self-consciousness is what makes a person a sentient organism through the psychical expression of feeling. To speak is not to communicate an emotion to someone else, but rather to express an emotion of a particular kind through a controlled body action in which the idea is expressed. He believed expression is speech: The speaker is the first hearer and, in speaking, becomes aware of having an idea that he or she hears in expressing it. Thus, we can only know what we feel when we can express it in a word; only by expressing feelings is it possible to know what our emotions are. As to someone hearing the speech and understanding it, this occurs through the hearer's ability to reconstruct his or her own consciousness of the idea expressed in the words heard.

In discussing language as symbol, Collingwood held that a symbol is language yet not language and, whether mathematical or logical, its purpose is scientific. Symbolism is intellectualized language because it expresses emotions that are intellectualized simply because they are used for the expression of intellectual emotion. Language as intellect has both expressiveness and meaning. Symbolism, in contrast, refers beyond emotion to the thought behind the emotional charge.

The Gombrichian View

Ernst Gombrich, previously cited as an example for interpreting art as idea, is conceptually committed to art as schema and accepting of many Gestalten ideas as well. His text, *Art as Illusion* (1989), is one of the most extensive 20th-century efforts to lay out a possible psychology of pictorial representation. Although biased as an art historian in accepting that pictures come from other pictures, he also offered a number of well-reasoned explanations for why pictures looked as they did at various periods in history and how these various forms of pictorial representations were shaped by discoveries in the psychological sciences of perception. His ideas are important to the psychology of perception mostly because he opened up the possibility that the art and science view of perception may be more alike than different (Gombrich, 1989).

Gombrich claimed that the classic rabbit–duck image, which is used to describe the nature of the ambiguous image often associated with works of art, is an example of the failure of the viewer to know the meaning of a shape apart from its interpretation (Fig. 4.6). To convey meanings, images are the result of the artist's effort to alter shapes in such a way that meaning is possible.

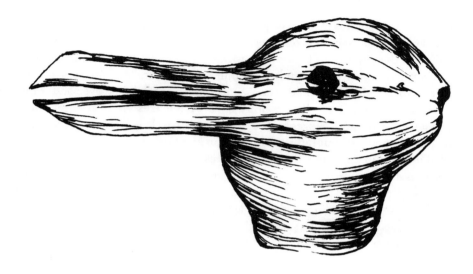

FIG. 4.6.   A version of Gombrich's Rabbit or Duck? image that, as an ambiguous figure-ground reversal, can be seen as either a rabbit or a duck.

To illustrate, he used an image that begins as a circle. It is later modified by an attached semicircle to become a shopping bag with a handle. By adding two little squiggles, it becomes a purse. Still later, by adding a tail at the bottom, it is a cat. He believed this shows the power of an image metamorphosis, where a tail destroyed the purse and created the cat (Fig. 4.7). In Gombrich's view, when art teachers fail in their efforts to get their pupils to look at nature and render it accurately, the problem is not with the student's ability to copy nature but rather an inability to see it (schematically). Nothing visible is understood by the sense of sight alone. Even the simplest sense impression is already a mental fact and what we call the world is really the result of a complex psychological process. Therefore, the artist can neither overcome the mental images they possess nor do without them as a means to get in touch with the memories that enable them to constitute three-dimensional form in their minds. He also believed that the study of art history has helped psychologists discover that the naive images of primitives or children are not the product of childish thinking, but rather a conforming to cultural ideals of representation and the power of memory.

Gombrich also challenged the notion of the mind as a bucket of sense impressions to be processed. He agreed with R. K. Popper (1957) that the mind never ceases to probe the environment and, over time, become more articulate and differentiated. He noted that there is no distinction between perception and illusion: Perception seeks to weed out un-

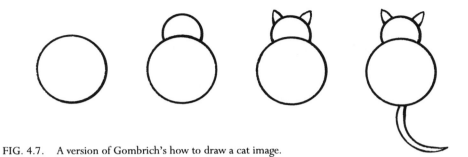

FIG. 4.7.   A version of Gombrich's how to draw a cat image.

satisfactory or harmful illusions through perceptual trial and error, which artists discover through the process of making and matching. In such a process, artists apply mental schema first and corrections in light of visual discoveries made later.

According to Gombrich, all imitation relies on guided projection, such as when we see that patches of color on a canvas create an impressionist landscape or when we hear someone speaking from a page of print. What we actually see and hear is supplied by our memory, which turns the patches of color into a landscape and the sounds of the speaker into thought. Expectation creates an illusion where one selects from an ensemble of possible states. The greater the probability of a symbol's occurrence in any given situation, the smaller its content. When we anticipate, we need not listen or look; it is here that he believed projection will do for perception.

Artistic images are also assisted by what he called the *etc. principle,* where a few detailed figures and heads with some additional fuzzy figures and heads suggest a crowd of people at a racetrack or ball game. This effect was described by Vasari (Gombrich, 1989) as hovering between the seen and unseen. Such devices speak to the problem of knowing what the eye cannot see in the distance and reporting what the eye does see if it does not see it at all. Oculists, he noted, test our eyesight with random letters because where we can guess we cannot separate seeing from knowing.

Perception.   Gombrich also believed that, because what we know in seeing is also what we expect to see, it is the power of expectation rather than the power of conceptual knowledge that molds what we see in life as well as in art. What psychologists refer to as *mental set* is, in Gombrich's view, a state of readiness to start projecting; what we call reading an image may in reality be better described as testing (i.e., to try out to see what fits). Once we discover that fit, it is also difficult to detach it.

Therefore, in viewing art, we first grope for the artist's intention behind the communication, especially so when we are thought to interpret art as records of artistic intentions. In such cases, we react to the work because we identify with the artist; if the meaning is incomplete, we are willing to believe that we will find the meaning in other works. This suggests that our acceptance of the artist's work, where a work does not make sense, will do so in some later work. In such instances, it is clear that meaning in art differs from meaning in visual perception generally because we also introduce the social factor of the artist creating his or her own elite and the elite its own artists. Such notions also reflect art being an idea or concept.

Pictures also differ from real-life experience in another way, which Gombrich illustrated through the Saul Steinberg drawing of the hand drawing the hand. We have no clue about which is meant to be real, and each image and each interpretation is equally probable but neither, as such, is consistent. There is no limit as to what pictures can represent without differentiating between what belongs to the picture and what belongs to intended reality. Pictures can also refer to other pictures, such as used in Steinberg's cartoon of an artist painting an enlarged thumb print, which appears as a landscape by Van Gogh. The thumb print appears to be a real landscape with a tree on the horizon and a ploughed-up field leading into space with a dark hedge showing against a swirling sky—a case where the real is imaginary and the imaginary real.

The Bottom–Up Aesthetic Model

The bottom–up model of artistic perception is different from the top–down model of Collingwood and Gombrich. The former is more like the bottom–up view in psychology, which admits to a direct perception devoid of mental schema or other systems for ordering perceptual clues into meaningful vision. Thus, direct perception is an immediate and relatively unfiltered vision, which Gibson identified in the law of affordances to permit human beings to function in an environment without the need to invoke beliefs, attitudes, or mental effort. The ideas of both the aesthetition Susanne Langer and psychologist Rudolph Arheim are used to address higher cognitive abilities from this perspective.

The Langerian View

Perception.   Susanne Langer's view of perception, although essentially bottom–up, shares a lot of the ideas of empiricist philosopher John Locke—where insight into the nature of relations through which we discover differences, identities, and contradiction are the laws of logic, which Locke called *natural light* (Langer, 1953). She noted that it is in the mind that we perceive the truth: The eye is directed to it with the mind, mostly perceiving that white is not black, that a circle is not a triangle, and that three are more than two and also equal to one plus two. In her view, such truths are what the mind perceives at the first sight of the ideas together by bare intuition and without the intervention of any other idea nor proof of that which is apparent to direct vision. For her, intuitive knowledge is essentially: the perception of relations in general, the perception of forms or abstract seeing, the perception of significance or meaning, and the perception of examples.

Langer also believed these intuitive functions are either logical or semantical and are not a revelation of metaphysical reality, which neither reason nor intuition finally reveals. They are data derived from sensation and reflection. Thus, for her, reason is a systematic means of getting from one intuition to another and for eliciting more complex and cumulative intuition. As such, there is no possible conflict between intuition and discursive reasoning. She concludes that there is also no distinction between insight achieved by reasoning and insight immediately enjoyed. Thus, intuition becomes a fundamental intellectual activity that produces logical and semantical understanding and compresses all acts of insight or recognition of formal properties, relations, significance, abstraction, and ex-emplification. It is also more primitive than belief, which is true or false because intuition is simply present to us.

The perception of an art work or its artistic import, Langer believed, is also intuitive and can never be stated in discursive language. A work of art is an expressive form and a symbol that refers to nothing outside of itself being also an idea of felt life. The difference between rational insight and artistic insight, Langer noted, is due to the way the intuition is elicited. Thus, artistic perception is directly intuitive in communicable yet rational terms.

The relationship between what is perceived as actual experience and pictured as artistic experience is also addressed by Langer through her explanations of virtual space. Langer believed the purpose of all plastic art is to articulate visual form and present that form in such a way as to be charged with feeling. She noted that space in the practical world has no shape, and pictured space is not experiential space that can be known by sight or touch. In her view, virtual space is the pictorial space that is the primary illusion of art having no con-tinuity with the space we live in and that is entirely self-contained and independent of ac-tual space.

Pictorial space is also substitute or inferential space, which is not normally given to vi-sion. On the topic of aesthetic space, she accepted the notions of Hildebrand, which is that such space is a concept of a visual field or picture plane. Thus, in pictorial space, sight is similar to what we earlier described as occurring in the rods and cones of the eye, where the perception of objects, distances, and planes are perceptible as our vision focuses on new and different visual planes. Visual planes in pictures are what she would call the *motifs,* in which forms are made and related to define space and exhibit its character.

According to Langer, pictorial form is also a semblance of things being an illusion and entirely independent of actual space, which is to awaken in the viewer an idea of space that the artist presents. What an artist presents is the semblances of objects, people, land-scapes, and so on, which are the visual values of perceptual space. Therefore, representa-tion in art is for the sake of creating individual forms, which, through the act of imagination, establish virtual proportions, connections, and focal points. The suggestion of objects in pictures becomes a mechanism not to suggest reality, but rather to construct volumes, distances, planes of vision, and space.

Langer believed that creation in art is found in the modifications artists make to the ap-pearance of things by selection and emphasis. These selections, as well as radical distor-tions of actual form, are for the purpose of making space visible and its continuity sensible. It is like a projected image, where everything pictured serves to define and organize.

Language.   Langer viewed language as being an entirely different system than the symbolic system of artistic expression. For her, language is a symbolism (i.e., a system of symbols governed by conventions of use). Its basic symbols are also equivalent to each other and may be used to express the same meaning. Language, as such, can be used to de-fine and explain things to pass from one expression to another and build up an idea from a group of simpler ideas.

To the contrary, a work of art is a symbol (form) and is not a product of symbolism with no meaningful units making it up and where its meaning is derived as an intuition of total import and one that cannot be conveyed through language. Art as imagination, as William

James (1955) noted, breaks up the confusion of sense perception into units and groups, events and chains of events, things and relations, and causes and effects. In Langer's view, primitive conception is imagination, where language and imagination group together in a reciprocal tutelage. She believed that language in its literal use does for the awareness of things about us what the arts do for our awareness of subjective reality—feeling and emotion. They give inward experiences of form and thus make forms conceivable.

The Rudolph Arnheim View

In looking at the act of perception, Arnheim began by looking at thinking itself, noting that thinking consists of intellectual operations on cognitive material. The material becomes nonperceptual through the act of thinking, which transforms raw percepts into concepts. Such thoughts reflect Arnheim's general view that cognitive processes, whether carried out consciously or unconsciously, voluntarily or automatically, are no different in principle. What matters is the direct ability of the mind to grope for information about the inner and outer world—a capacity present in the early beginnings of animal life and not dependent on consciousness or even the presence of a brain (Arnheim, 1969).

For Arnheim, sensory responsiveness is intelligence, which is the capacity of the various senses to obtain information about what is going on at a distance, including hearing, vision, and smell. As distance senses, they not only provide what is known but also remove the perceiver from the direct impact of the explored event. Because of this, the viewer is able to go beyond the immediate effect of the event, thus making it possible to probe the behavior of events more objectively. The observer is then concerned with what *is* rather than merely what has been done or with what he or she is doing. As a result, vision is detached, beholding contemplation.

He also believed that intelligent behavior depends on how articulate the data are on a sensory area. One can indulge in the senses but cannot think in them. Therefore, in learning and seeing, shapes, colors, movements, and sounds are susceptible to complex organization in space and line. He claimed that vision is helped by the sense of touch and muscle sense, but these senses, unlike vision, must explore shapes inch by inch rather than sense it as the eye does—all in one sweep. The great virtue of vision is that it provides a highly articulate sensory medium as well as being inexhaustibly rich in information about objects and events in the outer world. Thus, vision is the primary medium of thought.

Arnheim also argued that because the senses are biological aids for survival, perception is both purposive and selective. Active selectivity is basic to vision. He noted that when something appears or disappears, moves, or changes shape, size, or color, the viewer will find his or her own condition altered. This provides, in moments of danger, that which is signaled to be obeyed. Change is absent in immobile things, but in both humans and animals constancy stimulates efforts to change or vary what is seen, reorganizing the grouping of things or switching from one view to another. These human reactions to monotony are an elementary form of intelligent contempt for indiscriminate attention, which ultimately needs to be attended to and noticed because humans refuse to be bored. However, such changes do not only help in gaining wisdom but also restrict it.

Neurologically, the eyes are moveable in their sockets, with selective explorations being affected by movements of the head and body. In that process, eye photochemistry proceeds by abstraction to produce, in conscious perceptions, colors as variation and combinations of a few primaries. This kind of simplified vision is accomplished with only a few kinds of transmitters—a task that is relatively complex, imposing physiologically a conceptual visual order in the material it records. This built-in selectivity is useful because it avoids wasting effort and restricts choice to make reactions faster and surer.

Arnheim believed that selective attention is built in by heredity and applies to various species as a whole. In humans, the choice of stimuli and the reaction to them are controlled with selective eye movements that target a vision somewhere between automatism and willful response. Because retinal sensitivity is restricted, the eye can and must single out a particular spot that becomes isolated, dominant, and central. What this means is that the eye picks up one thing at a time, distinguishing the primary objective from its surroundings, and selects a particular object for attention because it stands out against its background or meets the observer's needs. He noted that ocular fixation can be described as a move from tension to tension reduction, where a conflict between the inner or outer worlds is the cause of tension and is eliminated, through the movement of the eyeball, to resolve the conflict—thus adapting the inner to the outer. In his view, this action is a form of cognitive behavior called *problem solving,* wherein the action occurring requires the restructuring of a given problem situation. Although such ocular restructuring is of a rather simple kind, it cannot, in his opinion, be at such a level that thought and perception become separate. Perception is the direct exploration of what is out there; in contrast, thinking begins with the task and the modifying of a given order so that it fits the requirements of the solution to a given problem.

According to Arnheim, ocular fixation also shows that the individual is searching to find its objective in a perceptual field that has an order of its own. Such an interplay between the structure of a given field and individual needs is characteristic of the psychology of attention. Selectivity and attention are also involved in the perception of depth, where psychologists have discovered that the image the eye receives is not part of the object, but rather an equivalent of it. Because the size of the image depends on the distance between the object and the eye, choosing the proper distance is a cognitive task. Intelligence is operational when animals or humans blocked from a certain course of action choose another to meet the situation. The observer's attention is in searching to find its objective in a perceptual field, which has an order of its own.

Arnheim also believed that shape recognition is a form of highly cognitive concept formation. Response to shapes are a response to patterns of shapes, rather than conforming to the traditional view of vision mechanically recording the elements of stimulation, which are then suitably conglomerated into shapes on the basis of the perceiver's past experience. If the later theory were true, shape perception would be a cognitively inferior operation.

Thus, in Arnheim's view, perception begins with a problem-solving act that is not a passive recording of stimulus material, but an active concern of the mind. In this act, sight operates selectively, with perception involving an application of form categories called *visual concepts.* When an image of an object changes, the individual must know if the change is due to the object, its context, or both. Thus, the object observed is abstracted from its context and judged mentally by observing its behavior in or outside its context. The generally accepted view is that perception is where the mind aims at and achieves abstraction through separating the object from the environment. Arnheim rejected this, believing instead that perception involves both levels (i.e., that which occurs in the mind at a selective level and that which later occurs in the mental manipulation of basic sight). Only because an object has a graspable shape can it be distinguished from its environmental context. In his view, perception is capable of abstracting an object from its context only because it grasps shape as an organized structure rather than as a recorded mosaic of elements.

To view an object as separate from its context in a pure unimpaired state is, in Arnheim's view, to see the object as a constant, subtracting the effect of the context from the character of the object itself, which is to view it scientifically. The opposite view is to see the object aesthetically, such as what occurred in impressionist painting—where an object was viewed at different times of the day under different light. The first view leaves us with an untouched figment of high generality, which is only useful because it facilitates definition or classification learning. The second encourages productive thinking, which allows human beings to have a continuing contact with a variety of phenomena. The thinker, whose concepts are limited to traditional logic, is, in his view, in danger of performing in a world of paralyzed constructs.

Arnheim's view of art is seen principally in his ideas on impressionism, which he called an example of abandoned constancy. He noted that impressionist painting shows local color and local brightness modulated by the influences of the color and brightness influences in a variety of situations, which a painting could not possibly have through adopting the procedures used in color photographs. His view is that the impressionists were not involved with true hue or brightness of color, but rather with a different notion of abstraction and one that was a more sophisticated cognitive operation. This is a form of abstraction that does not rely on extracting common elements, but rather on the capacity to see an object that is not limited to the view it receives at a given moment, but rather as a integral part of a greater whole, which unfolds as a sequence. This is illustrated also in cubist works, where visual shapes embrace multiple appearances, partial concealments, head-on flatness, and pronounced volumes, where the portrayal of the object depicts a variety of human experience—as seen in variations in viewing contexts and distortions under pressure.

Distortion of the kind evidenced in impressionist and cubist works are, in Arnheim's view, distortions that call for abstraction. Projective distortions not only make the discovery of a prototype possible, but also call for it. Thus, projection produces a dynamic distortion rather than a static deviation. It is perceived as attention toward a simpler form from which it deviates, thereby being an abstraction not drawn from but rather found in the object that calls for the abstraction.

Distortions such as those found in a diamond-shaped parallelogram, which appears as a leaning rectangle, suggest that the rectangle needs straightening or is under pressure, which may encourage a feeling of tension, distortion, or drama in the mind of the observer (Fig. 4.7). The distortion is perceived as a logical consequence of the object's position on the picture plane. Similarly, a distortion of a cube can be seen as a geometrically simple slanting or convergence of its unvariant shape, which, as an imposed modification, makes it possible for the mind to distinguish between what belongs to the object's shape per se and what is due to projective distortion.

Arnheim argued against Gombrich's notion of mental images in the mind as a screen for perception, taking the view that the nature of thinking should be determined by what it

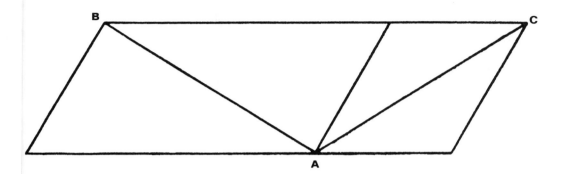

FIG. 4.8.   A drawing of the Sandler parallelogram where identical-length diagonal lines AB and AC appear unequal.

accomplishes. Because psychologists cannot demonstrate imagery existing in consciousness, he sided with the view of the psychoanalysts—that many mental processes occur at what he called the *threshold of awareness,* which questions whether all sensory experiences are conscious. If images exist in the mind, they would be more like the strokes rendered by the expressionist painter, which are responsive to what he described as a pattern of visual forces. In the arts, the reduction of the human figure to an expressive gesture can sharpen an image through the sharpening of essentials. Why, he questioned, can it not do the same in mental imagery?

In Arnheim's view, the art image is the highest form of cognition. For him, it is a symbol and is not a sign that signifies the content of a thing or picture, which portray things. The image in art acts as a symbol to the extent that it portrays things that are at a higher level of abstractness than the symbol itself. Therefore, a symbol gives particular shapes to things, constellations, or forces, which makes art something far removed from being a replica or something faithful to reality or likeness. A painting or sculpture, he argued, intends to evoke an impact of the configuration of forces with references to subject matter being only a means to that end. Any abstraction is a good one when it does not portray the external shape of physical objects, but is closer to the pure forces it presents symbolically.

In Arnheim's view, language fails to move to the level of a pictorial symbol because it functions indirectly through pointing to the referents of words and propositions and is not indispensable to thought. Detached, theoretical thinking can function without words, and the ability to think about a question without confronting a particular object or event speaks more to the human use of cognitive functions than to the nature of these functions. Language, although useful in thinking, is not thinking itself and is furthermore hardly productive thinking. For Arnheim, pure verbal thinking (speech) is the protype of thoughtless thinking that is an automatic response to memory. The visual medium, he pointed out, is superior to other senses because it: (a) offers structural equivalents to all characteristics of objects, events, and relations; (b) can be ordered according to readily definable patterns; and (c) is polydimensional, which provides good thought models of physical objects as well as the dimensions needed for theoretical reasoning.

Language is also a perceptual medium of sounds or signs, which by itself provides few elements of thought because it refers to imagery in some other medium. Because it suggests relation by sequence, it has no function in thought. Imagery achieves what dreams and writings do not because it can combine different and separate levels of abstraction in one sensory situation. He concluded that the role of language is a mere auxiliary to the basic vehicles of thought, which are better for representing objects and relations by articulate shape. According to Arnheim, the function of language is conservative and stabilizing, and therefore tends to make cognition static and immobile. One cannot take pictures or pieces of pictures and put them together to produce new statements as easily as one can combine words or ideographs. Pictorial montages, he noted, show their sense, whereas images produced by words do not.

CHILDREN'S ARTISTIC DEVELOPMENT
1905–1962

One of the most extensive efforts to survey the research literature on children's art was accomplished in the early 1960s by Dale Harris at Pennsylvania State University. Several hundred studies of children's drawings were reviewed by Harris (1963) as part of a collaborative effort with Dr. Florence Goodenough to revise her well-known draw-a-man scale.

In general, Harris believed the research on children's development and drawing specifically supports the following overall generalizations (Harris, 1963).

Children's General and Drawing Development

Children's General Development

- Children's mental performances become more numerous and broaden in range and scope over time.
- Mental performances that involve symbolization and problem solving increase in complexity as a result of associative processes.
- The development of mental abilities is best described as a negatively accelerated growth curve.
- Changes in the growth curve reflect the differential effect of stimulation on growth.
- Cumulative changes in the growth curve depend on repetition or reinforcement, not merely the lapse of time.
- Intellectual maturity includes the ability to perceive likeness and differences, to classify objects, and assign objects to a correct class which are the processes involved in concept formation.
- Older children specify properties in greater detail, recognize essential properties of a class, and form more precise and specific concepts.

Developments in Drawing

- A child's drawing of an object is an index of the child's conception of an object.
- A child's drawing of any object will reveal the discriminations the child makes conceptually.
- Maturity increases the ability to draw relevant and significant features of concepts both as ideas about objects and as class concepts.
- Drawing tests can assess intellectual and conceptual maturity from 4 to 14 years but have less value as a study of personality.

Harris organized his review of studies of children's drawings from 1885 to 1962 into four classifications: (a) descriptive developmental studies, (b) the draw-a-man technique, (c) projective studies of children's drawings, and (d) studies involving perception and cognition.

In his review of developmental studies, he included the drawing classification studies of Kerschensteiner (1905), Burt (1921), Rouma (1913), and Rabello (1932). Kerschensteiner is noted for his child drawing classifications of (a) schematic, (b) visual, or ideoplastic drawing, and (c) dimensional drawing. Rouma is noted for his conception of two stages of development: the preliminary stage and human figure stage. Burt is noted for his classification of seven stages of development: (a) the scribble stage, (b) line stage, (c) descriptive symbolism stage, (d) realism stage, (e) visual realism stage, (f) depression stage, and (g) artistic revival stage. Harris valued these studies because he believes they have furnished a picture of the developmental aspects of drawing that have remained unaltered up to this time.

Draw-a-Man Test

Harris viewed the Florence Goodenough draw-a-man technique as a crowning achievement in the evaluation of children's drawings because it demonstrated that drawing for children had more cognitive than aesthetic meaning (Goodenough, 1928). Harris supported her scale by reviewing a number of Goodenough's fellow researchers who found the scale to be reliable, revealing of differences in drawing ability, successful in the diagnosis of behavior disorders, valid in measuring the effect of art training and art ability, and able to relate well with other measures of intelligence (Fig. 4.9). He noted that scores on the test by children between the ages of 5 and 14 correlate between .70 and .80 with other measures of general mental or scholastic ability. He believed the reason for such high correlations is that its concrete mental operations reflect elemental cognitive concepts that, in turn, logically make up more complex concepts.

In his review of clinical and projective uses of childrens drawing, he referenced studies by numerous researchers (e.g., Alschuler & Hattwick, 1947; Buhler, Smitter, & Richardson, 1952; Harms, 1941; Hevner, 1935; Krauss, 1930; Lowenfeld, 1947). Lowenfeld's analysis of the stages affirmed that children's drawings tell us about motivation. Buhler and colleagues' study helped teachers analyze and understand child personality, motiva-

Short Scoring Guide *

WOMAN POINT SCALE

1. Head present
2. Neck present
3. Neck, two dimensions
4. Eyes present
5. Eye detail: brow or lashes
6. Eye detail: pupil
7. Eye detail: proportion
8. Cheeks
9. Nose present
10. Nose, two dimensions
11. Bridge of nose
12. Nostrils shown
13. Mouth present
14. Lips, two dimensions
15. "Cosmetic lips"
16. Both nose and lips in two dimensions
17. Both chin and forehead shown
18. Line of jaw indicated
19. Hair I
20. Hair II
21. Hair III
22. Hair IV
23. Necklace or earrings
24. Arms present
25. Shoulders
26. Arms at side (or engaged in activity or behind back)

27. Elbow joint shown
28. Fingers present
29. Correct number of fingers shown
30. Detail of fingers correct
31. Opposition of thumb shown
32. Hands present
33. Legs present
34. Hip
35. Feet I: any indication
36. Feet II: proportion
37. Feet III: detail
38. Shoe I: "feminine"
39. Shoe II: style
40. Placement of feet appropriate to figure
41. Attachment of arms and legs I
42. Attachment of arms and legs II
43. Clothing indicated
44. Sleeve I
45. Sleeve II
46. Neckline I
47. Neckline II: collar
48. Waist I
49. Waist II
50. Skirt "modeled" to indicate pleats or draping
51. No transparencies in the figure

52. Garb feminine
53. Garb complete, without incongruities
54. Garb a definite "type"
55. Trunk present
56. Trunk in proportion, two dimensions
57. Head-trunk proportion
58. Head: proportion
59. Limbs: proportion
60. Arms in proportion to trunk
61. Location of waist
62. Dress area
63. Motor coordination: junctures
64. Motor coordination: lines
65. Superior motor coordination
66. Directed lines and form: head outline
67. Directed lines and form: breast
68. Directed lines and form: hip contour
69. Directed lines and form: arms taper
70. Directed lines and form: calf of leg
71. Directed lines and form: facial features

* For use only after the scoring requirements have been mastered.

FIG. 4.9. "Short Scoring Guide" from *Children's Drawings as Measures Of Intellectual Maturity: A Revision and Extension of the Goodenough Draw-A-Man Test* by Dale B. Harris, copyright (c) 1963 by Harcourt Brace & Company and renewed 1991 by Dale B. Harris. Reprinted by permission of the publisher.

tion, and readiness for learning. Harm's study contributed to the study of neurotic children, and Hevner's work showed that lines and forms express feelings stated in adjectives. Krauss advanced the notion that children understand the emotional states of their fellow students through their drawings. Alschuler and Hattwick used drawings as an index of children's emotions. Harris also believed that, although the results of these projective studies were in some ways problematical, they also indicate that drawings show not what the child knows, but what the child feels.

In his review of studies on affect and cognition, Harris maintained that drawings primarily express cognitive practices and that research should concentrate more on the sequences of drawings rather than on individual drawings. Also, as children grow older, they become more concerned about relationships than appearances; without mastering the techniques that suggest these relationships, they must also abandon attempts to portray concepts and understandings graphically.

In an attempt to reconcile these divergent psychological viewpoints and formulate what he called a psychology of young children's drawing activity, Harris effectively pointed to this research as suggesting the following:

1.   Early scribbles are more than random markings and are patterned more by their physical development than visual observation and by relations within the drawing field.
2.   The majority of young children show a directionability in drawing simple forms, which is probably related to motor development.
3.   Children's drawings represent objects as they perceive them, which as a whole contain discernable parts and over time show more detail and organizational complexity.
4.   Central or cognitive factors appear to be crucial in determining developmental features in children's drawings.

With regard to the relationship between early scribbles and physical development, visual observation, and drawing field, he also noted that the research suggests: (a) early scribbles are circular, (b) early scribbles can be classified into at least 20 different types, (c) manipulative patterns are characteristic, preferred, or habitual rather than selective, and (d) these patterns show orientation in space with early development in drawing and writing, showing analogous patterns and similar origins.

On the research dealing with directionality in drawing, he made five specific observations: (a) directionality in drawing shows development trends, (b) figure positions are related to handedness, (c) features other than handedness are also influences, (d) motor behavior in preschool drawing guides production, and (e) motor influence declines and comprehension and cognitive influences guide work after the acquisition of speech. The studies on directionality and the influences in motor development and handedness made after the development of speech seem to suggest a much closer relationship between drawing and intellectual development in preschoolers.

The studies he reviewed also suggest that young children interpret their drawings in much the same way as they draw them, children from ages 7 to 11 respond better to pictures with familiar organizational pattern, and children's picture preferences differ from adults due to differences in comprehension.

Studies reviewed by Harris support that children's drawings represent objects as they perceive them and that their perceptions are holistic or Gestalt in character. They also provide evidence that, in young children, relative size or spatial relations develops more slowly than awareness of parts; younger children depend more on tactual and kinesthetic clues than older children; drawings become increasingly more differentiated as children mature; highly detailed drawings seem to develop along recognizable patterns; and cognitive factors are crucial in the development of drawings. With respect to cognitive factors in drawing, he also noted that children are limited in their ability to draw from three-dimensional models, it is easier for young children to copy an image they are familiar with, copying is more closely correlated to form perception than to motor skill, and copying skills correlate more highly with mental age than with chronological age.

Harris' analysis of these studies notes that there is evidence that young children perceive the world like Gibson's analysis of Gestalt perception. For example, he noted that the research confirms that concepts replace visual clues with absence of the object, language influences form perception in drawing, drawings are influenced by sensations felt at the time they are drawn, and children vary in their approach to drawing from wholes to parts and from parts to wholes. Although he also concluded that no universal statement can be made in regard to the tendency to add or omit elements in a drawing, it is still hard to escape the notion that a person's cognitive content is fundamental in both simplifying and amplifying that which gives meaning or conceptual character of the object drawn.

DEVELOPMENTAL RESEARCH STUDIES AFTER 1962

Child development in art studies attempted after 1962 include efforts to continue the study of child art development and introduce some newer areas of study. Because of a greater involvement of art education researchers, investigations into the unresearched claims of the art education textbooks of the 1940s and 1950s were attempted. The newer research topics included study of: (a) relations between drawing and language development, (b) instructional factors influencing art skill development, (c) effects of perceptual training in drawing, and (d) effects of tool and media choice.

General Development

Some of the post-1962 research that continued the study of child development that included research conducted by Lewis and Livson (1967), Brittain (1969), Mann and Lehman (1976), Colbert and Taunton (1988), and Clare (1988). Lewis and Livson (1967) studied the tasks of drawing a cube, pyramid, pentagon, and cylinder by observation using students in Grades 1 to 6. Their study concluded that, as children grow older, they become better in depicting three-dimensional spatial relations and that change is more rapid in the earlier grades. In his study of nursery school children, Brittain (1969) found that 5-year-old children's art has pictorial content that can be recognized by adults, that adult intervention lengthens the amount of time children spend in drawing, that the "what is it?" question is effective, and that mastery of a few materials may be more effective than messing around with a broad range of media (depth vs. breadth).

Mann and Lehman (1976) studied the use of x-ray techniques by 4- to 9-year-olds, finding that these transparencies are more advanced representations, younger children using them score higher on IQ tests, they constitute a simplification of task, and are not due to one single cause. Colbert and Taunton (1988) studied 70 preschool to 3rd-grade children on the problem of drawing from a three-dimensional model. They found that preschoolers are able to use sophisticated depth conventions in drawing, are comfortable in doing such drawings, and use a variety of approaches including redefining of the task. Clare (1988) conducted four experiments on 2- and 3-year-olds, finding that the location of scribbles are relevant to handedness and paper size, relative size of figures is related to emotional involvement, omission of the torso in drawing is more a matter of choice than intelligence, and using larger paper produces more detail in drawings.

Drawing, Memory, and Language

Studies by Lansing (1981), Colbert (1984), and Caldwell and Moore (1991) focused on relationships among drawing, language, and memory behaviors. Colbert studied 160 students, Grades 3 to 10, on the relationship of language and drawing in description and memory tasks. The study rejected that language first enhances and then defeats drawing ability and supported that memory is improved when preceded by drawing description tasks, drawings from memory were smaller than those made through observation, and children's descriptive abilities show a relationship between language and drawing systems.

Caldwell and Moore studied the effects of drawing as preparation for narrative writing in primary grade children, concluding that drawing is a viable and effective rehearsal for narrative writing, a more complete form of rehearsal than discussion, and shows there is a mutual support between forms of expressing. Lansing studied 200 kindergarten children for the effects of drawing the mental representations of students, determining that drawing is better than tracing for mental representations, is progressive, and improves memory.

Skill Development

Studies on the effects of various interventions for the purpose of teaching drawing skills were attempted by Clare (1983), Rosenstiel and Gardner (1977), and Nelson and Flannery (1961). Clare studied the importance of utilizing the whole brain in learning to draw realistically, seeking to test the suitability of providing rules for realistic drawing instruction. Clare's study of 61 eighth-, sixth-, fifth-, and fourth-grade students suggested that familiarity with drawing rules makes realistic drawing easier for amateurs and that students 9 years and above should be taught to draw realistically.

Rosenstiel and Gardner sought to answer the questions of why older students decline in their amount of artistic activity and whether they were discouraged by seeing work of better quality. In their study of 99 first-, third-, sixth-, and tenth-grade students, they found that students will spend more time on a second drawing after seeing a drawing that is a higher standard than their own and will show more care and work harder. Older children are more negative in the evaluation of their work and also tend to pick things that are easier to draw.

Nelson and Flannery studied the effects of teaching drawing techniques to improve the drawing potentials of 6- and 7-year-olds. In their study of 74 children, they concluded that the drawing abilities and inabilities of first graders are rather stereotyped, instruction helps children reach their maturational level, not all types of instruction are of equal value, instruction emphasizing the edge of the drawing is more feasible as age increases, self-criticism is an effective avenue of improvement, and attention paid to proportion and/or sheer practice is detrimental.

Perceptual Training

Studies focusing on perceptual training include those by Salome (1965), Kensler (1965), Salome and Reeves (1972), and Marshalek (1986). Salome studied the question of whether perceptual training in conjunction with drawing instruction would increase the visual information content of fourth- and fifth-grade student drawings. In his study, Salome found that perceptual training in the use of visual clues would increase the amount of information in a child's drawing and that IQ was not related to differences in accomplishing drawing tasks.

Kensler also studied the effects of perceptual training and modes of perceiving on individual differences in the ability to learn perspective drawing using fourth- and fifth-grade students. Kensler also found that perceptual training increases the amount of visual information in fifth graders' drawing, that IQ is not relevant to drawing tasks at either grade level, and that field-independent and field-dependent tendencies did not affect perspective drawing ability.

Salome and Reeves studied the effects of perceptual training on 4- and 5-year-old kindergarteners, finding that the perceptual training of kindergarteners does improve their drawing differentiation. Marshalek focused on the effects of context on elementary children's attention to contour and interior patterns of shapes on color drawings. Studying 60 children in Grades 1, 3, and 5, they discovered that children were able to discriminate between an isolated shape and the shape in a full drawing, the visual material attended to is dependent on the context of the material and the age of the viewer, young children attend to multiple aspects of shapes when shapes are isolated, and contour awareness may be developed in children in Grades 1 to 5. Overall, the study supports the principal Gestalt notion of bottom–up processing, noting that attention to such matters improves with age and that attention and memory of the same material is different from adults in both kind and quality.

Copying

Studies concerning the influence of copying on student art performances were conducted by Pariser (1979) and Dowell (1990). Pariser studied two methods of teaching drawing skills by comparing a blind contour problem with a copying problem. His study of contour drawing with fourth, fifth, and sixth graders suggested that blind contour exercises help children modify schema, their contour drawings are more advanced than their ability to read them, some children reject contours as images, foreshortening can occur in blind contour, copying does not always result in stereotypes, and no single theory of the origins of graphic form can account for variations. He concluded that technical instruction should be a first step and that not all drawings come from previously learned conventions.

Dowell attempted to study the effects of visual referents on representational drawing of the human figure. His study compared drawings made from photos or from life with respect to drawing quality, proportion, foreshortening, and value on the figure drawings of 25 high school students. The study concluded that a student's drawing done from a copy (photo) was not significantly different than one drawn from life, and that both sets of drawings were about the same in what the students learned about proportion, foreshortening, value, and so on.

Media and Tools

Studies attempted on the uses of art media include those of Salome (1967), Seefeldt (1973), Golomb (1976), and Griffin, Highberger, and Cunningham (1981). Salome did a comparative analysis of children's drawings, using crayon and colored pencil, in an attempt to reveal the effects of a fine-pointed tool on kindergarten children's drawings. His study involving 45 kindergarten children concluded that there was no difference in drawing detail between children who used crayons and those who used colored pencils. It also showed that larger shapes and more feeling of space occurs when children used crayons, and lines made with crayon appear to be more definite, freer, and heavier.

Seefeldt studied the validity of the exclusive use of wide paint brushes by 5-year-old kindergarten children. Forty-eight children were involved in the study. The results indicate that narrow brush drawings contain more detail, are more complex, more often portrayed a theme or story, and contained more design patterns and texture, and that brush size was not related to mental or social development.

Golomb studied the effects of the medium, task, and instruction on the child's representation of the human figure. The results of this study suggest that the human figure varied systematically as a function of the medium, task, and instruction; representation does not rest on simple imitation or perceptual correspondence of parts; drawing ability is not an index of maturity or increasing intellectual capacity; the development of form is not much affected by the kind of tools the child uses; and children do more when assigned a task superior to that of a free position.

Griffin, Highberger, and Cunningham conducted a study comparing the effects of horizontal and vertical painting surfaces for the purpose of determining whether a table or easel surface is more important developmentally for 3-year-olds. The study included 20 boys and girls between the ages of 33 and 50 months. The results indicate that 3-year-olds show greater variety in paintings done on a table rather than an easel, painting behaviors differ in boys and girls with no differences in time spent, and skill buildings indeed related to age and developmental level.

SUMMARY

The analysis of the philosophical, aesthetic, psychological, and child developmental literature in the arts suggests that many of the same philosophical assumptions undergirding the cognitive sciences are also evident in the psychological and aesthetic premises underlying arts cognition as approached by philosophers, aesthetitions, and scholars in the psychology of art. This is evident both through the top–down and bottom–up positions advanced by arts scholars and their comparability, with the top–down and bottom–up positions advanced by the cognitive sciences in chapter 2 with regard to the mental processes used in cognition. The notion that there is more than one possible explanation of the cognitive act in artistic forming also provides ample room for there being several equally viable definitions of art, such as the ones advanced in this chapter (i.e., art as idea, art as form, and art as language).

This chapter's review of the empirical research studies spanning nearly a century, which were conducted in the area of child development in art, generally confirms that a child's drawing of an object is an index of the child's conception of that object, children's drawings reveal discriminations of a conceptual nature, vision dominates the conceptual processes the child acquires, maturity increases the child's ability to grasp concepts as ideas about objects and as class concepts, and drawing tests can be used to assess intellectual and conceptual maturity from 4 to 14 years of age.

Although the research on child art development conducted after 1962 produced some findings that, at times, appear to contradict some of the pre-1962 studies, in general it confirmed what the early studies reported on the nature of early cognitive development and art. These newer studies also introduced several different research possibilities. Although some seem to narrowly target troublesome pre-1960s sacred cows, most affirm the cognitive nature of art learning and, in particular, the importance of art instruction as a determining factor in child art growth.

Especially notable in the post-1962 research is the participation of art educators as researchers. This has come about primarily because of the increase in number of doctorates in the field during the 1960s and the employment of art educators with doctorates in research universities. It should also be noted that, after 1962, the National Art Education Association did provide a forum for the reporting of research studies at its annual conventions and through its publication of *Studies in Art Education,* a journal of issues on research.

However, providing such a forum and a publication outlet has also encouraged some resistance to using empirical research methods in the study of art education. For example, resistance is being felt from those in the field who are still wedded to the creative self-development point of view of the 1940s and 1950s and also by newer forces in the field that embrace conceptions of art derived from an art world rather than from art itself. These are clearly evident in the decline of empirical studies appearing in *Studies in Art Education,* where no quasi-experimental studies were published in that journal over the past 3 years and only four were published in the past 6 years.

Chapter 5 addresses the issue of concept development and art to understand the nature of artistic cognition as defined by how artists think and what it is they do in the process of bringing new art objects or events into being. The focus of chapter 5 is on the meaning of art, its quality, and what forms of cognition are necessary for the creative activity, that generates the aesthetic object, the phenomenology that creates it, and the epistomology that gives it meaning in the lives of creative human beings.

REFERENCES

Alschuler, R., & Hattwick, L. (1947). *Painting and personality, a study of young children.* Chicago: University of Chicago Press.

Arnheim, R. (1969). *Visual thinking.* Berkeley: University of California Press.

Bertalanffy, L. (1968). *General system theory.* New York: Braziller.

Brittain, L. W. (1969). Some exploratory studies of the art of pre-school children. *Studies in Art Education, 10*(3), 14–24.

Buhler, C., Smitter, F., & Richardson, S. (1952). *Childhood problems and the teacher.* New York: Holt, Rhinehart, & Winston.

Burnham, J. (1974). *Great western salt works/essays on the meaning of post formalist art.* New York: Braziller.

Burt, C. (1921). *Mental and scholastic tests.* London: P.S. King & Sons.

Caldwell, H., & Moore, H. B. (1991). The art of writing: Drawing as preparation for narrative writing in the primary grades. *Studies in Art Education, 32*(4), 207–217.

Clare, S. M. (1983). The importance of the whole brain for learning realistic drawing. *Studies in Art Education, 24*(3), 126–139.

Clare, S. M. (1988). The drawings of pre-school children: A longitudinal case study and four experiments. *Studies in Art Education, 29*(4), 211–221.

Colbert, C. B. (1984). The relationship of language and drawing on description and memory tasks. *Studies in Art Education, 25*(2), 84–91.

Colbert, C. B., & Taunton, M. (1988). Problems of representation in preschool and third grade childrens observational drawings of a three dimensional model. *Studies in Art Education, 28*(2), 103–114.

Collingwood, R. G. (1975). *The principles of art.* New York: Oxford University Press.

Dowell, M. L. (1990). Effects of visual referents upon representational drawing of the human figure. *Studies in Art Education, 31*(2), 78–85.

Golomb, C. (1976). The child as image maker: The invention of representational models and the effects of the medium. *Studies in Art Education, 17*(2), 19–21.

Gombrich, E. H. (1989). *Art and illusion: A study in the psychology of pictorial representation.* Princeton, NJ: Princeton University Press.

Goodenough, F. L. (1928). Studies in the psychology of children drawings. *Psychological Bulletin, 25,* 272–283.

Griffin, M. E., Highberger, R., & Cunningham, J. L. (1981). A comparison of horizontal and vertical painting devices. *Studies in Art Education, 23*(1), 40–47.

Harms, E. (1941). Child art as an aid in the diagnosis of juvenile neuroses. *American Journal of Orthopsychiatry, 11,* 191–200.

Harris, D. B. (1963). *Childrens drawings as measures of intellectual maturity.* New York: Harcourt Brace.

Hevner, K. (1935). Experimental studies of the affective value of color and lines. *Journal of Applied Psychology, 19,* 385–398.

James, W. (1955). *Pragmatism and four essays from the meaning of truth.* New York: Meridian.

Kandinsky, W. (1979). *Point and line to plane.* New York: Dover Publications.

Kensler, G. L. (1965). The effects of perceptual training and modes of perceiving upon individual differences in ability to learn perspective drawing. *Studies in Art Education, 7*(1), 34–42.

Kerschensteiner, D. G. (1905). *Ole Entwickelung der zlichnerkschen Begaburg* [The development of talent for drawing]. Munich: Gerber.

Krauss, R. (1930). Uber graphischen ansdruck. Eine experimentelle untersuchung uber das Erzeugen and Aus deuten von gegenslandfreien dinien [Graphic expression. An experimental study about the creation and interpretation of lines without objects]. *Beih.z. Angeiv Psychol, 48,* 39.

Langer, S. (1953). *Feeling and form.* New York: Scribner's.

Lansing, K. M. (1981). The effect of drawing on the development of mental representations. *Studies in Art Education, 22*(3), 15–23.

Lewis, H. P., & Livson, N. (1967). Spatial representation in children's drawings. *Studies in Art Education, 8*(2), 56–51.

Lowenfeld, V. (1947). *Creative and mental growth.* New York: Macmillan.

Mann, B. S., & Lehman, E. B. (1976). Transparencies in children's human figure drawings—a developmental approach. *Studies in Art Education, 18*(1), 42–47.

Marshalek, D. G. (1986). The effect upon elementary children's attention to contour and interior pattern of shapes in color drawings. *Studies in Art Education, 28*(1), 30–36.

Nelson, T. M., & Flannery, M. E. (1961). Instruction in drawing techniques as a means of utilizing drawing potential of six and seven year olds. *Studies in Art Education, 10*(3), 58–65.

Nordland, G. (1967). *Richard Diebenkorn.* New York: Rizzoll International Publications.

Pariser, D. A. (1979). Two methods of teaching drawing skills. *Studies in Art Education, 20*(3), 30–42.

Popper, K. R. (1957). The philosophy of science: A personal report. In C. A. Mace (Ed.), *British philosophy in the mid-century* (pp. 155–194).

Rabello, S. (1932). Caracteristicus do dencho infantil [The characteristics of childhood]. *Psychological Abstracts, 8,* 1247.

Rosenstiel, A. K., & Gardner, H. (1977). The effect of critical comparisons upon children's drawings. *Studies in Art Education, 19*(1), 36–45.

Rouma, G. (1913). *Le langage graphique de l'enfant* [The graphic language of the child]. Paris: Mish. et Thron.

Salome, R. A. (1965). The effects of perceptual training upon the two dimensional drawings of children. *Studies in Art Education, 7*(1), 18–33.

Salome, R. A. (1967). A comparative analysis of kindergarten children's drawings in crayon and colored pencil. *Studies in Art Education, 10*(3), 19–36.

Salome, R. A., & Reeves, D. (1972). Two pilot investigations of perceptual training of four and five year old kindergarten children. *Studies in Art Education, 13*(2), 3–9.

Sarup, M. (1989). *An introductory guide to post-structuralism and post-modernism.* Athens: University of Georgia Press.

Scruton, R. (1981). *From Descartes to Wittgenstein: A short history of modern philosophy.* New York: Colophon Books.

Seefeldt, C. (1973). The validity of the exclusive use of wide paint brushes in the five year old kindergarten. *Studies in Art Education, 14*(3), 48–53.

Weitz, M. (1959). The role of theory and aesthetics. In M. Weitz (Ed.), *Problems in aesthetics.* New York: Macmillan.

KEY TERMS

Metastyle	Imagination
Appropriative	Sensum
Motif	Intuition
Abstraction	Virtual
Formalism	Fixation
Parallelism	Affect
Structuralism	Directionality
Conceptualism	

STUDY QUESTIONS

1. Describe the three contending theories of arts: art as idea, art as form, and art as language. Why, philosophically, is it important to know that there is more than one theory of art? How would accepting multiple theories affect the way we teach art? Which theory comes closest to your philosophical beliefs and why?

2. Discuss the top–down and bottom–up explanations of thinking about and making art. How do these systems differ in the ways we perceive visual form and use our imagination, sensation, and consciousness in the perception of art? Do some of your art instructors use one or more of these approaches in their teaching? What things do they do in their teaching that gives you a clue about their point of view?

3. Based on your experience, do we draw what we see, draw what we know, or both? Can it be said that seeing is believing or that believing is seeing? What arguments and which of the aestheticians discussed in this chapter come closest to your point of view? Use some quotes from the text to support your claims.

4. What do the experimental studies of children's art growth tell us about what to teach in art and when to teach it? How do these researchers view art learning in relation to the overall intellectual development of the child?

5. How does the draw-a-man test stand up with other measures of intellectual ability? Do you think that effective art learning experiences will positively affect student performances in other areas of the curriculum? If so, what evidence did you find in this chapter supporting your point of view?

6. What do post-1962 experimental studies on drawing, memory, and language suggest with regard to the learning relationship between art and language? Do the results of these studies suggest that art helps or hinders language development? Cite some studies that support or disagree with your position.

7. What do the post-1962 studies on skill development, perception, and copying suggest about the use of advanced organizers in teaching art? Do these studies encourage you to believe that art instruction should be free from the teacher's direction or that preparing students to notice certain perceptual clues actually improves their art performances? Is copying always a bad practice or can it help students to more closely observe? Cite some examples for and against.

5

Conceptual Behaviors in Art

CONCEPT FORMATION
Concepts Defined
Concepts as Directional
Concepts of Consciousness
Concept Measurement

CONCEPTUAL THINKING IN ART
The Intuitive Process
Decision Making
Thought in Action
Resemblances and Parallels

ARTISTS FORMING CONCEPTUALLY
Absract Art
Realist Art
Pop Art

SUMMARY

The preceding chapter presented an overview of the mental processes involved in artistic thinking and making as described in the literature of philosophy and aesthetics and in the research on the artistic development of young learners. That discussion included addressing art from three different philosophical-aesthetic perspectives: art as idea, art as form, and art as language, which is accepting of the notion that artistic thinking and making cannot be relegated to a single unified concept but is rather shaped by differing philosophical and aesthetic frames of mind.

The previous chapter also addressed the top–down and bottom–up interpretations of both the frames of mind and the results of the experimental methods used in both the cognitive sciences and visual arts. The similarities pointed out in the interpreting of the experiments in both disciplines not only suggest that the same philosophical argument guides interpretations for practice but also what most divides these conceptions of cognitive activity are the differences in the logical systems and the supporting evidence used to reach and verify their respective claims. Put another way, the sciences seem constrained to mostly inductive–deductive forms of logic and linguistic modes of verification, whereas aesthetitions seem equally constrained through the use of mostly intuitional thought and the perceptual evidence revealed in aesthetic objects and events.

The aim of this chapter is primarily to examine concept development as it relates to the creative process, which recognizes that, to understand the nature of artistic cognition, it is also necessary to understand how artists think and what they do in the process of bringing new art objects or events into being. Thus, the process here is to look at the creative process not only from the viewpoint of what aesthetitions and scholars say about it but also from the point of view of the written and silent speech of the artist and the processes the artist uses in the visual decision-making process.

Of course, there are certain risks in relying on what artists say about their work and in what they report about the processes they use in artistic forming, which is to acknowledge that artists do not always know the results or the meaning of a work until it is completed and, in some cases, not even then. Therefore, there are some good reasons that the artist's speech may not lend itself to arriving at a thoroughly objective analysis of cognition in art. To avoid relying solely on artists' statements of intent, the claims made in this chapter on the role of cognition in artistic forming are supported by the biographies of 10 major American painters, all of whom worked in the last half of the 20th century and all of whom were clearly influenced by the New York School abstract expressionist tradition and yet chose individual and separate paths in the development of their imagery. What should also be made clear to the reader is that, although the artists chosen may not include all the artists working during that period, they are at least representative of the major stylistic developments in American painting occurring in the last half of this century.

The decision in this chapter to use bibliographical references viewing the artists' work over time, rather than using historical or critical descriptions of individual works, was a conscious choice. It was based on the notion that, even if a critic or historian is also the biographer, he or she must, in fulfilling the biographical task, review an extensive body of work covering most of the artist's creative life. He or she also must make connections between an artist's images and what it is they say about that process, which goes beyond merely meeting the professional paradigms that art historians and critics use to satisfy their own particular canons of scholarship.

The evidence offered in support of artistic cognition in this chapter is presented in the form of what artists tell us about their working method, in the thoughts they offer in retrospect about their work, and in the visual evidence presented and supported by their work. Because this is not a picture book, much of the visual proof will have to come from the reader's own recognition of these well-known artists' work and/or their willingness to do a separate review of their work over time. Such evidence is, of course, critical in support of any claims made about the nature of visual cognition, which can be verified only through the artistic image and not through the language we can use to describe or explain it.

One additional problem in organizing this chapter was to find a framework for addressing cognition in art other than the highly idiosyncratic ways biographers and artists tend to organize their thoughts. Therefore, the discussion has been framed around two conceptual points of view: one that makes the case for an objectivist, epistemological approach to art concept formation and one that philosophically addresses the phenomenology of designing and making expressive objects.

CONCEPT FORMATION

Concepts Defined

The objectivist view of conception is that what constitutes a mental concept is found in the mental interpretation of two or more perceptive units possessing the same distinguishing character(s), but with their particular measurements omitted (Benswanger & Piekoff, 1979). What this means is that a concept cannot be formed at random, but is rather formed by differentiating two or more existants from other existants. This means no concept can be formed by attempting to distinguish long objects from purple objects. Hence, tables are different from chairs or beds and have particular kinds of shapes that distinguish them from one another. In such a concept, shape becomes an attribute that reveals differences and yet can ultimately be reduced to some form of linear measurement. However, one does not need to know all the furniture shapes that are possible or even how to measure them to form a concept; one only has to recognize the element of similarity.

In objective parlance, similarity as a shape concept is grasped perceptually and does not have to involve measurement. However, like mathematics, concept formation does need to identify relationships through perceptual data. For example, in forming concepts of colors, one can observe that the various shades of blue are similar as opposed to shades of green, yellow, or red, which becomes an essential element in distinguishing a range of blue from a range of yellow.

Thus, new concepts are formed when earlier formed concepts are integrated into wider or narrower categories, becoming ultimately reducible to their common perceptual character. Children's beginning concepts normally focus on a single attribute and are mostly understood perceptually rather than conceptually. It is only after the child has grasped a number of concepts of entities that they can advance to the stage of abstracting entities and forming new concepts of attributes. However, concepts do also vary in their formation; concepts of materials are formed by observing the constituent materials of entities, such as a plank of wood or drop of water, and concepts of motion are formed by specifying the distinctive character of a motion and of the entities performing it or the medium in which it is performed. For example, walking denotes a form of motion associated with legs and not with the motion of a snake or automobile.

In explaining the links between concept development and mathematics, objectivists point out that (a) concepts need not specify all possible concretes, specifying only certain defined units; and (b) in concept formation, measurements need to exist only in some quantity (e.g., as in algebra, where each symbol x or y must have some numerical value, but where any value will do). In objectivist thought, perceptual awareness becomes the arithmetic and conceptual values—the algebra of cognition.

Concepts as Directional

From the objectivist view, cognition generally moves in two interactive directions: (a) toward more extensive and intensive knowledge, wider integrations, and more precise differentiations, and (b) toward smaller concepts being integrated into wider ones or subdivided into narrower ones. In concept formation, children need not originate and develop every concept, but must learn to differentiate and integrate perceptual concretes to grasp the understanding of words. From this perspective, learning to speak permits the child to grasp meanings where the referents of words accelerate the child's cognitive development but are not a substitute for concept formation. In children's conceptual development, there is no particular order required to learn new concepts nor the words attached to them, provided the child first understands their meanings. However, objectivists do claim that for fully independent conceptual development to occur, the child must ultimately be able to form sentences that are required to be able to think. Prior to such time, children retain concepts in predominately perceptual or visual form.

Also from the objectivist view, it is necessary to understand the meaning of words to achieve an understanding of a concept; what needs most to be avoided is substituting memorizing for understanding. Children in the early stages of integrating narrow concepts into wider ones observe that concepts such as table, chair, or bed have certain similarities but are still different from objects labeled as a door, window, or drapes in that they can also later be widened into the more encompassing concept of furniture. What happens in the process of concept formation is that categories of shape—such as something that has a flat level surface with supports (legs) used first to define the concept of table—can later be reorganized to conceive of all things called furniture as having a shape that later can be subsumed into the wider concept of furniture.

Therefore, when narrow concepts are integrated into wider ones (i.e., a flat surface with support becoming a concept later defined as a shape of a particular kind and then subsumed into the concept of furniture), the distinguishing characteristics of early discipline units are omitted and are united by what all these units have in common to develop a new concept. Conversely, when a concept is subdivided into a narrower one, the number of constituent units involved are reduced in the process of forming new concepts.

As children grow, their knowledge of, for example, the concept of animal expands; it can then be subdivided into newer and more abstract concepts, as evidenced in terms *mammal, amphibian, fish,* and so on, which can later be even further subdivided into narrower subcategories. However, the basic principle of concept formation remains the same, where the concept of animal is still retained even if later qualified by the addition of other anatomical physical facts, which now form the distinguishing characteristics of the new concept.

More important, the formation of wider concepts from narrower ones requires more knowledge or perceptual evidence than is needed for the beginning concepts they subsume. For example, the concept *hue* requires more knowledge than the concept *color* because it seeks a new and broader concept within the constituent concept of color. Therefore, when a concept is widened, it does not contain less cognitive content, but rather, through the process of abstracting an abstraction, requires one to know the distinguishing characteristic of a unit, which has to remain unknown until one examines the characteristics of all the units involved and the extent to which they can be differentiated.

Objectivists also point out that it is not possible to grasp a concept through memorizing definitions, but only through retracing the process through which the concept is formed and, therefore, grasping at least some of the units that it subsumes. The formation of a concept is the means for identifying it as well as all other concretes of that kind, which one might encounter in the future. The forming of wider concepts becomes possible when the child learns to speak; it becomes progressively more difficult as the child's concepts move further away from perceptual evidence. From the objectivist view, the process of forming and applying concepts involves the fundamental methods for cognition: induction and deduction.

Concepts of Consciousness

According to objectivists, consciousness is the faculty for perceiving what exists through an awareness of that which makes concept formation possible. It is our capacity to become aware of an environment that makes it possible for human beings to find some kind of object or content in experience. This comes both from extrospection, which is a form of cognition directed outwardly toward the environment, and introspection, which is cognition directed inwardly—as in being aware of one's psychological reactions through thinking, feeling, reminiscing, and so on. Therefore, awareness is an awareness of something and is thus synonymous with consciousness.

Objectivists describe the two fundamental attributes of awareness as content and action, which refer to how the content of the awareness and how the action of consciousness are used in revealing that content. To objectively form concepts of consciousness, it is necessary to separate action from content through an abstraction is (e.g., to see a work of art as a *perception,* to decide that it is beautiful as an *evaluation,* to feel the action of consciousness as an *emotion,* to examine the action of consciousness as *thought,* to later recall it as a *reminiscence,* and then speculate on alternatives in its appearance as an act of *imagination*). To examine the similarities between acts of consciousness and apply it to other objects or events is to form concepts of consciousness, where the measurable attributes of this psychological process are made evident through its content and intensity. According to objectivist belief, although the content of object or event may be measurable through some discrete measurement, a psychological process of consciousness must also include evidence of a number of other concerns, including its clarity, cognitive, or motivational context and the degree of mental energy or effort required.

Unfortunately, there is not any exact method for measuring the intensity of all psychological processes, such as is the case in forming a concept of *color*, which does not require an exact measurement. Also, although degrees of intensity of emotion can be measured through one's hierarchy of values, it varies according to the intensity or importance of the event. Objectivists believe that the intensity of a process of thought and the intellectual effort required varies according to the scope of its content, such as in first understanding the concept color and then the concept of hue, later to grasp the idea that certain colors together create a color harmony and then are further affected through their interactions.

A concept pertaining to consciousness, unlike one attached to an object, is thus a mental integration of two or more psychological processes, with the same distinguishing characteristics only with the contents and measurements of the action's intensity omitted. However, this is founded on the principle that the omitted measurements must exist in some quantity (i.e., that a given psychological process must have some content and some intensity while still requiring that it exist at some level).

Thus, higher order thinking or higher levels of psychological cognition can be distinguished objectively by noting the extensiveness of their scope and the level of the intensity contained in the psychological processes used. With regard to concepts such as observation, reasoning, learning, and so on, scope is determined by the range of the factual material involved and the length of the conceptual process used to deal with that material. Thus, scope refers to the levels of abstraction needed to know how to reach that level. Concepts pertaining to evaluation, such as those dealing with emotion, feeling, or desire, however, do require a hierarchy of a different kind—where objectivists prefer to use what they call *teleological measurement*.

Concept Measurement

According to objectivists, measurement is achieved through the identification of a relationship using some measurable standard. Teleological measurements, unlike discrete measurement, do not deal with cardinal, but rather ordinal, numbers, which have more to do with establishing a relative position on a graded scale toward achieving a particular end or goal. In this sense, moral codes can be evaluated teleologically—especially where it requires the participant to use abstract principles in choosing the particular goals and values to be pursued. Such acts require establishing a hierarchy of values on which one can act and then acting so as to establish the relationship between a given choice and all other possible choices yet be in accordance with one's established hierarchy of values. The concept of morality used here is not one based on an absolute standard of "thou shall not," but rather on a rational process one might use in deciding to purchase a particular item in a store—where the decision to be made is seen in the context of all the other goals, desires, and needs of the purchaser.

Thus, a moral standard becomes measurable not in discrete or ordinal terms, but in terms of choices made in relation to one's values as weighted against other competing values. Thus, matters such as love or beauty involve the most desired alternative among hierarchial states, the values one uses in making such a decision, and the intentions that drive that decision. Therefore, love for an object or person could vary in intensity according to one's evaluation of appearance, utility, or status and can be ranked hierarchically from simply a liking for something to believing that it is the best possible. The emotions felt in such evaluations are obviously not of the same intensity or direction. For example, a positive aesthetic experience could result from one's valuing an object for its craftsmanship, its monetary value, the name recognition of the artist who made it, or its relative position among other objects of acknowledged aesthetic worth.

The measurement of consciousness in the objectivist sense involves the identification of a numerical relationship, which exists even if the appropriate standards of measurement are not always apparent nor are as precise as might be applied in the measurement of some discrete matter. For objectivists, everything including consciousness is measurable because for something to be immeasurable it would have no relation to the rest of the environment, it would not affect or be affected by anything else, and it would enact no causes, bear no consequences, and, for that matter, not exist.

With certain exceptions, objectivists believe every concept can also be defined and communicated in terms of other concepts. One exception is concepts that refer to sensations, which are the primary material of consciousness; they cannot be communicated through the feeling states, which are their products. For example, no one can actually communicate what a color is like; one can only point to it and say, "This is what I mean." Therefore, definitions are not descriptions, but rather imply the characteristics of a concept's unity and identify the nature or essential characteristics of a unit, which links it to others of the same kind. Concepts are not formed in a vacuum, but are rather formed in a context. Concept formation in consciousness involves observing differences and similarities in a context and organizing them accordingly. *Context* can be defined as what one is mentally aware of at any level of cognitive development. However, these concepts are not subjective, but rather selective, in that they are determined by individual choices about how much knowledge is needed and what conceptual complexity will be reached. The lack of contradiction between the facts used and the reality of the context in which they are applied is more important in objectivists' cognition than the complexity of either the facts or contexts. However, concepts do, at the preverbal level awareness, differ from those that occur in early childhood and those later achieved in adolescence—when it can be observed that general definitions no longer suffice. When new knowledge becomes available, these steps are not always the steps required for cognition, but this pattern of growth is what makes intensive study and growth in knowledge possible.

For objectivity to exist, there must also be an act of discovery because one cannot know more than that which has been discovered. Truth becomes the product of recognizing the facts in context as concepts, which are then retained in the mind through definitions and later organized into propositions. However, conclusions, inferences, and thoughts do rest on truthful definitions, where an invalid concept invalidates every proposition or process of thought used in a cognitive assertion. Therefore, to know the meaning of the concept being used, one must retrace the specific logical steps through which it was formed and demonstrate their connection with perceptual reality.

In objectivist terms, the perceptual level of awareness is the basis for all conceptual development. Concepts must be formed whenever the scope of the perceptual data becomes too great for the mind to handle. Thus, a concept becomes an open-ended classification including yet-to-be-discovered characteristics of a given phenomenon. Therefore, concepts and the language used to connote them are, according to objectivists, only a tool of cognition and are neither a language nor a system for communicating or arriving at public speech. In this sense, communication is a consequence of making definitions, words, or speech and is neither the cause nor the purpose of concept formation. For the most part, language is used to attain cognitive understanding and is not a means to seek propositional truth communicated in unambiguous terms. In this sense, cognition precedes communication, with the primary purpose of language being to provide a system of cognitive classification and organization to acquire and manipulate increasingly larger amounts of data.

Thus, the function of language in objectivist epistemology is to facilitate thought; it is not to use linguistic analysis as a device to arrive at publicly agreed on meanings in social contexts. The goal of language is primarily to enable advanced cognitive development through abstractions, which integrate more information into broader and narrower concept formation, more consciousness of the level of awareness, and facilitate rational thought.

The objectivist epistemology as defined here offers a number of conditions defining the process of concept development: concept development is ultimately a process of abstraction, the role of language in conception is private and personal, and every event in the environment exists in some quantity and over some duration. Objectivist epistemology, as previously noted, also recognizes the important role of consciousness in cognition, which is to know the content of awareness (attention) and the action of awareness (metacognition) in revealing that content. Such conditions make it possible to conceive of cognition in art as being evident in the levels or degrees of abstraction in images, in the silent speech of the artist, and in teleological measurements of pointing out things such as meanings evidenced in virtual form.

CONCEPTUAL THINKING IN ART

The question that still needs to be examined is whether an objectivist epistemology coheres with the forms of cognition used in art making. These forms have been variously described as involving the creation of imaginary objects of sense experience, where meanings are reflected in common cultural agreement or disagreement, made from some tangible material shaped by someone who modifies, alters, shapes, and molds as he or she constructs and who may or may not know the meaning of the object until it is completed. As in my previous work, *Thinking in Art,* I am indebted in this discussion to Harrison (1978) for his ideas on the process of making and thinking in art.

As a philosopher, Harrison not only accepts the notion that creative activity is intelligent, but he also speaks the language of the studio artist—a language familiar to those who think about and make art. Harrison described the process of designing while making as one where the artist has no clear idea of what he or she wants to say, builds forms in the context of what his or her materials will do, and, when questioned about what he or she is trying to achieve, can tell us no more than that the activity is purposive, intentional, and rational. He explained the artist's method as a process in which something is being discovered and where the artist can only show what, if successful, it will look like when it is completed, which is to say what it is to express something. Further, the artist has goals even if they are only to paint a picture of a certain sort on a specific topic made with certain self-imposed standards, which is to offer a goal or intent based on what the artist is doing in the process of making.

The Intuitive Process

Although Harrison's overall view may be overly romantic—because not all artists, as is pointed out later, work in such a vague manner—he at least laid out the general nature of the creative artist's intuitive experience, which is certainly the primary form of cognition used in the making of most works of art. This intuitive process, which, according to Harrison, is a rational one, also makes it possible for the artist to recognize the following: that the work has been successfully completed, what thoughts have led to its accomplishment, what it is like to make an object in this way, and to achieve something that is part of a whole in the realization of one component in a total policy.

Harrison's notion of a policy is that which the artist deals with in the work, which may be symbolic, illustrative, or a manner in which to tell a story. It is generally found in the arrangement of shapes and colors the artist uses to interest or disturb us and which invites us to pay attention to seeing shapes and colors in ways that we have never seen before. In Harrison's view, how the artist has spread the paint and what conventions are used, modified, or exploited all play a part in how a picture is seen, how it works on us, and how we arrive at an understanding of it. For example, we may observe that the artist began with a random streak of paint and later responded by liking or disliking it, having unconscious associations with shapes of this sort and preserving some favorably received shapes, painting over others that are disliked, and ending such alterations when the result is a satisfactory one. This process may then resume again with some shapes destroying or enhancing others and with the process of choosing, which features to preserve or suppress continuing throughout its forming. The result of all this is to invite the viewer to a way of seeing or attending to the picture plane, to see a shape in this way or that, and/or to pay more attention to some shapes rather than others. It tells us more about the degrees of attention paid to certain elements in the picture than to its historical or critical contents.

This process results in an artistic image that is a representation of something or another and that imposes a pattern of intelligibility on something or another as a form of pattern aspecting. What is actually seen as a result of this act is more about the process of what kind of attention the artist pays to the shapes he or she invents, the choices and preferences made between preserving or destroying them, the decisions made to modify or retain what has been done, and the spatial considerations needed for the ending of that process. In this sense, a work of art is something built up through a pattern of decisions of increasing complexity and abstraction; these decisions concern what to keep or change and what to include—both the intentional and accidental marks that occur in the process of its making.

Decision Making

In this process, Harrison believed that the artist may abandon both attempts to preserve, even with modifications, what he or she has already done or made or attempt to achieve what is not yet done. In this sense, to abandon is, like levels of abstraction, to abandon a goal yet not discard what already is but give up on an attempt to make it otherwise. What the artist pays attention to in this selection process also answers what is being articulated (i.e., what patterns of shapes, colors, and textures are being developed in regard to what already exists and how destroying or enhancing a particular shape or color determines how another shape or color is seen). All these actions involve a number of mental acts that are interesting in their own right, and all are involved with how the artist comes to know what he or she earlier had been concerned with, which also becomes a process of self discovery. According to Harrison, in the end, the artist comes to know not only what it was he or she was concerned with all along, but also something that he or she was previously unaware of and how the choices made did not make nonsense of what had gone on before—a process that is not so much about knowing something about the unknown, but rather a process of making that which is already known more vivid.

Not all that is contained in the work is built up through a pattern of activity. The artist's skill in letting the tool do its job, how the way things go together to build a pattern of decision making, and the way things are built up reveals the order of the maker's decisions. This permits us to see the object as being designed in a particular way, to see the elements of the design that correspond to how the artist may be supposed to have done so, or invite us to do so.

All of the foregoing claims about artistic forming are, in Harrison's view, conceptions that are clearly evident to anyone viewing the artistic object. These are made evident through the patterns of shapes that have been developed and modified through the decision-making process that the artist uses, the natural shapes that are modified in terms of certain goals or abstractions, and what forms of attention the artist has paid to particular details. The object makes us sense these things and respond to them—requiring us to think conceptually.

All works of art involve the making of abstractions or concepts that vary in their scope and intensity. To enter the mind of the artist in the process of making requires us to imagine how he or she sees one shape as modifying another or how he or she anticipates future modifications and what past events need to be recalled to make these decisions and anticipate future courses of action.

Thought in Action

This artistic model of conception challenges the conventional wisdom that intelligence is limited to knowing, in advance, exactly what one wants to achieve in creating a concept or abstraction—where thought is, in effect, divorced from action. Artistic thought in action offers a way to react to what one has done, acted on, and reacted to, which is a creation that reveals what one's goals are, what one is concerned about in the world, and what principles need to be observed in the process of its creation. The thought in action process verifies that any theory of intelligence should begin with a theory that notes the role of creative activity and acknowledges the critical part it plays in the development of human intelligence.

In essence, this model is a process that pays attention to particulars and perceptually leads to ways these particulars as concepts can be widened or narrowed into what objectivists label as *abstracted abstractions*. This process begins with an awareness of the environment and goes beyond thought; it follows an activity in that it also contributes to the individual's knowledge of his or her own growth and development. It does not involve a dereliction of will, but is rather will itself, which is to take responsibility for what one chooses to do and adopt it as one's own. It is then about both attending to what has been done and imagining how things should or could be done.

Resemblances and Parallels

Furthermore, as a search, the creative process involves not just looking but rather looking for something such as resemblances and parallels. As noted earlier, that search process is evidenced in the thing constructed, its visual characteristics, and what it visually attends to. It is more than an observation because it is an interpretation—a thing created and an abstraction. Therefore, to make a painting is to make a pattern, structure, or design that represents a concept of the thing pictured and to show a structure of how something should or could look and how a thing of that order could be structured. Moreover, all pictures, when divided into progressively smaller units, reveal both the level of their abstraction and the pictorial units or subunits discarded in the process. This can be empirically discovered by attending to the work itself through noting what the artist attends to in its making, which is not about what something looks like but rather about how the artist looks at it. How a work is designed, what constraints or choices are made in the process of making, and how the object is represented are forms of understanding and perception. To understand something in this manner is to construct a concept about it and gain an understanding of it through its making, which is the process by which the creator comes to know or understand what is seen in that process.

ARTISTS FORMING CONCEPTUALLY

Although Harrison clearly makes us aware that, in making art, the artist is mostly concerned with the making of things that are not real but rather abstractions or concepts, and that the process used is one of discovery through making, it is also apparent that individual artists are not all alike in the way they achieve such ends. What follows next is a brief look at this process through the creative activity of 10 American painters, all of whom lived and worked in the last half of the 20th century and were either involved or lived in the shadow of the 1960s New York painting scene, which was dominated by abstract expressionism.

As previously noted, these 10 artists do not represent *all* the artists who worked during that period. Rather, they are representative of the modern painting styles that emerged and that still hold credence as continuing movements in American painting. Some of these artists are no longer living; others continue to work and, although not as well recognized, are at least a major influence on those who are.

These artists were also selected because they have long and distinguished careers in art and have a corpus of work. Readers can see what has influenced the artists' work over time and how their earlier images have been either modified or sustained over time. As noted earlier, this was a conscious choice driven by the inadequacies of criticizing or analyzing a single work in the hope it will reveal the artist's true method or intent. This is supported by the notion advanced earlier by Ernst Gombrich, which debates whether any work of art is a complete statement or one that leaves some questions unanswered—to be revealed later in some following work. Also as earlier noted, in judging the perceptual growth of children's art, we find ourselves on much firmer ground when we review several works over time (a portfolio approach) rather than basing our conclusions on a single work. As Gombrich noted, artists are influenced by other artists; they, in turn, influence the expectations their viewers have of their work over time (Gombrich, 1989).

The choice to limit these examples to just one medium—painting—may weaken some of my argument. However, that choice was also a conscious one. I did not want to further complicate my analysis by comparing the differing concepts posed by two-dimensional versus three-dimensional space and those introduced by the need to explain the problems inherent in photography, crafts, printmaking, and other art media.

The artists to be discussed here include: George Tooker, symbolic realist; Jacob Lawrence, realist; James Rosenquist, pop; Audrey Flack, superrealist; Robert Motherwell, abstract expressionist; Ellsworth Kelly, postpainterly abstractionist; Helen Frankenthaler, modernist; Fairfield Porter, realist; Wayne Thiebaud, realist; and Richard Diebenkorn, abstract expressionist.

The terms *symbolic realist, realist, pop,* and so on are ones I believe those artists would agree with, but may not be ones that now or in the future conform to how historians or critics choose to classify them. However, my goal here is to provide an idea of how they go about making an artistic concept or abstraction rather than about how we might classify them. Hence, my primary goal is to focus on the methods they employ to arrive at an image, rather than on what they or their biographers claim about the meaning of their work or their artistic intent. In pursuit of this task, it is necessary to discuss matters relating to the artist's working method, including the techniques and materials used, assumptions made about pictorial form, process used in creating visual abstractions, and the decision-making process used in determining the progress and completion of the work.

Although I previously claimed that artists tend to pursue different approaches to image development, for purposes of organization I have ordered the artists presented here into three different visual modes, in part, because those who work in a given manner tend to be more alike than different. For this reason, I have grouped Diebenkorn, Frankenthaler, Motherwell, and Kelly under *abstract artists,* Porter, Lawrence, Thiebaud, and Tooker under *realist artists,* and Flack and Rosenquist under *pop artists.* Although such an arrangement has some stylistic problems, it does address the paradigms in which these artists work: for realist artists, real objects, people, and events; for abstract artists, form itself; and for pop artists, the ordering of popular images. The order of presentation is as follows: abstract artists, realists, and pop artists.

Abstract Art

Abstract art has been defined as art that does not attempt to represent the appearance of objects, real or imaginary (Piper, 1984). Abstract art is not normally referred to as a style, but is rather a description of art that rejects representation. Abstract art is said to have first appeared in the second decade of the 20th century and was first noticed in the works of Delaunay, Kandinsky, Kupka, Malevich, and Mondrian. Sometimes referred to as *nonrepresentational painting,* its characteristics are the (a) reduction of natural forms to essentials, and/or (b) combinations of colors, lines, or shapes without representational intent. A number of stylistic terms have also been used to describe such work, including *constructivism, destyl, suprematism, abstract expressionism, orphism,* or *tachisme.*

The New York abstract school of the 1960s is most closely associated with abstract expressionism, which placed emphasis on spontaneous personal expression, including aspects of surrealism with its stress on the unconscious. Also associated is the movement called *action painting,* as practiced by Pollock and others. Other artists associated with abstract expressionism include Gorky, Tobey, and DeKooning. Another title applied to abstract art is the term *postpainterly abstraction.* This description was invented by American critic Clement Greenberg in the 1960s to describe the work of Noland, Stella, Olitski, Kelly, and others. This was considered to be an alternative to the extreme painterlyness and subjectivity of abstract expressionism—through the featuring of hard-edged pictures, high-keyed colors, and the two dimensionality of the picture plane.

Robert Motherwell, 1915–

Motherwell has been an extremely influential figure in American art since World War II, both as a painter and writer. Considered part of the New York school, Motherwell was considered a pioneer in abstract expressionism; his early work reflected the traditions of Dada and the images of Picasso and Matisse (Fig. 5.1).

In the late 1940s, his work became increasingly more abstract. In 1949, he painted the first of his *Elegies to the Spanish Republic* series using a recurrent motif of vertical bands and oval shapes in black and white. In 1968, in his *Open Series,* he introduced work that included large fields of saturated color spatially controlled by charcoal lines (Ashton & Flam, 1983).

Working Method.   Motherwell's method of working appears to be closely associated with the surrealistic method of automatic drawing and the methods of Japanese calligraphy. Motherwell has described Japanese calligraphy as a means to let the hand take over, to watch it as if it were not one's own, and to look at what happens critically while noting the making of more or less rhythmic jumps and driving off the edge at certain moments. He also once reported taking 1,000 identical sheets of Japanese rice paper, an English watercolor brush, and common American inks and working at a session without conscious preconceptions and with no revision, which he considered to be the rule of the game.

Motherwell also favored using black and white, as contrasted with color, in much of his work. When he used color, he considered it to be mostly symbolic, using ocher for the earth, green for grass, and blue for the sea and sky, with black and white playing the role of protagonist. He also preferred simple technical means, setting the hand moving to create marks that later became the forms emerging in the painting.

He also called himself an Egyptian painter because of his flat, linear, local hue. The subjects of his paintings, he claimed, emerge out of an interaction between himself, his persona or "I," and his medium, with the images in the paintings coming from these and various other preoccupations. Conceptions, gestures, and his own imagery, which first comes out, make the picture, which he names afterward. Motherwell also claimed that he never starts with an image. Rather he starts with a painting idea or impulse: sometimes im-

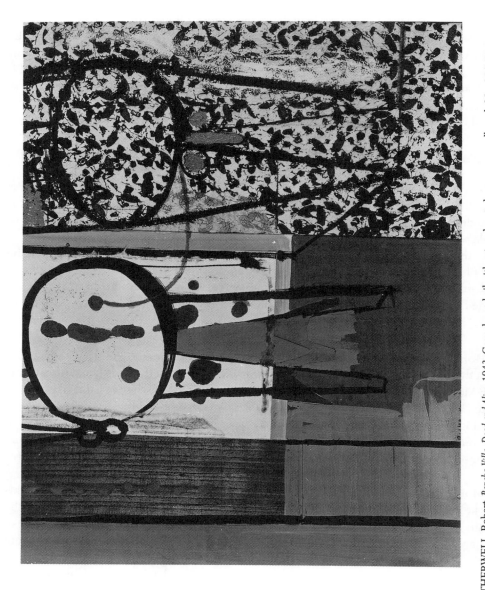

FIG. 5.1. MOTHERWELL, Robert. *Pancho Villa, Dead and Alive*. 1943. Gouache and oil with cut-and pasted papers on cardboard, 28 x 35 7/8" (71.7 x 91.1 cm). The Museum of Modern Art, New York. Purchase. Photograph (c) 1998 by The Museum of Modern Art, New York. (c) Dadelus Foundation/Licensed by VAGA, New York, NY

ages emerge as if in a dream or they unconsciously develop, where a certain kind of experience is necessary to perceive it.

Motherwell considered himself a modernist. He saw this movement as a critical act of rebellion against the *corny academic art* so admired by the bourgeoisie and the working class for its compromising anecdotes, sentimentality, religion, and so on. He also felt it was the task of modern art to find a landscape closer to the structure of the human mind—one that could express the complex physical and metaphysical realities that modern science and philosophy make us aware of.

Being both a writer and an academic, Motherwell believed the university was a place strongly interested in abstract painting and one where his ability to talk about the movement would be appreciated. Because he was originally trained in philosophy, he felt he had, by default, become the spokesperson for abstract expressionists.

Motherwell basically agreed with the notion that most good painters do not know what they think until they paint it. Speaking to what he is aware of in the act of painting, Motherwell feels he is always dealing with an unrelational structure that gives him the permission to be abstract and avoid any anxiety about whether his painting has a given meaning.

Reacting to someone's question at an exhibition, Motherwell noted:

> . . . a middle aged man approached me and asked what the picture was about, what it "meant." Because we happened to be standing in front of the actual painting, I was able to look at it directly, instead of using an after-image inside my head. I realized that the picture had been painted over several times and radically changed in shape, balances and weights. At one time it was too black, at one time the rhythm was too regular, at one time there was not enough variation in the geometry of the shapes. I realized there were about ten thousand brush strokes in it, and that each brush stroke is a decision. It is not only a decision of aesthetics—will this look more beautiful?—but a decision that concerns one's inner I: is it getting too heavy or too light? It has to do with one's sense of sensuality, the surface is getting too coarse, or it's not fluid enough. It has to do with one's sense of life: is it airy enough or is it leaden? It has to do with one's own inner sense of weights: I happen to be a heavy, clumsy, awkward man, and if something gets too airy, even though I might admire it very much, it doesn't feel like myself, my I. (Ashton & Flam, 1983, p. 12)

Helen Frankenthaler 1928–

Frankenthaler is an American painter who is credited with marking the transition between abstract expressionism and color stain painting. In the 1950s, Frankenthaler studied with Hans Hofmann. Her work was first discovered by Morris Louis and Kenneth Noland in 1951. She is considered an abstract painter with some suggestions of landscape by using a method consisting of washes of thinned paint poured and stained into unprimed canvas (Fig. 5.2). From 1958 to 1971, she was married to Robert Motherwell. In the early 1960s, she changed from oil to acrylic paint, which permitted her to use more intensely saturated color (Rose, 1973).

Frankenthaler was also a student of Rufino Tamayo and, in her student years, was also influenced by Cubism, Picasso, Cezanne, and Matisse. In 1951, she was exposed to the work of Jackson Pollock and was impressed with the extraordinary physical impact of his paintings—especially in the manner in which they appeared to surround the viewer, which, in her view, established a more intimate and direct contact between image and

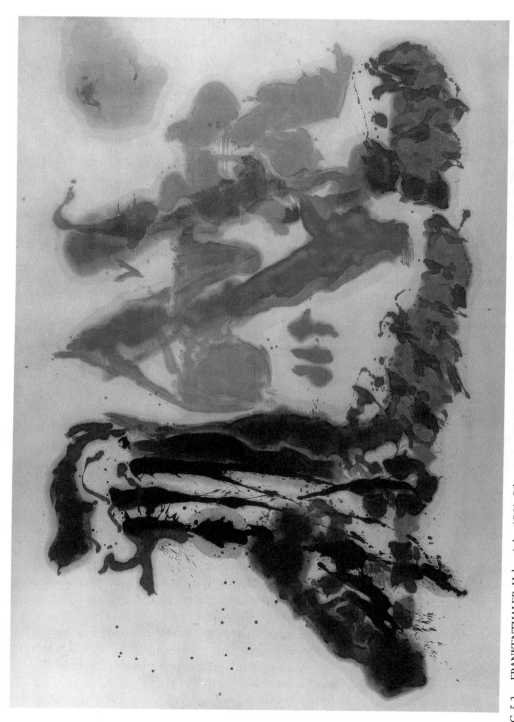

FIG. 5.2. FRANKENTHALER, Helen. *Arden*. 1961. Oil on canvas. 87 1/2 x 128″ (222.3 x 325.1 cm). Collection of Whitney Museum of American Art, New York. Gift of the artist. 69.170.

spectator. Although she liked de Kooning, whom she felt she could copy, she did not feel the same about Pollock, whom, she felt, moved painting from the easel to the floor to work on it from all sides, abandoning the traditional brushes and oil for enamel and a variety of dripping instruments. de Kooning, she noted, made enclosed linear shapes and applied the brush, whereas Pollock used his shoulder and ignored edges and corners. She claims to have learned from Pollock how to compose without recourse to the cubist grid, which was frontal and parallel to the picture plane.

Like Motherwell, Frankenthaler understood the method of the cubists—automatism—but was considered to be a more intuitive painter than an intellectual one, which she credits to Pollock. Most of all, she viewed the canvas from Pollock's view, which was to work on the studio floor, putting herself visually above and in the center of the work. Therefore, she did look down on the image when she painted. When viewing it on the wall, later vestiges of the aerial view she had when she created it remain. Often the illusion is of an oblique tilting away from a flattened mass, which may resemble an island on its side.

In talking about her unique aerial view of the image, she suggested that it offers a number of possibilities:

You might look, for example, at a roomful of chairs or a table top of apples, or a hillside of trees and without ever graphically referring to those chairs, apples or trees you might do a play on the color, shape and positioning of these objects. You might put a green "A" shape here and below it a green "A" shape there which, while they are very much the same, are also totally different just as a tree in a stand of trees is different from each other tree and different in its relation to the whole image. (Rose, 1973, p. 67)

In her early stained pictures, Frankenthaler created a stained image that was not illusionistically on top of or behind the picture plane, but rather came in and out of the ground. The obvious link between image and ground allowed her to create an illusion of depth that did not work against its flatness because it could be perceived that the image was embedded in and supported by its contiguous relation with the surface. It is said that she imitated the processes of nature by allowing an image to grow spontaneously and evolve from the method, materials, and process she used in creating, allowing paint to flow, spread, and unfold to create an image.

In her working method, a color is chosen and put down on the canvas with the hand, sponge mop, rag, brush, a combination of these tools, or simply poured and blotted. Accidents in the process are permitted but controlled. Frankenthaler admits most accidents are predetermined—where she might want a blob of blue two-foot square or throw the blue paint on the canvas to achieve an "S" shape, which creates a still different image. She then proceeds from or works with that or abandons it, only to come back to it in a few weeks or months.

In deciding when a picture is good or finished, Frankenthaler stated that a really good picture appears as if it happened at once—such as in seeing an immediate image. When her work looks labored or overworked, or when one can read in it that she did this then did that, in her opinion, it makes it not beautiful and requires her to throw it out. She estimates that it takes 10 of these overlabored efforts to produce one really beautiful wrist motion that is synchronized with her head and heart.

However, Frankenthaler admitted that she would also risk an ugly surprise rather than rely on images she knows she can do. As a result, some feel her strength is in her ability to create a Gestalt image immediately and directly—a "one shot" image, as Noland once called it. As a result of her trial-and-error method, Frankenthaler has destroyed many paintings, noting that for every one she shows, many more end up in shreds in the garbage can.

Frankenthaler also noted that her study of Pollock's paintings on the floor of his studio and Greenberg's analysis of it gave her a sense of being open, free, and surprised as possible. She learned her own sense for knowing when to stop; when to labor; when to be puzzled; when to be satisfied; when to recognize beautiful, strange, ugly, or clumsy forms; and when to risk a final edit by trimming some edges off the work after it was completed.

Richard Diebenkorn 1922–

Richard Diebenkorn was a California-based abstract painter who developed his particular style in response to Stella and Rothko, fellow teachers at the California School of Fine Arts where he worked in the 1940s. Over the years, he has alternated between abstract and figurative work, but is mainly known for his abstracts, with simplified colors and gestural brush work. In 1967, he began a series of abstract painting entitled *Ocean Park,* which are in all probability his best known work.

His overall style of working is considered abstract expressionist. His earliest influences come from the work of Hopper, Cezanne, Matisse, and Miro. He also studied with and was influenced by Baziotes, Mendelowitz, and Hans Hofmann. In the 1950s, when he taught at the University of New Mexico, his work was described as being drum head flat, strongly evocative of the desert landscape, and activated by linear tracery that relates to the old Hassel Smith exchange and the influences of reproductions of works by Gorky and de Kooning (Nordland, 1987).

His painting method could be described as both painterly and direct. He described his painting method as putting down how he feels regarding the overall image and then perhaps being disappointed by it the next day, only to alter or destroy it partially or wholly and then work back into it to pull out something that makes sense. Each new painting, he feels, is *sue generis*—true only to itself as an effort to find a new approach to both form and color. In the process, Diebenkorn's devices of horizontal banding (Fig. 5.3) appear or are omitted, and signs of earlier approaches and still life images from earlier pictures emerge later, only to be systematically painted out.

Diebenkorn resists being described as an abstract painter because he believes his paintings grow out of a mood—out of relationships with things or people and out of complex visual impressions. For Diebenkorn, abstract means literally to draw out or separate a concept, which is something he feels all artists do anyway. Whether one initially uses a realistic or nonobjective approach makes little difference; it is the result that counts. Speaking about his general mode of working, he noted:

> I keep plastering it until it comes around to what I want in terms of all I know and think about painting now, as well as in terms of the initial observation. One wants to see the artifice of the thing as well as the subject. Reality has to be digested, it has to be transmitted to paint. It has to be given a hoist of some kind. (Nordland, 1987, p. 89)

His work has been described as spontaneous, energetic, and emotional. He is said to subject himself to self-torturing criticism, pursuing the creation of a work over long periods of time and subjecting the work to countless repaintings and revisions. "Everyone

FIG. 5.3.   DIEBENKORN, Richard. *Ocean Park 115*. 1979. Oil on canvas, 8'4" x 6'9" (25.4 x 205.6 cm). The Museum of Modern Art, New York. Mrs. Charles G. Stachelberg Fund. Photograph (c) 1998 by The Museum of Modern Art, New York.

makes mistakes," he is noted to have said. At times, he also has admitted to being ashamed of some of the pictures and thus to obliterate them so no one could see his mistakes.

In his use of materials, Diebenkorn liked to work thinly, but he also wanted to see a density in the layered pigments. Although scraping the surface and overpainting did result in his making some compromises, he would also push the painting into chaos to see what would happen—yet with the hope of finding a unity that was fresh and surprising.

In starting a work, Diebenkorn believed a premeditated scheme or system to be out of the question, noting that a drawing cannot be translated into a painting. The artist must begin anew with each new painting, feeling out the size of the canvas and the rhythms that seem right to the particular proportions chosen on a given day. He has also said that he did not believe one could design a painting in his head.

In describing his thoughts as he paints, he noted in the early states of the work that certain forms appear promising as they emerge in graphite, charcoal, and color. However, he distrusts the easiness with which these early forms emerge yet likes to pursue the possibilities they allow. Each decision relates to every successive one; at every stage in the development of the work, the artist must work with the conviction that this could be the final stage and that the work is nearing its completion. He noted that, at the next session, he could find a weakness to exploit and could even decide to reenter the work through that weakness. At that point, the painting becomes fluid again and the feelings engendered are the same as in the final stages of the work. At the final stage, he is also freed of both the emotion and effort made in expressing it.

Like many other artists, Diebenkorn finds out what he wanted to accomplish only after the work has been completed. What objects or forms remain in the work when it is finished indicate what objects remain important to him. The idea of the work comes at the time the picture is done. "There seems," he noted, "something a little immoral about touching up ideas" (Nordland, 1987, p. 69). Unlike Frankenthaler and despite his claims of being ashamed of his mistakes, overworking is Diebenkorn's admitted method of working, and the evidence of his overworking is left exposed on the canvas. Part of the painting is physical, whereas another part is intellectual; the balance between them changes intuitively with each painting.

Ellsworth Kelly 1923–

The fourth abstract American painter to be discussed is considered part of a group of American artists engaged in postpainterly abstraction. Kelly's work has been described as employing regular, irregular, geometric, and curved formats, sometimes with multiple planes—as is seen, for example, in his work entitled *Blue, Green, Yellow, Orange, Red,* which was completed in 1966. He uses pigments applied flatly, choosing bright colors, black and white, and, in more recent times, shades of grey. The large, simple, hard-edged forms appearing in his work (Fig. 5.4), which comes from observation, contain extreme contrasts of positive and negative shapes and extend into three dimensions.

Kelly is considered by some writers to reflect a European style of working, and he admits to liking the work of Picasso, Matisse, and, in particular, Mondrian. Like Mondrian, he claims he rarely makes a painting without a formulation in his mind of the specific shapes of the canvas and the problems and aesthetic issues it was intended to resolve (Coplans, 1973).

FIG. 5.4. KELLY, Ellsworth. *Atlantic*, 1956. Oil on canvas, two panels, overall: 80" x 114" (203.2 x 289.6 cm) Collection of the Whitney Museum of American Art, New York. Purchase. 57.9.

141

Unlike Motherwell, Frankenthaler, and Diebenkorn, Kelly notes that he never finds an image in the process of creating the work, but rather in prior analyses of the work's preliminary drawing or collage, some of which are used immediately in the creation of the work and others held over for a later work. He is said to build on an existent body of work whose terms were already accepted and, through the process of refection, makes his own additions.

Kelly's method of abstraction is to see abstractions in nature, photograph or draw them, and use these as the model to be followed in the actual work. In 1949, Kelly began to make drawings of the random effects he found when observing cast shadows, as well as what he noted in the dead branches of trees and other forms of vegetation. He also developed work from automatic drawings—sometimes with his eyes shut and at other times using subject matter revealed in his blind contour drawings. Later in his career, he began to tear and cut up discarded drawings and collage the pieces together.

Instead of making a picture, he has been noted as saying that his drawing was an interpretation of a thing seen or a picture of invented content. This includes making a painting of five white stones found on a beach to make a face in his hand, works made from the markings of a tennis court, a kilometer marker plate, seaweed, or from a window pane. None of his pictures are arrangements, but are rather divisions of a whole, where colors are arranged and where his intention is to divide the space rather than arrange forms.

Inspiration for his initial drawings comes from a variety of sources in the environment. At the Museum of Modern Art in Paris, he was more interested in the large windows between the paintings than in the art work exhibited. According to Kelly, that event really changed the way he painted; he made a drawing of that window and designed his first object, called *Window—Museum of Modern Art Paris.* From then on, painting as he had known it was changed for him.

A number of his earlier paintings were wholly inspired by similar events. One, a painting called *Gateboard,* was inspired by the metal driveway gates he saw in rural France. In this work, he copied the gate using a panel for the doors of the gate and lacing strings dyed black through the holes in the panel. By leaving several of the holes unlaced, he avoided making a symetrical design, which resulted in a work using an unfinished drawing with five lines missing.

Another painting, called *Window V,* was inspired by the projection of light from a street lamp shining through an irregular shaped window into the wall of his room at night. The horizontal bands in the painting are the shadows of telephone wires and a piece of paper was placed into the image and traced exactly. The projection of light was also made palpable by cutting the form out of wood the same size and painting the telephone wire bands black on a white ground. That image, he claims, had been on that wall for many years and probably still is.

Conceptually, Kelly rejects any kind of verbal framework or philosophy as having guided his work over time. In looking back at his work, he notes it is almost impossible to trace any kind of linear development, except to note that nearly all of his later work is tautologically reflected in his earlier work.

Technologically, Kelly's materials and mode of working are highly deliberate. In laying on his color, he uses several coats of slightly modified color to change the density, strength, and brilliance of the first and successive coats of color. The optical characteristic of a

Kelly-constructed color is of a color bound up in the interpenetration of layers that modify each other. In addition, each color is further modified by its reciprocal relation to adjoining colors and as seen in a context, where any given color cannot be seen in terms of its hue color characteristics but rather as exists in the Gestalt formed by all the colors used in the work.

Kelly never begins a painting until he has systematically probed a particular idea and its possible variations in drawings. Before proceeding to paint, Kelly forms a sharp mental image of the final work—especially its prospective, size, and scale. It is at this point that Kelly orders the canvas stretchers, which are then used for a specific image and no other. He is said to carry a series of different images in his mind over a considerate period of time and then, some time later, order enough stretchers to paint a run of work.

Kelly's ideas for a work or a series come from what he sees in the external environment. Coplans (1973) claimed that, in just looking, he does find a variety of things to be made exactly as he sees them, with nothing to be added and nothing to compose. Coplans quoted Kelly as saying,

> I could take from everything . . . it all belonged to me. A glass roof of a factory, with its broken and patched frames, lines of a road map, the shape of a scarf on a woman's head, a fragment of the Corbusier's Swiss Pavilion, a corner of a Braque painting, fragments in the street. (p. 28)

Realist Art

There are, in effect, several definitions of realism, but it is most often described as unidealized and objective representation associated with the realism movement in 19th-century France, where painters of the period rebelled against the idealized subjects and/or mythical and historical painting. These artists include caricaturists like Daumier and genre painters such as Bonvin and Corbet.

Today, realism includes a broad range of painting styles ranging from the figurative work of Beal, Morandi, Pearlstein, and Wellover to the more abstract works of Katz, Avery, and Freilicher. Realism has also been used interchangeably with the term *naturalism,* which describes a style where the artist attempts to render a subject accurately and objectively rather than stylizing or applying intellectual or extraneous considerations to the work. The artist Meissonier is most often associated with naturalism.

Both Realism and Naturalism need to be distinguished from Illusionism, which is the pictorial technique used to create a convincing or deceptive sensation of real space or form on a two-dimensional surface. The use of perspective and minute naturalism are the most common techniques employed by illusionists. Quadratura and Trompe L'oeil are the specialized branches most often associated with this way of working.

Another form of realism discussed here is called *magic realism,* which was initially applied to the work of the French surrealist Pierre Roy and to the German painter Neue Sachlichkeit. Magic realism gained currency in America at the Museum of Modern Art's (MOMA) 1943 exhibition entitled *American Realists and Magic Realists,* which included the work of Albright, Shahn, and Wyeth. The term is generally applied to works that which depict disquieting, fantastic, or surreal themes in a sharply focused style. This term has also been used to describe the work of the American painter Paul Cadmus, whose work is similar to the work of George Tooker—using a polished Italian Renaissance figurative style. The subject matter of American magic realism is of contemporary society viewed satirically or with a jaundiced eye.

Jacob Laurence

Jacob Laurence is a realist painter who has also been described as one of the first African-American painters. Laurence studied in the Works Progress Administration (WPA) classes of the depression and was influenced by the social consciousness of the 1930s. He drew on African-American culture for his subjects and is most famous for his series of 60 paintings on *The Migration of the Negro* 1940–1941, shown at New York's MOMA and the Washington Phillips Collection. In this work, Lawrence worked in tempera, combining a simplified handling of flattened forms with the kind of primitive angularity most often associated with Ben Shahn (Piper, 1984).

In the Migration Series, Laurence created abstracted, expressive figures with exaggerated, masklike features acting out causes and consequences in shallow, stagelike spaces. In this series, Lawrence created a text that incorporated history, sociology, and a kind of poetry in a visual narration while breaking out of the typical categories of modern art. Critic Alain Le Roy noted that, in this series, there was no kind of social propaganda and no slighting of the artistic problems involved, such as one tends to find in most social theme painters (Elizabeth, 1993).

In Panel 45 of the series, which shows a migrant family on its first view of Pittsburg, Laurence used the colors of their clothes—especially their hats and the color and pattern of food baskets—to suggest southern designs and bright hues. Using smiling faces and dramatic gestures, he successfully conveyed the excitement of these southern migrants as they enter the northern industrial civilization. Thus, the bright colors and patterns are used symbolically to represent the hopeful expectations the migrants must have felt when they first faced the urban north.

In an earlier work entitled *Interior Space* (1973), Laurence created the illusion of three dimensionality through the use of a flat, stylized design with sculptural qualities. Sharp angles and bold color contrasts are used to suggest a three dimensionality of the picture and create a surreal stage on which stage characters play out scripted and somewhat comical roles.

Laurence's method of working is both deliberate and authoritative; he backs up pictorial content through library research and spontaneity while ignoring the visual records that document that research. Before Laurence began the migration series and before he even picked up a brush, he went to the library and researched and wrote the text for the story he was preparing to tell in the series. It has also been noted that, while browsing the catalogue looking for story references to be used in the series, he could not recall using any of the extensive photographic files in the collection to stimulate his imagination for the images. He did research, read numerous books, took notes, and went through the notes up to three times to eliminate unimportant points, believing that history paintings should be based on actual recorded events.

The sources for Laurence's images are found mainly in his home community of Harlem (Fig. 5.5). His inspiration to draw came from the streets around him, which were a kind of

FIG. 5.5.   LAWRENCE, Jacob. *Tombstones*. 1942. Gouache on paper. Sight: 28 3/4" x 20 1/2" (73 x 52.1 cm). Collection of the Whitney Museum of American Art. Purchase. 43.14.

theater offering a range of personalities—from barefoot prophets to shell-shocked World War I veterans, from street corner Garveyites who advocated that African-Americans return to Africa, to the soap-box communists who predicted the worldwide triumph of the proletariat. He acknowledges that he and the other artists of his time were inspired more by the Harlem community than by each other, both socially and formally. He saw African-American urban communities like Harlem as kaleidoscopes of pattern, color, movement, and design.

Laurence's Migration Series is an attempt to resolve two central competing modes of representation in the African-American tradition that struggled for dominance in the 1920s and 1930s: (a) naturalism, which reveals how individual choice was both shaped and curtailed by environmental forces, and (b) modernism, which sought to chart the relation of the individual's will in a chaotic environment—a concern Laurence expressed through a form of expressive cubism.

Laurence noted that his painting method does not include dragging a painting out; rather, her prefers to work directly. His style is to paint one layer at a time to create a strong sense of movement and space by strong lines, varying the brush work, and juxtaposing flat opaque passages next to more transparent ones, in which his brush work is expressive.

Fairfield Porter 1970–

Fairfield Porter, another American realist painter, holds an entirely different view of the sociology of art than his contemporary Jacob Laurence. According to Ashbery and Moffett (1982), Porter has a horror of "art as sociology"—that is, of the artist who treats art as if it were the raw material from a factory that "produces a commodity called understanding" (p. 9).

Porter has been influenced by deKooning, Johns, and Lichtenstein. He also likes the traditional work of Rubens, Giotto, and Piero della Francesca. Among the impressionists, he likes Vuillard; he admires impressionist works mostly because of their emphasis on paint and color rather than on contour and shading. He does not like Cezanne because he was too conceptual and too involved with ideas. Porter feels that abstract expressionism was the movement most closely aligned with impressionism because it was both empirical and respective of its means.

Other artists he admires includes Jane Freilicher, deKooning, and Alex Katz. He admires Freilicher because, when confronted with the life of the painting and the rules of construction, she would decide to let the rules go. Although he feels that at times her articulation of figures were impossible and awkward, it is a smaller fault than pure murder. In Porter's view, deKooning's work was an affirmation of painting being both a physical and material thing. With Alex Katz, his paintings reminded him of a first experience in nature or a first experience in seeing.

As to what constitutes a work of art, Porter has been quoted as saying that aesthetics is about what connects one to matters of fact. Considering himself to be an ecologist, he also views idealism as technology, with technology becoming idealism put into practice. He feels subject matter should be normal so that it does not appear sought after so much as simply happening to someone (Fig. 5.6). As to the artist's identity, he feels that you are simply what you have been saying all this time and not any less than that. In effect, you are not only what you are, but also somebody you know and who other people know as well.

FIG. 5.6.   PORTER, Fairfield. *The Garden Road*. 1962. Oil on canvas, 62" x 48" (157.5 x 121.9 cm). Collection of the Whitney Museum of American Art, Gift of the Greylock Foundation 62.55.

As to his method of working, Porter views compositional order as coming from the search for disorder and the awkwardness of searching for harmony and likeness. The truest order, he believes, is in what you already find there or that will be given to you if you try for it. When you arrange, he notes, you fail. About the arrangement of a still life, Ashbery and Moffett (1982) noted him as stating:

> Often in still lifes—almost always in still lifes—I don't arrange them. This still life was arranged. But usually it's just that the way the dishes are on the table at the end of the day strikes me suddenly. And so I paint it. Part of my idea or my feeling about form that's interesting is that it is discovered—that it's the effect of something unconscious like, you know, the dishes are in a certain arrangement at the end of the meal because people, without thinking, have moved things and then have gone away. (p. 57)

As to his painting method, Porter complains that he had to learn to paint from scratch, in part, because of America's lack of a developed painting culture, which, in his view, made him a late bloomer. When working, Porter does not simply delineate a tree, shoreline, house, or dishes on a table. Rather, he defines these subjects by drawing the space around them. Because he perceives form backward, his shapes and arrangements become as abstract as a Kline, deKooning, or Baziotes.

Commenting on one of his paintings, he admits that the shadows of the tree, the figure, the house, and the chimney may all fall in different directions, but he also points out that the same may be seen in a Titian, Caravaggio, or Rembrandt. As to why such things happen, he feels he cannot be distracted from paying attention to what he is doing by evaluating it ahead of time. According to Porter, the artist does not know what he knows in general, but rather specifically. What can be known in general, he claims, has to become apparent later.

George Tooker 1920–

George Tooker, as previously noted, is sometimes referred to as a symbolic realist. Some have called Tooker a classicist because he was trained in the virtues of intellection, having received the benefits of a knowledge of art history and believing that art comes from other art. Tooker has acknowledged his debt to the sculptors of classical antiquity, to the Italian painters and sculptors of the 14th and 15th centuries, and, in particular, Uccello, Piero della Francesca, the Flemish painters of the same period, as well as the Dutch and French 17th-century paintings and Americans Paul Cadmus and Edward Hopper. Tooker received his formal training in art in 1943 while a student at the Arts Student League, where he studied with Reginald Marsh.

Tooker's paintings in egg tempera depict clothed and unclothed figures in juxtaposition, where nudity may symbolize visionary truth as opposed by symbolic agents of obstruction, doubt, and conventionality. In his paintings, he uses architectural settings, classical manipulation of perspective, formal goals of order and containment, deep and shallow spaces played against one another, and deep open space at the left rapidly compressed by strong diagonal or step forms to much shallower space at the right hand side of the panel.

In his best known work, *Subway* (1950; Fig. 5.7), the figures are all swathed in layers of clothing and every face has the look of nameless dread. One critic noted that it is as if these

FIG. 5.7.   TOOKER, George. *The Subway*. 1950. Egg tempera on composition board. Sight: 18 1/8" 36 1/8" (46 x 91.8 cm). Frame: 26" x 44" (66 x 111.8 cm). Collection of the Whitney Museum of American Art. Purchased with funds from the Juliana Force Purchase Award. 50.23.

people were frozen in space, unable to extricate themselves from a seemingly endless maze of white-tiled corridors and dim grey stairways in which they are trapped; even those he painted in motion appear paralyzed.

All three of Tooker's major political works—*Subway, Government Bureau,* and *Waiting Room*—share his interest in precise geometric order as an intellectual and physical construct, against which protagonists clothed in heavy coats and hats are completely intimidated by the governmental structures built to serve them. Lincoln Kirstein, an early champion of Tooker's work, characterized Tooker's brand of symbolic realism as exemplifying an intellectual rather than an emotional or manual profession or responsibility. In his view, symbolic realism assumes that its durable product is found in the expression of ideas rather than in craft or the demonstrations of self-love or self-pity, which are expressed in the subject matter. In his view, such painting also reflects the triumph of the orderly, intelligent, and achieved rather than being the victim of the decorative, fragmentary, or improvised.

Tooker's working method, perhaps more than anything else, tells us about his disciplinary and deliberate approach to painting. Since 1945, only one of Tooker's paintings has been executed in a style other than one using egg yolk tempera on untempered pressed wood board previously brushed over with five or six coats of gesso—a fine white, plasterlike ground made of powdered chalk mixed with rabbit skin glue. Tooker plies his trade six days a week, where the pigment is mixed and applied so the image can grow in density, richness, and depth. In this process, Tooker applies layer after layer of color to achieve the luminosity he desires, working on a painting intensely for two or more months, six hours a day, to complete it.

Tooker reportedly begins each day in his kitchen cracking eggs, separating the white from the yolk, and draining the yolks into small plastic cups, to which he adds enough cool water to double the volume. Later in the studio, he decides which areas of the painting he will work on that day or for the next day or two; he then prepares his palette accordingly.

In the painting process, Tooker will work on a 23" × 17½" painting for up to two and a half months. His meticulous mode of working has been described by Garver (1985):

> Using powdered pigments, he takes two parts ultramarine blue, two parts of ivory black (Mars black is too cold) and one part of titanium white and puts them on a white glazed tile on the taboret tray to mix the color for the day. A few drops of water are sprinkled on the pigment and the colors are rubbed together into a paste. The paste is then transferred into one of thirty nine deep round depressions or "pots" of a water-color palette. Using an old sable brush ("one that doesn't hold a point anymore") Tooker adds several brushes full of the thinned egg yolk, swirling the egg and pigment together until the mixture is the texture of thin cream. (p. 7)

During the painting process, Tooker claims his images develop by trial and error. He prefers to limit details in his preliminary drawings because he feels he can discover more when involved in the actual act of painting. In selecting the images remaining in the work, Tooker claims he is not interested in a surreal look, but rather to depict a reality impressed in his mind so hard that it returns as a dream or fantasy. Like Laurence, Tooker's images also rely on literary references or even imagery from the past, but these, he claims, come into effect after the idea of the work is formed.

Wayne Thiebaud 1920–

Wayne Thiebaud, the last of the realist painters to be discussed here, began his career as an army artist and cartoonist, working both on training films and doing set designs. In 1956 to 1957 he moved to New York and became the art director of an ad agency. While working in New York, he became attracted to abstract expressionists including deKooning, Kline, Newman, Pearlstein, and Wolf Kahn. Because he also liked representational work, he became interested in the 19th-century Italian school, which involved the opulent handling of paint and coarselike applications of paint. He especially liked the work of Velasquez and Goya. Later on he became associated with and was influenced by the so-called "bay area painters," Elmer Bishoff and David Park, who, along with Diebenkorn, fused abstract expressionism with representational imagery (Tsujimoto, 1985).

Thiebaud's images have undergone a number of changes over time. While teaching at University of California–Davis in 1960, he painted hamburgers, plates of bacon and eggs, roast beef dinners, hot dogs, barbecued chickens, salt and pepper shakers, cakes, pies, and candy machines (Fig. 5.8). As he once noted, he could make art out of anything. In 1962, in his first New York show, he was assigned to pop art status and was considered a stylist in the vein of Jim Dine, Roy Lichtenstein, Andy Warhol, Claes Oldenburg, and James Rosenquist. In 1964, at the urging of his bay artist colleagues, he briefly returned to figure painting, which he claimed he attempted to do without affectation, sentimentality, or evasiveness. In 1966, Thiebaud turned to painting landscapes that were influenced by Morris Louis. He explored Louis' stain techniques using waves of thinned acrylic paint to describe the shape of a mountainous ridge.

In the search for things to paint, Thiebaud says he looks for things that are overlooked, avoiding such objects as a lollipop tree, copper pots, or the clay pipes such as appear in the painting of Chardin or Cezanne. He feels that to sentimentalize or adopt a posture more polite than our own is not taking a real look at ourselves for what we are. Thiebaud's main preoccupations in painting are found in his explorations of repetition and variation, which he views as expressing the duality between the conceptual notion of conformity in the rows of pies he paints. He is also preoccupied with the effects of light, which is closely related to his interest in halation, which is what happens to the edges of objects when brightly illuminated. Technically, he believes, halation is the consequence of the imperfect binocular vision in the human eye when two images are merged but not exactly. As a consequence, Thiebaud does not make distinctions between such things as landscape or figure painting because, for him, both deal with the same problems (i.e., lighting, color, structure, etc.).

Thiebaud views the painting problem as an attempt to distinguish between objective, perceptual information to distill, codify, or find a symbolic reference as opposed to memory, fantasy, and other references. What he fears most is a mind filled with conventions that offer convenient ways of doing things or a search for a cliche. While avoiding any symbolic references in subject matter, he is committed to the formal problems of painting, but not so formal in his selection of subject matter.

As in his food paintings, his primary goal is to eliminate busy expressionistic surfaces to focus on four rudimentary shapes: rectangle, triangle, circle, and ellipse. He selects subjects that mimic these shapes, such as seen in a club sandwich, which can be seen simply as

FIG. 5.8.   THIEBAUD, Wayne. *Pie Counter.* 1963. Oil on canvas. 30" x 36" (76.2 x 91.4 cm). Collection of the Whitney Museum of American Art. Purchased with funds from the Larry Aldrich Foundation Fund. 64.11.

a series of triangles on a round platter. Once he determines his subject, he explores it in endless compositional variations. He experiments with changing the number of pie slices, their size, or their placement within the canvas, moving them close to the edges, moving them into the middle, or covering them with glass.

In his figure drawings, Thiebaud draws more on historical schema, where he finds it possible to think through the hands and minds of others (i.e., to sense the origins of a Degas back, Holbein's profile lines or the eye spacing of Picasso or Utamaro). By studying both the history and practice of drawing, Thiebaud believes it is possible to reexamine the variations and novelties of prime origins. Borrowing the figure drawing method of Nicoliades, his interest in the figure centers more on what the figure is about to do rather than what it is posed as doing.

In his landscapes, Thiebaud sees another kind of compositional problem: to eliminate the horizon line to get a landscape image divorced from a horizon fixation. Instead, he establishes a positional directive for the viewer, whether up or down a helicopter view, world view, or valley view, to get some sense of the loss of the convenience and comfort associated with just standing and looking at things normally.

Pop Art

The last category of painters to be described are included in the movement called *pop art,* which began in the mid-1950s in Britain and came to its zenith in New York in the 1960s. The term was coined by critic Lawrence Alloway to describe works that were focused on and used the techniques of the mass media, advertising, and popular culture. Pop art was said to be a reaction to abstract expressionism. It was pursued in England by Hamilton, Kitaj, and Blake and in the United States by Warhol, Lichtenstein, Oldenburg, Wesselmann, and Rosenquist. Rosenquist was first credited with employing collage techniques; air brush, industrial printing press, and silk screen.

This movement shares concerns with other painting trends of the 1960s, including minimal art, photorealism, and superrealism. Superrealism is generally described as a style of figurative painting or sculpture prominent in the United States and Britain in the late 1960s. Its subject matter has been described as being banal, static, and contemporary, reproduced with minute exactitude a high finish and a smooth, bland finish. Superrealism's aim is to generate a sense of unreality by presenting the subject with hallucinatory particularity, where the scale is often altered, such as is seen in Chuck Close's magnified snapshots and Duane Hanson's slightly less than life-size facsimiles of contemporary Americans at work and play.

James Rosenquist 1933–

Rosenquist first worked as a commercial artist painting billboards from 1941 to 1960. Although his early work was primarily abstract, his work gradually began to emulate the style and subject matter of commercial billboard painting. His most famous painting, *F-111* (1955), uses a montage of blown-up sharp images of billboards juxtaposed in unfamiliar suggestive arrangements. This work finally covered four walls of a room, thus creating a powerful bombardment of images.

Rosenquist began his artistic development as a sign painter in rural Minnesota and Iowa, where he learned the hard way to use the best materials—brushes with Chinese bristles that hold paint and cut a straight line. He learned to lighten his colors and black by mixing them with white, which was called *adding milk,* and to mix long paint that flows like cream, much like Picasso and deKooning preferred. His formal study included stints at the Art Students League and the Art Institute of Chicago, where he studied with Will Barnet, Edwin Dickinson, George Grosz, and Morris Kantor (Goldman, 1985).

What first attracted the critics' attention was his sign painter style, the collage technique, and the disjunctive couplings of images. There was much to connect Rosenquist to pop art, including his imagery; his palette, which reflected commercial inks; and his slick handling of paint. What separated him most from the movement was his avoidance of ordinary images. One critic noted that his pictures were hard to understand and never attracted the critical following of his colleagues Lichtenstein, Dine, Oldenburg, and Warhol. He was even referred to by one critic as being the "dark horse" of pop.

In 1962, on the occasion of Rosenquist's first New York exhibition in the Green Gallery, one critic described his work as being nonliterary and without a trace of Dada (Goldman, 1985). This critic noted that a painting might include a broad pun, but that was never the point. Further, although he took his imagery from the debris of a consumer culture, "his art did not judge that culture" (Goldman, 1985, p. 12).

Rosenquist's painting style has also been described as painterly and fluid, defining his forms through modeling and containing shapes within softly painted edges. He is best known for painting fragments of things in unlikely combinations (e.g., coupling a woman's face with a tomato, and using the funeral profiles of a man and woman with the front bumper of a 1950s Ford and a field of spaghetti (Fig. 5.9). Thus, his visual vocabulary became known by his fields of spaghetti, car fenders, toothy grins, and even the rose signifying his name.

In explaining his work, Rosenquist is quoted as saying that he wanted to make fragments of pictures (i.e., images that would spill off the canvas instead of recede into it, like in a medicine cabinet). He hoped that each fragment would be seen as moving at a different rate of speed and to paint the fragments as realistically as possible. "I am interested," he is noted as saying, "in the contemporary vision of the flicker of chrome, reflections, rapid associations, quick flashes of light, and 'bing bang.' I don't do," he claims, "anecdotes, I accumulate experiences" (Goldman, 1985, p. 46).

Rosenquist's most famous work, *F-111,* was painted in fragments reportedly because his Broome Street studio was too small for the painting. However, in his view, this fragmentary conception was appropriate to the picture's politics, claiming that he made the painting as a joke, using an image of an as yet undeveloped but already obsolete bomber painted in fragments. It was his plan to sell the picture in fragments so that collectors who bought pieces of the picture would be acquiring a souvenir of something they had already paid for with their taxes. If one collector decided to buy the whole picture, it would still be a joke because he would have to be very, very rich and could have probably bought a couple of F-111s with his income tax anyway.

Another painting by Rosenquist, which sold in 1981 for $285,000, entitled *Star Thief,* created a controversy. The painting, which was 17 × 46 feet, pictured strips of uncooked bacon, industrial gear, and a red and green grid with fragments of a woman's head split

FIG. 5.9.   ROSENQUIST, James. *Fahrenheit 1982 Degrees*. 1982. Colored ink on frosted mylar. Sheet: 33 1/8" x 71 1/2" (84.1 x 181.6 cm). Image: 27 1/8" x 65 5/8" (68.9 x 166.7 cm). Frame: 40 1/2" x 78 1/4" (102.9 x 198.8 cm). Collection of the Whitney Museum of American Art. Purchased with funds from the John I. H. Baur Purchase Fund, the Mr. and Mrs. M. Anthony Fisher Purchase Fund and The Lauder Foundation—Drawing Fund. 82.35. (c) James Rosenquist/Licensed by VAGA, New York, NY.

open and filled with wires floating across a star-studded celestial ground. Said Frank Borman, former astronaut and then president of Eastern Airlines, "I have had some exposure to space flight and I can tell you without any equivocation that there is no correlation ... between the artist's depiction and the real thing" (Goldman, 1985, p. 12).

Rosenquist claims his work involves a search for a metaphor, which involves the scary process of putting a new vision together that can change his own or somebody else's thinking. It is much like the unraveling of your sweater—where all of a sudden it comes off because of one loose thread. He also feels that the metaphor was more important than the imagery he pictured because he wanted to use the imagery as a tool, not as an object for recognition. He claims his work has nothing to do with popular images like chewing gum.

Audrey Flack 1931–

Although at times Audrey Flack has been classified as a realist, she is characterized here as a pop artist who, like Rosenquist, uses photographic images, airbrush techniques, popular images, enlarged scale, and arrangement of images on the picture plane. Flack denies she is a realist primarily because she believes a realist is one who faithfully mirrors reality, which she claims she does not do. She also rejects the term *photorealist,* preferring to be called a *superrealist*—one who exaggerates reality by bringing it into sharp focus at some points and blurring it at others. She also believes her work exists at many levels, including recognizable imagery, which she believes serves as a gift of the artist.

In the late 1950s, Laurence Alloway noted that Flack had a desire to get away from the broken edge of Cezanne and that early on she was interested in the gestural mode of painting. Alloway believed her adoption of photographic sources also did not conflict with her old master interests because both modes use mediated images as a screen to preexisting conventions already avowed by the arts (Flack, 1981).

Flack claims she was influenced early on by the work of Pollock and the art of the Spanish Baroque. In 1963 to 1965, Flack began a series of large portraits using older women from a family album, Mexican women with sun-dried faces, and a group of public personalities, including Rockefeller, Hitler, Churchill, Roosevelt, Stalin, and John F. Kennedy. She also did a portrait series of movie stars including Marilyn Monroe. However, it was not until 1977 that she first began using the airbrush.

Ann Harris has described her first encounter with Flack's painting as depicting the baptistery of Pisa, which looked like a giant blow-up taken from a cheap color postcard, and her copy of the *La Macarena Madonna* sculpture by Luisa Roldan, where its weeping face brings comfort to the pilgrims of Seville. Her technical equipment, she notes, was formidable, but there was something about each work that made it hard to like, including the raw colors, the use of popular images, and the formalist overtones of popular art (Flack, 1981).

Flack's earlier portraits soon changed because of an incident involving a portrait commission, where she reportedly discovered the idea of projecting the slide image directly on the canvas. She noticed that the figures she had originally drawn in her sketch were within a quarter inch of the projected image. She also notes that, up to that time, she could scale easily but was uncomfortable with the grid process. Using a grid slowed the process and made her painting look too mechanical, which worked against her abstract expressionist interests.

Jeanne Hamilton, a neighbor of Flack's, is the one who photographs the still-life forms Flack uses to construct her paintings. Commenting on Flack's still life arrangements, Hamilton noted:

> Audrey does not, no matter what anyone says, believe in gravity. She wants to paint objects as if they were flying off the canvas (because we live in a space age, I think), and therefore, the objects we photograph have to be one in front of the other in space, not on the table. We have flown not only toy airplanes but bunches of grapes, pairs of dice, hour-glasses and anything else that needs to be out there in front—using strings hung from clothes racks or from the ceiling, common pins stuck into pieces of fruit and chunks of plasticene, (Flack, 1981, p. 96)

Flack's method for creating abstracted images, unlike painters who work directly on the canvas or those who see abstractions in the environment, occurs through the way she arranges the kitsch objects she photographs. Her photographer, explaining the way the objects were arranged when she shot *Royal Flush,* speaks of Flack's disappointment with the arrangement used in her first photograph of that set-up. According to Hamilton, Flack found the still life to be too spread out and not effective in conveying the drama of a poker game. Consequently, they shot it again and again, each time pushing the objects closer and closer together until they worked compositionally.

In photographing the still-life arrangements, Flack likes the brightest light possible because she wants a brilliance in the paintings and also because she wants sharp slides from which to paint. However, some critics have noted that she is not a woman photorealist because she never allows her analysis of the design to dominate, which makes her work more about the content of the images than about how they are composed.

Flack's images play with illusionist appearances through such objects as shiny beads, drinking glasses, gilt and lustre cups, perfect roses, ripe pears, and glazed petit fours (Fig. 5.10). Some critics feel that, in the process, she celebrates the sensual pleasures of food to make her paintings a kind of allegory of greed. Flack's paintings are also affected by her use of scale, where the delineation of objects in her immense close-ups still do not reveal the flaws and fissures that exist below the level of ordinary vision. Some have characterized her blow-ups as nondestructive enlargements that celebrate the integrity of objects.

Conceptually, Flack views her work as being both highly symbolic and iconographic (e.g., where an apple becomes a color, a weight, or a density within an abstract circle specifically positioned in space). She sees her compositional arrangements as forcing objects to come forward and break the picture plane, such as is seen in her painting *Spaced Out Apple.* Her choice to use projected images rather than photographs reflects her observation of the differences in brilliance between these two kinds of photographic images. For her, the photograph is dull, whereas the slide makes her paintings as luminous as possible. How her work looks has also been influenced by her experiments with color, light, and the airbrush.

Flack's work is often developed in a series, including the *Gray Border Series* and the *Vanitas Series.* In the *Vanitas Series,* she claims to have exploited that which was popular in the 17th century. She considers that series to include some of the most important paintings in her career.

The *Gray Border Series* was created to establish a medium plane and a medium tone through the domination of the edge to measure space, depth, and light. She also notes that

FIG. 5.10.   FLACK, Audrey. *Leonardo's Lady*. 1974. Oil over synthetic polymer paint on canvas, 6'2" x 6'8' (188 x 203.2 cm). The Museum of Modern Art, New York. Purchased with the aid of funds from the National Endowment for the Arts and an anonymous donor. Photograph © 1998 by The Museum of Modern Art, New York.

she used a specific shade of gray for each painting to keep in balance with the tonality of the painting. In addressing her goals in the series, Flack (1981) noted:

> In the Gray Border Series I was dealing with volumetric objects. I wanted to move backward and forward in space. The space in these paintings is measured, controlled and finite. In Spaced Out Apple I inverted, reversed and flopped the photograph in order to disorient the viewer . . . eventually objects began to float and appear to be lifting off the surface. (p. 69)

SUMMARY

This chapter's review of concept formation as specificized by objectivist thinking reveals that concepts (a) are identified through perceptual data, (b) vary according to the age of the percipient, (c) are measurable, (d) consist of both wider or narrower perceptual evidence, (e) are aided by speech, and (f) are developed through the process of discovery. A *concept* has been defined as a mental interpretation of two or more perceptive units possessing the same character but with their measurements omitted.

Concept formation, as it would apply to creative forming, involves both the discovery and manipulation of discrete visual data and acts of awareness, where mental actions combine smaller observations into larger ones or reduce larger observations into more simplified or limited ones. This process varies according to the perceptual data being experienced and the age of the person experiencing it, and it follows no specific order in its development.

Therefore, concepts are also a form of abstraction or an abstraction of an abstraction, which vary in the amount of factual material used and in the length of the perceptual process. Longer perceptual processes, whether involving the development of either wider or narrower concepts, subsume constituent units yet contain more knowledge or perceptual evidence than the individual units subsumed in the original concept.

Also revealed is the notion that concept development is furthered through the use of silent and public speech, the use of words, and through understanding the meaning of words, which makes the accumulation of more and more data possible. The artist's speech can relate to both the discrete visual data observed and the acts of consciousness or awareness involved in thinking and feeling, as well as the formulation of concepts of consciousness that integrate psychological states.

Objectivism also suggests that all concepts contain material that can be described as existing in some amount or over some duration. Although some of this data can be measured cardinally, not all data lend itself to such measurement; they can be said to exist only as perceptual acts of consciousness (i.e., in thinking and feeling states, which can only be measured teleologically) or ordinally through its psychological content and intensity, its clarity, cognitive, or motivational content, and/or through the mental energy or effort involved.

Further, it can be noted in this chapter's review of the creative act and the image-forming processes of the 10 artists described that the creation of artistic form involves the discovery and manipulation of perceptual data, acts of awareness in the creation of visual abstractions or concepts, and the mental actions of reducing larger amounts of perceptual data into smaller or simplified abstractions or expanding limited visual data into larger and more complex visual meanings. Also, the artistic process varies according to the visual data being experienced and follows no distinct, agreed-on method or sequence of development. The visual abstraction evident in the artist's work reveals the amount of perceptual material employed and the length and depth of the perceptual process. Further, the perceptual processes revealed in the work, whether conceptually wider or narrower, all subsume constituent units into abstractions or visual metaphors containing more knowledge or perceptual evidence than the visual perceptual units subsumed in the formulation of the final work.

The manner in which the discussed artists work also suggests that the abstractions created contain content that exists in an amount or has sufficient duration to be evaluated perceptually in terms of psychological content and intensity, clarity, cognitive or motivational content, and/or the mental energy or effort involved. It is through such evaluations that the artists' decision-making processes occur and the act of completion is made possible.

What all this suggests for educational practice is a matter to be more fully discussed in the next chapter. It involves thinking about what artists do as well as how children grow in their conceptual development and the instructional environment that will maximize that development. Most of all, this chapter sets the stage for considering both intellectual and perceptual concept forming as not only related but as inextricably linked to higher order thinking skills and concept formation as a perceptual and consciousness process.

REFERENCES

Ashbery, J., & Moffett, K. (1982). *Fairfield Porter*. Boston: Little, Brown.
Ashton, D., & Flam, J. D. (1983). *Robert Motherwell*. New York: Abbeville Press.
Benswanger, H., & Piekoff, L. (Ed.). (1979). *Introduction to objectivist epistemology*. New York: Meridian Books.
Coplans, J. (1973). *Ellsworth Kelly*. New York: H. N. Abrams.
Elizabeth, H. T. (Ed.). (1993). *Jacob Laurence: The Migration Series*. Washington, DC: The Rappahannock Press.
Flack, A. (1981). *Audrey Flack on painting*. New York: H. N. Abrams.
Garver, T. H. (1985). *George Tooker*. New York: Clarkson N. Potter.
Goldman, J. (1985). *James Rosenquist*. New York: Penguin.
Gombrich, E. H. (1989). *Art and illusion: A study in the psychology of pictorial representation*. Princeton, NJ: Princeton University Press.
Harrison, H. (1978). *Making and thinking: A study of intelligent activities*. Indianapolis: Hackett.
Nordland, G. (1987). *Richard Diebenkorn*. New York: Rizzoli International Publications Inc.
Piper, D. (ed.) (1981). *The Random House Dictionary of Art and Artists*. New York: Random House.
Rose, B. (1973). *Frankenthaler*. New York: H. N. Abrams.
Tsujimoto, K. (1985). *Wayne Thiebaud*. Seattle, WA: University of Washington Press.

KEY TERMS

Concept	Invented content
Extrospection	Realism
Introspection	Magic realism
Cognitive scope	Halation
Cognitive intensity	Horizon fixation
Teleological measurements	Pop painting

Metacognition   Metaphor
Abstracted abstractions   Superrealist
Abstract expressionism   Gestural mode
Automatic drawing   Domination of the edge
Postpainterly abstraction

STUDY QUESTIONS

1. What are the main elements in the development of a mental concept? How does a concept differ from the language used to describe a concept? What is meant by widening and narrowing the perceptual data evident in a concept?

2. Describe how one goes about abstracting abstractions that directionally move toward more extensive and intensive knowledge and toward smaller concepts integrated into wider ones or subdivided into narrower ones. Do wider or narrower concepts involve more or less data and do they differ in their value?

3. What function does language play in the development of concepts? Do you think a vocabulary test would be an effective way to assess a student's grasp of a concept? Explain why you took this position for or against such an assessment.

4. How do objectivists view the need to measure a concept? Can a feeling or emotion be measured and, if so, would the form of measurement used differ from assessments that can be developed from the perceptual evidence contained in a product? Also, are there different standards involved in the measurement of feeling and form?

5. What causes a concept to develop in the mind and through what processes? How do concepts relate to one another and how would you determine which is a valid or invalid concept? What process does one use to determine the meaning of a concept that has been formed?

6. How does an artist know when a work of art is finished? What thoughts were necessary to accomplish it and what is it like to make an object in a particular way? In what ways do you think these knowledges relate to the formation of visual concepts and what part does the process of creating itself play in concept formation?

7. Referring to what has been described earlier as a bottom—up or top—down view of cognition, which view comes closest to your own way of working in art? Which artists in the chapter use a top—down or bottom—up way of

thinking? Does using one or the other of these approaches influence your own liking or disliking of their work? Provide some examples of which of these artists you like most and why their images are compelling to you.

8. Given Collingwood's dictum that art cannot be known in advance of its making, how would you explain to a parent or colleague in another discipline? How you would go about educating someone to make something you, as a teacher, could not know what it will be until the student is finished? How would you go about explaining the perceptual data the student acquired, how those data were used in concept formation, and how you would evaluate that effort?

6

The Conceptual Curriculum

CURRICULUM CONTENT
Organizing Perceptual Data
Developing Visual Strategies
Concepts as Content

SEQUENCING THE CURRICULUM
Sequence as Age Specific
Piagetian Stages
Lowenfeldian Stages
Piaget and Lowenfeld Compared

CONCEPT FORMATION
Concepts Related to Visual Forming
Concepts Related to Speech

INSTRUCTIONAL GOALS
Goals Related to Art
Goals Related to Art Practice
Focal Knowledge

THE CURRICULUM PLAN
Visual Concepts Evidenced in Performance
Preconceptual Stage Framework
Conceptual/Preconceptual Stage Framework
Conceptual Stage Framework

SUMMARY

The previous chapter strongly suggested that the development of mental/visual concepts in art involve the same cognitive functions of memory, consciousness, reasoning, and problem solving; the same perceptual/conceptual functioning are used in acts of cognition in other domains of inquiry, where units of data are converted into concepts or abstractions. What has yet to be examined is whether the conversion of units of visual data into visual concepts using larger amounts of perceptual knowledge and its quantification suggest that mental development can be one of the principal goals pursued in the art classrooms of American schools.

Should the conceptual processes used in forming visual abstractions in artistic learning cohere with the forms of intellectual activity addressed in the last chapter, it may be possible to conceive of a creatively focused school art program that offers some of the same kinds of intellectual challenges for growth as is offered by other academic areas of the school curriculum. Should such a notion prove supportable, it would also challenge the conventional wisdom that art is a *soft* school subject, lacking intellectual rigor with little to offer in the way of important cognitive growth or for improving the general intellectual development of school learners. Even if found true, however, it will still require new ways of thinking about art programs, new teaching strategies, and new ways of evaluating school art instruction.

Despite such obstacles, however, the introduction of a conceptual approach to art instruction has the potential to create a different view of artistic thinking, which could help students think more conceptually about the mental operations they employ in thinking and having commerce with the world in general. As a profession, the use of a conceptual approach to art teaching could move us closer to verifying what still remains, for the most part, the unsubstantiated claim that art learning leads to: (a) gains in the cognitive understanding of other school subjects, (b) elevated feelings of self-worth, (c) kids being retained in schools, and (d) improved school graduation rates. Such claims ring hollow, however, when the arts cannot convincingly demonstrate that they really do make a difference. Nevertheless, the realities are that, without strong conceptually based programs and valid and reliable ways to assess art learning in schools, the arts will never play a truly vital role in American schooling. Although we may want to reject the idea, it is still true that what cannot be evaluated in schools cannot be said to exist.

The conceptual ideas advanced in the previous chapter could, in the appropriate context, move us closer to realizing the greater intellectual potential of arts education in American schooling, especially if we are willing to rethink the objectives of art instruction, including what goals we need most to pursue and what methods we need to use to evaluate them. However, we must also understand that educational goals driven by efforts to improve school achievement, attendance, and graduation rates are also ones aimed at solving the social problems of children with disabilities, dysfunctional families, unemployment, drug abuse, and poverty. Such issues are what juvenile justice professionals view as the multiple risks that contribute to a child's proclivity toward violence and reflect the cycle of crime that begins early for most youthful offenders. This so-called trajectory toward violence involves ineffective parenting, poor school attendance, poor peer relations, school dropout, and exposure to violence in the home, neighborhood, and media—all of which increase the risk for children acquiring aggressive and violent behaviors. Although not all children with poor attendance or high drop-out rates become criminals, many are affected by the same social problems, including underemployment, poverty, welfare, teen pregnancy, and family breakup.

Of course, no single school subject, including the arts, can resolve all the social problems caused by ineffective parenting, drug or alcohol abuse, or teen pregnancy. Nevertheless, schools should be expected to develop programs that enhance student cognitive abilities, help kids to stay in school, and offer the necessary training and skills for achieving gainful employment or advanced educational training following graduation.

What those experienced with the life of children on the street tell us is that children who sell drugs rarely use them; ironically, the drug dealer usually becomes the only one willing to offer them a way of supporting the family. Although keeping children in schools and preparing them for the work world may not have been the principal reason most of us decided to teach art, these are extraordinary times requiring extraordinary efforts by teachers in every school subject. However, making the art curriculum meet these and other future school challenges will radically reshape school art programs in the 21st century. To change in this way is also to be accepting of this notion: No matter how good our art programs are, they are still diminished when the curriculum (a) does not help children to advance cognitively, and (b) fails to convince them to remain in school and believe that what they are experiencing in art is valuable both in itself and for achieving gainful and productive future employment or advanced schooling.

Although art instruction will always be considered inherently valuable, both for the life of the mind and for educating future audiences and enlightened cherishers of the arts, art as a school subject will never occupy its rightful place in schools unless it is also valued by those responsible for the delivery and financing of school programs and by the children and youth served in these programs. Although there are still valid reasons for art teachers to believe that art instruction improves students' self-esteem and that it is valuable for a general education, which teaches both art appreciation and connoisseurmanship, it still misses the mark unless the arts are valued by those outside the field as much as it is by those who work in it.

Therefore, this chapter focuses on relating the conceptual growth claims identified in the previous chapter, especially as they impact on the instruction of K to 12 students in art. In particular, this chapter examines how these claims impact on both the effectiveness of art instruction as an academic subject in schools and on the school's total effort to promote basic skills, keep students in school, and improve graduation rates. To achieve these goals, it is first necessary to determine the basic principles for guiding a K to 12 conceptually based art curriculum.

The following discussion argues that an art program focused on perceptual and cognitive forms of visual knowing, when properly assessed, will yield both quantifiable and practical verification that the students enrolled acquire new conceptual knowledge, skills, and behaviors that, over time, will increase in difficulty and complexity with respect to the higher order thinking achieved and enhance their ability to pursue advanced study or enter the world of work.

CURRICULUM CONTENT

The first part of this chapter outlines the general characteristics of a K to 12 concept-oriented art education program for schools. *Thinking in Art* noted eight different conceptual emphases that have been pursued in American schooling from the 19th century to the present. These include education as inquiry, education as reasonable learning, education as problem solving, education as discovery learning, education as discipline education, education as cognition, education as relevancy, and education as affect. All these emphases are present, to some degree, in the school curriculum today (Dorn, 1994).

It was further noted in the work that today's curriculum needs to be practical, based on theory, accepting of different curricular viewpoints, and also needs to demonstrate that the curriculum is working. It was also pointed out that, because curriculum situations and circumstances vary, a diversity of curriculum policies should remain a central premise in thinking about the art curriculum in practice today. This is also accepting of the notion that the key to curricular change is the teacher being open to alternative points of view and pursuing the particular view that makes the most sense within the context of the classroom where the teacher functions.

Because of what has already been said about the art curriculum structure in *Thinking in Art,* there is little need to repeat the general notions advanced in that work. Further, it is not necessary here to explain the paradigms, schema motif, art as form—Gestalt, and art as linguistic metaphor, except to say that what curricular paradigm is used is of less concern than deciding what learning experiences or activities are to be offered and how they are to be evaluated. Of particular importance is Tyler's (1950) notion that students need the opportunity to use what they have been taught (discovered) to enjoy and to have been taught something they can learn (Dorn, 1994).

Therefore, what follows is not about curriculum conception, but rather about what conceptual learning activities in art should be encouraged, how should they be taught, and in what sequence they should be ordered. Further, the challenge here is to go beyond the teacher's paradigmatic choice (i.e., to work toward the development of schema, form, or metaphor, and to focus rather on the particular cognitive processes that encourage visual concept formation in thinking about and making art in schools). The discussion that follows is organized around the four major principles of concept formation identified in chapter 5: (a) concept learning begins with the organization of perceptual data, (b) concept learning abilities vary according to the age level of the learner, (c) concepts are formed through the integration of perceptual data, and (d) concept development, especially in younger learners, is aided by the development of speech.

Organizing Perceptual Data

As revealed in the previous chapter, a mental concept is discovered through the mental interpretation of two or more perceptual units possessing the same distinguishing characteristics. A mental concept becomes evident in a visual work when it is organized in such a way as to form a conceptual/visual image. A simple illustration of this is found in Fig. 3.7, where Gombrich shows the process of the circle becoming the handbag, which then becomes the purse, which later becomes the cat. In this illustration, the circle with a half circle added becomes a hand bag, to which is added two small triangles, which makes it a purse, to which is added a curved line, which makes it a cat.

Developing Visual Strategies

However, even more sophisticated visual concepts occur, as noted in the previous chapter in the work of mature artists, where, for example, Ellsworth Kelly finds "ready-made" abstractions on the wall of a bedroom, Jacob Laurence discovers pattern in Southern people's dress, James Rosenquist finds form in the weathered and torn effects of a billboard, and George Tooker uses space as seen in Renaissance diptychs and triptychs. Other conceptual models can be seen in the nonobjective paintings of Bob Motherwell and Helen Frankenthaler, where abstractions are found in the arrangement of shapes and colors the artist forces us to pay attention to and that involve the deconstruction or substitution of one form or another in the process of making and deciding what shapes and colors remain, choosing what is preserved or suppressed, and discovering what organizations of pictorial space determine the completion of the work. All of these are concepts built up through a pattern of decisions of increasing complexity and abstraction regarding what images to keep, abandon, or change, including both the intentional and accidental marks used in the process.

Based on what was revealed in the artists' ways of working described in the last chapter, visual abstractions can be said to come from a number of different strategies, including the imposition of an abstract form on a visual environment, the integration or morphing of one pictorial style or schema with another, a mental discovery made during the act of manipulating forms and colors, or the synthesis of one artistic medium with another, such as is seen in the airbrush, photo, and graphic processes used by Flack and Rosenquist. As visual abstractions or concepts, it should also be noted that they occur before, during, and after the work is finished. This requires that we recognize that not all conceptual abstractions are evident in the work, but can be found in both the planning and execution of the work and in other works produced by the artist over time.

Concepts as Content

A work of art is a concept that, depending on its character, subsumes, modifies, replaces, alters, or, in some way, finds a way for two or more distinct real or imaginary images to be seen as having similarities, resemblances, and parallels. What we find in the final product is a visual form that reflects the artist's observations. It is also an interpretation that is accomplished through the imposition of a conscious pattern, structure, or design to form a visual concept or abstraction of a thing seen, felt, or imagined. This shows how the order of things might look and how it might be structured.

SEQUENCING THE CURRICULUM

Although it is important to know what constitutes visual and mental abstractions, it is also important for educators to know that all concepts are not always of the same order at all stages of human development and may not even be possible until humans reach more mature stages of life, if at all. Some recent movements in American art education, including the art disciplinary movement starting in the 1960s, generally avoided concerns for child development as a factor in art instruction. Inspired by the idea of Jerome Bruner—that any concept can be simplified enough to be learned at any age—and by Manuel Barkan's linguistic approach to art education, in recent years, theorists in the field have emphasized cognitive knowledge of art over expressive development through it. Unfortunately, this movement was also introduced as a repudiation of the child development view, which influenced the teaching of art in American schools from 1940 to 1960. Like all new movements that reject existing paradigms, the disciplinary movement sought to replace, rather than build on, the discoveries of the child development approaches developed at midcentury. As a result, interest in and knowledge of child development in art has radically declined among many newly educated art teachers who have had little or no contact with theories of how children learn and grow in art in Grades K to 12. For a truly effective art curriculum, teachers need to have a knowledge of both art and child development, especially if our goals are to move the art curriculum to a higher conceptual level.

Sequence as Age Specific

What follows next are some characteristics of the conceptual development of young learners as found in the research and theories of Piaget and in the work of Viktor Lowenfeld, who has written extensively on child development in art. The effort here is to use the Piaget and Lowenfeld research to reconcile theories of concept formation with what is known about child art development in Grades K to 12. The goal is not to argue for a *tides of development* approach to art teaching, but rather to assist the reader in understanding how artistic conceptual development normally occurs in the behavior of children of different ages. This section first describes the stages of concept development as outlined in the work of Piaget and then provides some comparisons with the same stages of development as supported in the work of Viktor Lowenfeld.

Piagetian Stages

According to Piaget, at times a concept is a mental image that represents an object or event. As a concept becomes more complex, it connects groups of objects and events sharing common properties. Before children can develop accurate concepts, objects or properties must be correctly distinguished according to size and shape; this process begins early on in life. Over time, youngsters learn to properly identify shapes and forms in their surroundings; shapes with ambiguous or hidden dimensions are especially difficult for them to perceive. Spatial concepts are particularly difficult for younger children to grasp; children often do not realize that an object can have various spatial appearances. For example, young children have difficulty telling whether an object is to the left or right, in front of or behind other objects, or right-side up or down. Piaget believes that these difficulties are due, in part, to their not knowing how to describe the object's various appearances.

According to Piaget, mental images representing object categories are known as *class concepts*. When young children are asked to group objects together, they are likely to categorize them by serialization or chaining—where, at first, things are grouped by color and later by shape. Children have difficulty deciding relationships between subclasses and classes. For example, when they are given four things of one color and two of another color, most children become confused because parts and wholes cannot be comprehended simultaneously. Children learn how to classify objects at these ages best through demonstration.

According to Piaget, mature cognition cannot exist without memory. At first children are capable of holding only a few words or ideas in their mind and have difficulty remembering events that happened weeks, days, or even hours before. Children gradually increase their overall memory span as they grow older and can increase the number of items that can be held in short-term memory; they learn how to remember (metacognition) by rehearsing events so that they can be remembered or by using other memory strategies to prevent forgetting. These strategies are sometimes referred to as *metamemory skills*.

Preoperational Stage—2 to 7 Years

Early Childhood. At this stage, motor skill development rapidly accelerates in the physical play activity of the child. Both gross (large) and fine (small) motor skills advance, including coordination of the hands in using scissors and learning to write. Before the preschool years, muscular development is proportionate to overall body growth while at this stage 75% of the child's weight gains are due to muscle development. Child psychologists at this stage question whether practice increases motor skill efficiency. Many psychologists believe the benefits of practice relate to the maturation state of the child, with certain kinds of motor skill activity being impossible to develop and where practice itself will not help. Therefore, motor efficiency is considered a product of maturation and experience.

According to Piaget, at this stage children are now able to use a variety of drawing media. In the end, children can produce recognizable pictures (Fig. 6.1). Shapes begin to emerge from concentrated scribbles, and the ability to draw certain shapes follows a pattern, with vertical lines coming before horizontal lines and squares, triangles, and diamond shapes appearing in that order. Shapes in drawings tend not to be combined or interrelated and have little or no association value. Therefore, children will note that a mixture of lines on a page is something that is separate and distinct from a circle that appears in the same drawing.

As children mature, they are more capable of using a rhythmical stroke, are more aware of the movements they can make, can associate values with shapes, and can combine circles, squares, triangles, and rectangles together to make numerous designs (Fig. 6.2).

Between the ages of 4 and 5, children create their first pictures, which are relatively unstructured. These early attempts use a variation of one or two basic shapes, such as is seen in the head–foot representation. At first, children use longitudinal scribbles to represent other body parts; later on, connected lines are added, moving from motor exploration of marks to symbolization of human form. Psychologists studying childrens' drawings note that the head is usually drawn first, resulting in a large head with smaller body parts. They believe this is more a problem with planning than with the child's lack of general body proportions (Fig. 6.3). Studies asking children to draw a man and a dog or a dog and a house suggest young children are able to draw them in proportional size (Silk & Thomas, 1988).

FIG. 6.1.   Angela Gruska, age 6. After Helen Frankenthaler, art teacher Susan Slavik, Livonia, Michigan Public Schools.

According to psychologists, the development of higher order thinking abilities is heavily influenced by a preschooler's continuing mastery of spoken language through using words and being able to understand what they represent. At this stage, spoken language is considered to be the essential link between meaning and sound and the transfer of thoughts from one person to another. Because of this, psychologists generally believe that language and thought are closely related developmental processes and are reflective of the child's general cognitive ability. It is believed that language reflects three cognitive functions: It allows children to (a) converse with one another socially, (b) internalize words into thought, and (c) have the internalization of action, which can be represented intuitively through pictures and mental experiments.

Preschoolers' thinking is more advanced, especially in regard to the refinement and elaboration of concepts. Thinking becomes more methodical and deliberate, and they are less easily discouraged by cognitive challenges. This suggests that a number of developmental forces interact in the development of cognition, which, at this time, is still dominated by perceptual processes that seem to be what logically they are.

Piaget also referred to this second stage of cognitive development as the *preconceptual thought stage.* He believed that preconceptual thought provided a foundation for later cog-

FIG. 6.2   First grade rainbow painting after an African myth, art teacher Susan J. Slavik, Livonia, Michigan Public Schools.

nitive functions, which are reconstructed experiences using existing mental schema, which places them into new mental categories. At this stage, children also begin to engage in symbolic functioning, which is the ability to differentiate signifiers (words and images) from significates (the objects or events that the signifiers refer to) and results in the construction of a mental image representing something not present (Fig. 6.4).

At this stage, concept development is encouraged through developing children's perceptual abilities, which are the cognitive activities allowing the detection and interpretation of relevant environmental information. Making accurate shape and size discriminations affects a number of perceptual conditions, including knowledge of distance and space relationships. Although children at this stage can discriminate among shapes and sizes, they still may not have a true perception of these categories. This may be due to their failure to remember the object by its characteristics, which can be improved by asking them to pay attention to details. Because of the lack of long-term memory, children may think a house becomes larger as it is approached and a cube changes its shape when seen from a new viewpoint.

Spatial concepts are also important for an accurate interpretation of an environment, but are limited in children during the preschool years. Egocentrism is seen as the main deterrent to comprehending such spatial discriminations as near, far, up, and down, which are usually interpreted personally as the toy or object being nearest. This also inhibits un-

FIG. 6.3. Self portrait by Haley Nunley, age 3. Garfield Preschool, Livonia, Michigan.

derstanding relationships relating to distance and direction. However, the research does suggest that the use of visual mapping can improve a child's ability to move in and understand spatial relationships and that children's map-reading abilities are more advanced than we realize. Using precise terminology and allowing children to see more than one spatial orientation can help preschoolers acquire more accurate spatial concepts. According to Piaget, the use of mirrors, maps, globes, and games requiring spatial analysis provides good learning opportunities.

Concrete Operational Stages—Ages 7 to 11

Middle Childhood. Middle childhood, also referred to as the school years including children ages 7 to 11, reveals gradual physical changes; children gain control and perfect motor skills they have been unable to master in the past. As a result, coordination, balance,

FIG. 6.4.   Mary Shereda, age 6. After Helen Frankenthaler, art teacher Susan J. Slavik, Livonia, Michigan
Public Schools CASS Arts 1996 Partnership Calender.

and refinement in physical skills occur, producing a positive effect on the child's psychological self-concepts, not to mention their acceptance into peer culture. Children of this
age are eager to participate in a variety of both gross and fine motor skills, which depend
on the rate of their physical maturity, the cognitive skills needed to master a task, and the
opportunity to engage in physical activity.

Increased mental ability, when connected with appropriate learning experiences, enables more advanced cognitive accomplishments to occur, such as having words and symbols take on new meaning and acquire increased problem-solving abilities that show
higher levels of insight and deliberation (Fig. 6.5). At this stage, children are better at expressing themselves through language and solving problems in math that involve concepts
of speed and distance. Comprehending and manipulating many different dimensions of
the environment are critical to higher mental functioning, although children at this stage
are still unable to think abstractly—as in making analogies. Although these abilities are
emerging, they may not occur evenly in all content areas.

In Piaget's stages of cognitive development, children between the ages of 4 and 7 enter
into the cognitive stage of intuitive thought, which is considered by psychologists to be
similar to preconceptual thought and a substage of preoperational thought, which lasts

FIG. 6.5   Collage by Ryan Gall, age 7, after Romare Bearen and Rene Magritte. Susan J. Slavik, art teacher, Livonia, Michigan Public Schools.

from ages 2 to 7. Children at this stage focus on immediate perceptions and experiences rather than on mental operations. They also tend to engage in centering, which means to concentrate on one outstanding feature of an object excluding other characteristics. This kind of thinking is often transductive (i.e., reasoning from the particular to the particular, rather than seeking generalizations that connect). Although such reasoning is at times correct, it is considered by psychologists to illustrate the child's mental shortcomings, which is to perceive the world intuitively.

The intuitive thought phase is characterized as lacking transformational reasoning, which makes it possible to observe sequential change or how one state is transformed into another. The lack of transformational thinking in art would make it impossible for a child at this age to make a drawing depicting the various stages of a falling form except to depict the beginning and final stages of this action. Another limitation would be the child's inability to reverse mental operations, which is called *reversibility,* or the ability to trace one's thinking back to where it originated—a necessary element in concept formation.

The stage of concrete operations is also a time when children begin to reason consistently. Children at this stage really do understand or comprehend things. These abilities are improved by such exercises as counting, manipulating, and sorting, which aid in the development of the mental operations of reversibility, seriation, and conservation. School subjects that teach the systematic obtaining of facts and social activities, which encourage children to appreciate the ideas, feelings, and opinions of others are encouraged.

At this age, children can understand the characteristics of objects but cannot understand abstractions and are therefore restricted to the immediate and the physical. As a consequence, youngsters cannot analyze their own thoughts or think about future problems, reason, about what is, and visualize what will be. However, they can understand the principle of conservation, which relates to the quantity of matter remaining the same even if the distribution of matter changes (i.e., not realizing the same amount of clay shaped as a ball or as an elongated form really contains the same quantity). Other cognitive advancements at this stage include the ability of children to engage in classification, which allows them to perceive the same element to exist in two classes of the same time (i.e., to recognize that shapes that are alike but of different colors are objects in the same class; Fig. 6.6). Seriation, which is ordering of objects of varying lengths and arranging them from smallest to largest, becomes possible by age 7 or 8.

During this period, children also learn to refine and elaborate on their concepts. They connect objects and events that are alike. They gradually become better organized in their concepts, which aids in their cognitive development. Developing perceptual abilities helps concepts become more mature; maturation enables children to develop attention and attending skills, which helps them examine the important features of a situation and decide what is and is not relevant. Their perceptions also become more economical; they learn to detect features that distinguish one object from another and what characteristics of objects are consistent. As to size and shape, they have a better understanding of size in relation to distance, recognize changes in form and location, and can detect shapes having ambiguous contours. Spatial concepts also improve; at this stage, children are able to understand how an object can occupy different spatial positions and have different locations in space. By the age of 7, children have an understanding of perspective and of how things look from different points of view (i.e., knowing things are left or right or opposite each other).

To solve problems, psychologists generally believe these abilities need to reflect on a distinct and more orderly sequence (i.e., to define a problem, propose possible solutions, and decide on a course of action). According to this point of view, children should know how to distinguish between knowing and thinking and knowing and guessing. Prob-

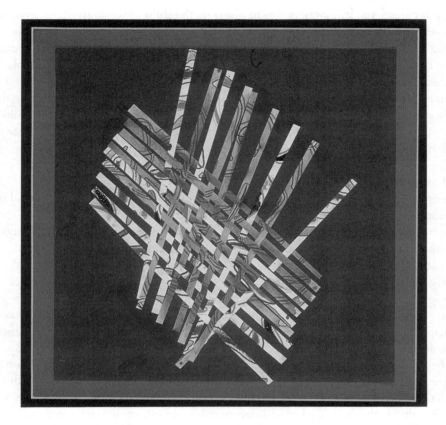

FIG. 6.6.   Andria Samsel, age 10, Constructionist collage, art teacher Susan J. Slavik, Livonia, Michigan Public Schools.

lem-solving abilities are also improved; through better work habits, children learn how to develop persistence, concentration, and independence in problem solving. Advancement also requires developing memory abilities and metacognition, which help children become better at organizing, searching for, and retrieving information encoded in memory and the ability to recognize the cause of an outcome and how successful one is in solving it. Intrinsic motivation in problem solving is an important development in this age child's ability to solve problems.

The Age of Formal Operations—11 Years to Adolescence

Adolescence is the life stage between childhood and adulthood where adjustments and adaptations are determined by pronounced physical change, the psychological search for identity, and heightened levels of socialization. The tendency is to wrongfully view adolescence as a stormy, stressful, and unstable time likely to produce uncertainty, doubt, and apprehension. This period coincides with Piaget's cognitive formal operations stage, which is the crystallization and integration of all previous cognitive stages: Thinking becomes rational and refined mental strategies can be applied to a greater number of problem-solving situations.

Psychologists believe that only about half of college students and adults reach this stage of mental functioning. Formal thinkers can perceive relationships between two ideas, perform complex tasks independently, and use information to offer interpretations and applications. However, not all students achieve mastery in every area, where some gifted can show greater flexibility in certain skill areas and in some cognitive operations. However, formal thought is most likely to be used in the disciplines adolescents are most familiar with. Unfortunately, at this age, even formal thinkers have trouble seeing the relationships between ideas, need to have things explained exactly, tend to interpret information literally, and usually cannot go from one task to another without specific instructions.

The attainment of formal operations also does not necessarily mean an increasing amount of creative behavior. Some studies have revealed a negative correlation between measures of creativity and the attainment of the formal operations stage. However, some psychologists believe that even these gains in creativity may be accidental because of the student's inability to change in light of new facts and because some adults see the omission of such facts as being creative. Generally, psychologists view the adolescent's larger capacity for creative behaviors as unrealized due to heightened pressures for conformity and increased cognitive development.

The adolescent's ability to move beyond mere physical properties of the environment is now evident in the growth of abstract thought, which involves the development of subjective concepts and ideas outside of the person's objective analysis of objects and events. Such abstract reasoning powers are needed to understand what cannot be seen. Teenagers can think more realistically about their identity, including future occupational and social roles; they can consider these issues from a variety of perspectives, including how these issues relate to the social environment in which they operate. When adolescents reach the formal thinking stage, it is believed that they imagine all kinds of possible relationships and can use both deductive and inductive reasoning to solve problems.

Researchers also believe that some adolescents achieve mental advancements that go beyond the formal operations stage, including systematic reasoning and abstract thinking, to create complex systems of mental functioning. Referred to as the *structural analytic stage,* adolescents at this level are able to compare relationships, representational systems, and models and use metasystematic reasoning, which is the ability to create new systems.

Lowenfeldian Stages

Viktor Lowenfeld's work is best known in the art education field through his so-called *stages of child art development* (Lowenfeld, 1964). Like Piaget, he also believed in the idea of schema, which he argues through a schema and correction theory not too different from the one argued by the historian Ernst Gombrich. However, Lowenfeld also believed that, although the child's art work is a representation of a thing seen, it originates in both the visual and nonvisual experiences of the child as determined by emotional and synthetic experiences, touching, impressions, and the function and behavior of objects.

Lowenfeld also believed that the art content of a child's work was the same as that used by the mature artist and that the child knows more about the world than is evident in the drawing, thus proposing a teaching strategy called the *activation of passive knowledge*. Like Piaget, Lowenfeld also believed in stages of emotional, intellectual, physical, social, perceptual, aesthetic, and creative growth. He believed that the adoption of schema or stereotypes answered the child's immediate visual, perceptual needs until growth made such schema inadequate and required the creation of new schema. Lowenfeld's method, like Piaget's, was to essentially activate the child's knowledge of objects and events in such a way that the child was encouraged to adopt new schema and abandon older ones. His ideas about how to do this have been criticized by some art educators as being dogmatic, suggesting to at least some that his notions of development in art were primarily a consequence of maturation, rather than being the result of effective teaching. Such arguments, although misleading, have led some in the field in recent years to question his child development approach.

Lowenfeld's students—Lambert Brittain (1979) and Kenneth Lansing (1976)—continued his legacy and even softened such Lowenfeld dogma as to never give young children colored crayons. Yet despite criticism, his basic observations on children's art development remain useful to anyone concerned with how patterns of growth and development affect the content, sequence, scope, activities, and motivation in the organization of sequential K to 12 art curriculum. Lowenfeld's methods, as indicated in *Thinking in Art,* were not too different from the drawing methods of Nicholaides (1941). He advocated schematic change through the child's experiential identification with the content being expressed, a metacognitive clarification of meaning in the progress of the work, and the role of media as offering new challenges.

Piaget and Lowenfeld Compared

Because most art educators are familiar with Lowenfeld's work and his book is readily available for more detailed study, Table 6.1 is limited to describing only some of the basic perceptual and conceptual growth characteristics of students according to his stages of development and as compared to the stages described by Piaget.

CONCEPT FORMATION

Although both the Piagetian and Lowenfeldian stages of development suggest what we might generally expect to see in the improvement of the student's mental abilities (i.e., to use tools and manipulate forms, lines, and colors in drawing), they do not help us decide on the specific nature and complexity of the visual concepts the student is forming. Although both Lowenfeld and Piaget agree that the child's ability to form concepts increases with age and maturation, neither deals with the specifics of how student images are affected or transformed by other images, which forms the basis for the visual concept being articulated to become either widened or narrowed by the perceptual data being used to form a new concept.

As indicated in the previous chapter, concepts are formed when one piece of perceptual data is integrated with another, so as to expand or narrow the amount of information needed to construct a new concept, which assimilates like perceptual data into a new form. This action moves in two interactive directions: (a) toward more expansive and in-

TABLE 6.1

COMPARATIVE DEVELOPMENTAL STAGES IN CHILD ART GROWTH AND PERCEPTION—JEAN PIAGET AND VIKTOR LOWENFELD

Piaget's Stages	*Lowenfeld's Stages*
Pre-operational, ages 2–7 years	**Scribbling Stage,** ages 2–4 years
The child:	The child:
• Uses an egoconcentric approach to space	• In disordered scribbles, has no visual control
• Observes one object at a time	• In controlled scribbles, has visual control
• Doesn't understand overlapping	• Discovers connections between motions and marks
• Has difficulty drawing shapes	• In unnamed scribbles, starts with an idea in mind
• Can learn to use scissors	• Is influenced by previous drawings
• May not benefit from practice	• Draws with intent
• Can use varied drawing media	• Does not anticipate finished results
• Can make recognizable pictures	**Preschematic,** ages 4–7 years
• Draws vertical lines first and horizontal lines second	• Consciously creates form
• Draws squares, then triangles, then diamond shapes	• Draws with representational intent
• Can combine shapes	• Reveals only what is important
• Creates pictures which are unstructured	• Cannot copy an object
• Can create human form	• Color is associational, not local
Piaget's Early Concrete Operational, ages 7–8 years	**Lowenfeld Schematic** Stage, ages 7–9 years
The child:	The child:
• Classifies objects	• Has schema concept that becomes a stereotype
• Shows concern for the real	• Creates a base line
• Draws objects related spatially	• Creates fold over drawings
• Creates objects as multiples	• Uses mixture of plan and elevation
• Can make one form contain another	• Uses space-time representations
• Draws lines with continuity	• Makes x-ray pictures
• Uses size and shape as working concepts	• Makes color related to object
• Cannot use perspective	• Finds logical order
• Uses realistic colors	• Increases detail
Later Concrete Operational, ages 9–11 years	**Gang Age,** ages 9–12 years
The student:	The student:
• Uses proximity, enclosure, and continuity	• Shows sex differences in drawing
• Uses Euclidian spatial relationships	• Finds geometric shapes no longer sufficient
• Uses single viewpoint perspective	• Gains details and loses feeling of action
• Shows differences in cognitive style	• Draws parts that have meaning in themselves
• Profits from seeing adult work	• Does not exaggerate or omit
• Tends to imitate life in art work	• Accumulates more details
• Is able to draw geometric figures	• Does not attempt light and shade
• Individualizes work	• Achieves true color differentiation
Formal Operation, ages 11–16 years	**The Age of Reasoning,** ages 12–14 years
The student:	The student:
• Can make accurate space judgments	• Increases criticism of work
• Is limited in pattern recognition	• Strives for greater naturalism
• Reveals that boys and girls differ in abilities	• Includes joints in figures

(continued on next page)

• Shows creativity slumps	• Shows effects of light and shade
• Can apply formal concepts	• Shows influence of distance
• Uses more asymmetry	• Can handle 1-, 2-, and 3-point perspective
• Shows more detail	**The Period of Decision,** ages 14–17 years
• Uses less color	The student:
• Uses subject matter that is rigid	• Likes products with utilitarian value
• Makes figures more proportional	• Can consider art as a career
• Uses increased media skills	• Understands terms such as warm, cool, and positive–negative space
• Is conservative in choices	• Likes specialization in media

(Table 6.1. cont'd).

tensive knowledge, wider integrations, and more precise differentiations; and (b) toward smaller concepts being integrated into wider ones or subdivided into narrower ones.

These interactive directions were evident in the ways in which the artists described in the previous chapter worked. Examples of smaller concepts being integrated into larger ones could be seen in the pattern abstracting of Motherwell, Frankenthaler, and Diebenkorn. In these cases, explorations of form and color began with a number of smaller units, where the amount of perceptual data introduced and the extensiveness and intensiveness of the concepts subsumed provides an image even greater than the sum of its parts. Examples of where wider concepts were subdivided into narrower ones were also seen in the efforts to reduce complex landscapes into simplified forms, such as can be noted in Kelly's abstract color shapes, Laurence's street scenes reduced to environmental pattern, Tooker's stagelike structuring, Fairfield Porter's flat use of color and shape, Thiebaud's geometric ordering of food forms, and Rosenquist's and Flack's structured arrangements of complex images. All these artists, whether expanding or narrowing the perceptual data employed, were engaged in the construction of a visual concept where one or more units of visual data were subsumed by others yet still presented as a unified, organized, cogent, and coherent visual concept. Each in his or her own way was creating an image where a number of visual concepts are integrated and subsumed in the process of creating a more extensive and intensive concept, revealing a pattern of decisions of increasing complexity and abstraction.

Concepts Related to Visual Forming

What should also be evident in reviewing these artists' work is that this concept formation is evident in the planning and construction of a work and even later on in other works. Some artists, like Kelly, Rosenquist, and Flack, for example, seem to complete their conception of the object before the actual painting is begun. For them, the act of painting is a means to test a concept already known in advance of when the work is created. Other artists, like Motherwell, Diebenkorn, and Frankenthaler, cannot know what their final concept is until the work is completed and the concept explored is revealed in the completed work. Still other artists, including Tooker, Laurence, and Porter, probably fall somewhere in between; they begin with a rough concept, which is only later revised in the act of completing the work, thus linking planning to execution. Recognizing that concept formation could involve both wider and narrower uses of perceptual evidence—and, further, that the process may not always be evident in every final product—may have important implications for the kinds of arts activities more advanced students should be expected to engage in. The following are offered as suggestions:

1. Art activities should vary in the time length required to complete them (i.e., to assign both short- and long-term projects).

2. Assigned art problems should offer opportunities for pattern abstraction involving both spontaneous and deliberate approaches to concept formation.

3. Problem solving in art should include strategies where both a pattern or schema are imposed on a product prior to execution and where pattern evolves in the process.

4. Students should be encouraged to use metacognitive skills, noting the processes for reducing or expanding the amount of perceptual data used in arriving at a concept (keeping a journal).

5. Opportunities should be given to students to reproduce patterns seen in nature or in the work of mature artists and crafts persons. The tracing of patterns from art reproductions and rubbings from natural objects should be encouraged.

6. Students should be encouraged to analyze the processes used in the creation of their art work. They should systematically review the body of work already completed over time to notice changes occurring in their pattern recognition and ways of working.

7. The evaluation of a work requires that all activities engaged in the process of planning, in the execution of the product and, in its relative position in the total body of work examined.

Concepts Related to Speech

The earlier mention of Vgotsky's silent speech of the child is a good beginning point for considering how speech affects concept development. As noted in chapter 2, Vgotsky saw the second stage in speech development as the point where the child shifts from naming a drawing after it is made to telling us "I am going to make a drawing of a _____," which indicates a shift from dependence on others to determining one's own course of action. Basically, speech, or the naming of objects and events, is what makes it possible for young learners to hold data in short-term memory and what makes long-term memory usable. As noted earlier, short-term memory is the capacity to remember what was just done or said to compare it with what is stored in long-term memory (Vygotsky, 1978).

Helping young children learn to remember, use, and understand what words mean helps link meaning and sound, transfer thoughts from one child to another, and develop concepts in art. This suggests that language and thought are related and that it moves words to thought and thought to action. Therefore, to differentiate words and images from objects and events is what makes it possible for children to imagine and what causes the images of things not present to exist. Over time, as Lowenfeld and Piaget suggested, children learn to remember, to describe an object's characteristics, and to learn the meaning of words; these steps help them learn to solve problems, develop concepts such as speed and distance, and make analogies.

In recent times, one of the positive effects of the so-called *disciplinary* approach to art teaching was to greatly increase general interest in the role of language in art teaching. This was evidenced mostly through the adding of language skills in art history and art criticism and through offering activities in describing, analyzing, and evaluating the work of mature artists. Some advocates, including Manuel Barkan, actually envisioned that the introduction of historical and critical study might eventually replace the production of art as a primary activity in art education programs.

However, not all linguistic systems are equally valuable in concept formation, most especially those of the logical positivists, who viewed language as a science where all concepts could be reduced to language. This was mainly responsible for approaches to art teaching emphasizing talk about art as being the key to unlocking the intellectual potentialities of art instruction as general education. This direction, which began with the socialization dialogues of Edmund Feldman, have now been expanded into some historical and critical methods, which have suggested up to 17 different strategies for students to analyze a given art work.

Modern linguists, especially Chomsky, Sausarre, and Vgotsky, whose ideas were discussed in chapter 2, have seriously questioned the structural approach to linguistics. Their approach does not view language mainly as public social speech or as an analogue for science, but rather a form of private speech that facilitates cognitive development, where cognition is not dependent on language. This point of view is also supported by the objectivists in chapter 5, who have noted that language should be used to connote concepts and as a tool of cognition to attain cognitive understanding rather than as a cause or purpose for concept formation. Therefore, cognition precedes communication, making the primary purpose of language being to provide the systems of cognitive classification and organization necessary for acquiring and manipulating increasingly larger amounts of data.

Language used in this way, unlike the uses posed by structuralists, facilitates thought and is not thought itself. As a result, one really should question whether the evaluation and use of descriptive or analytical language in art teaching is, in itself, important evidence of conceptual knowledge, much less being objective knowledge detached from social discourse. Although structuralist approaches to language may still have a place in art programs, where social reconstruction is valued as a goal, the social uses of language may have little to do with educating students conceptually.

INSTRUCTIONAL GOALS

To fulfill this chapter's goal, the process of concept formation addressed in the previous chapter needs to be looked at from the viewpoint of both what we want to accomplish in our art classrooms and from what we hope to achieve in the overall schooling process. This requires looking at visual concept formation from the viewpoint of what it means for the art curriculum. Unfortunately, this risks the possibility of saying too much on this, which is to suggest all art projects one might use or offer in schools, or too little, ignoring the varied philosophical values of both the teacher and school. The problem in doing too much (i.e., to list all the activities possible) is that it goes far beyond the scope of this effort. It is also redundant in that this has been accomplished in dozens of art activities books already on the market.

A second problem is how to develop a conceptually based art instructional program when there are several equally viable paradigms for teaching art and several competing but equally well-argued approaches for the integration of art in the school curriculum. In art education today, this includes, but is not limited to, the Getty-based Discipline Based Art Education Program (DBAE) and the newer Goals 2000 effort, as seen in Gardner's seven intelligences integrative curriculum model. Why such approaches are appropriate in some situations may not be due so much to their science, but rather to the need, at various levels of schooling, to make learning age specific and to provide classroom teachers with a *raison d'etre* for teaching art in schools. Whether art teachers believe that art is best taught through students altering existing artistic schema, through the articulation of form/Gestalt, or through visual metaphors are matters that are more about one's aesthetics or one's philosophy of art rather than about the conceptual act of image formation. Moreover, whether one believes the goals of art education are to develop enlightened cherishers of the arts or to use the arts to serve the interests of general education in schools, these concerns are more about the art world than about what makes art a conceptual activity.

Goals Related to Art

What truly makes a conceptual approach to art teaching different from other curricular approaches is that it does not come from art world explanations of the production, distribution, and utilization of art, but rather from the creative act, which is not the deontic-based, value-loaded, normative definition of *art* described by theorists detached from the creative act. Furthermore, the conceptual approach is also not about how an object becomes a work of art, how that art is deployed in some struggle for social prestige, nor about legitimate art or why art develops the way it does. Rather, the approach to artistic conception proposed here is focused on art meaning, quality, and intelligence, not on what functions art might serve or which belong in the analysis of processes in the art world and/or to the processes in which an art work and a viewer are involved. Therefore, we are most concerned with understanding the creative activity that generates the aesthetically testable object (i.e., the art work itself) and not about the process of its labeling, which, for the most part, only generates social definitions and norms of art.

The purpose of pointing this out here is not to deny the existence of an art world. Rather, it is to note that, no matter how important that world is, it is not a necessary precondition for art nor is it what makes art possible. Were this the case, there would not be a single art world, but rather many simultaneous art worlds or systems. Although art worlds make it easier to produce (and sell) art, they are not necessary preconditions for art even if they create the sufficient conditions for art productions to become possible.

What this suggests, then, is that we need to view the art curriculum in schools as something that makes creative art production possible and not as a precondition for the creation of works of art. Art education programs that assume a priori that artists and audiences share conventions, that suggest how a work can be best executed, actually arouse emotions that can obstruct emotional identification. In the process, they fail to recognize that it is not the nature of the work, but rather the process of its production that really matters.

In short, art is not made possible by an art world any more than fishing is made possible by a fishing industry. As such, one cannot provide a description of art through the artworld processes that bring it into being, but rather only through the phenomenology that creates it. A real problem exists when we seek social constructions of art, such as is found in constructivist analysis of constructivism, which presents perfect circularity through its own deconstruction. A socially constructed view of art, as Van der Tas (1990) noted, is more like viewing the flight of an airplane as an act of God rather than to explain why a plane equipped with wings and a propeller is safer than one without them.

Thus, to view art from the viewpoint of the sociologist who stresses art as social reconstruction and who pursues a profound analysis of the art world is to accept definitions of an art world where sociological ideals and interests are paramount. Moreover, it makes art an activity accomplished by sociologists who are forced to deal with an art world where they do not know what art is nor are even sure that it is socially constructed. Therefore, to increase our knowledge of the processes of art, we need to define our subject not as an essence or in the context of social reconstructions, but rather at the epistemological level of scientific ordering.

To construct a conceptual art curriculum that can be used in schooling requires the following: defining art as those objects and events created by men and women that express meaning and artistic quality and refer to specific aesthetic values, where the form of that art work is a meaningful aesthetic object functionally related to human motivations and interactions between humans and their environment through an act that is both cognitive and emotional in nature. Also, it is one where its practice is fulfilling because it satisfies expressed needs and cultural functions; it is a product in the real world, which is to say it is not the same as an art world, which cannot exist as a perceptible object.

Hence, a work of art is not an alibi for the pursuit of other objectives; it need not be labeled to be called a work of art and need not be legitimized through pursuit of certain other interests, class factions, or individual positions in the art world. Unfortunately, norms in art defined by sociological constructs require evaluation by the same means used to construct them. As such, they are valueless norms that cannot guide artistic and aesthetic actions and are consequently the result of a strategic practice used in the struggle for dominance, power, and status. In such a process, art is never evaluated in its own right, but rather becomes a strategy of a professional art world determined by an institutionalized sociology of art.

Goals Related to Art Practice

To envision what an activity-centered conceptual curriculum would look like in schools, it is necessary to examine the artistic process, which helps bring meaningful aesthetic objects into being. In doing this, I am indebted to the work of Vernon Howard (1977). In defining conceptions of artistic practice, Howard noted both what practice is and is not. He believed, practice in action involves repeating an action guided by specific aims to solve various kinds of problems and to build skills and abilities. To practice an action is to repeat it with the aim of improving and eventually mastering that action. That process may range in complexity from the mere elimination of errors to capturing the proper mood of an expressive form. In his view, practice is not the mere repetition of exercises until the performer gets it right and can do it without thought, which is to arrive at doing something without thinking.

Rather, in Howard's view, the cognitive aim of practice is to acknowledge that one has succeeded or failed to perform at a given level as well as why this is the case. To incorporate practice as part of teaching, Howard believed it is far more important to have a clear concept of the practice and what is to be accomplished by it than understanding mastery or greatness, except to the degree that this form of understanding gives direction to practice.

Howard viewed awareness as part of a conceptual topology of practice, including the roles of knowledge, awareness, and routinization. Here, he divided the issue into two major parts forming the strategic distinctions between types of awareness involved in the routinization of behavior and in the epistemological sorting of ordinary practice concepts, including habits, facilities, and skills. This includes traditional concerns for propositional knowledge that is what you need to know and procedural knowledge which is to know *how* to do it. He noted that the traditional historical, critical, philosophical, or psychological study of the arts takes the form of propositional knowledge about art, and performance competencies are considered to be those involved with procedural know-how. He believed procedural knowledge includes skill acquisition, routinization, and the development of skills, which may involve but cannot be reduced to propositional judgment. Knowing how to do something propositionally is neither necessary nor sufficient to knowing how to accomplish the task itself, where propositional knowledge is limited to standards of belief, truth, and evidence, and procedural knowledge is the result of repeated trials as well as newly discovered standards of achievement. Thus, for Howard, awareness is both cognizance of what circumstances are necessary for determining what behavior is needed and also what occurs in carrying out that behavior—one being a symbol-based awareness and the other a behavior-based awareness. Both are necessary for the routinization of a skill, which in turn becomes a process of both ceasing to be propositionally aware and becoming newly aware of a relevant bit of know-how. Much of what we know never crosses the threshold of awareness, yet controlled improvement suggests some things are brought to awareness and some forms of awareness suppressed in the efforts of efficiency.

In art performance, Howard believed that both a focal and a peripheral awareness are the most relevant, which means to be aware of what one is doing—to be able to describe it and explain one's actions in a detached, scientific manner. This aspect of knowing is what he called knowing *what* to think about (i.e., what precepts, percepts, images, or sensations to keep in consciousness at any stage of a skilled performance). Using a nailing activity as a metaphor, he pointed out that, when we drive the nail, we pay attention to both the nail and hammer but in a different way. We watch the effect of our strokes on the nail and we wield the hammer so as to hit the nail squarely. This means to be both physically aware of the sensations associated with the hammering and focally aware of driving a nail.

For Howard, the artistic problem is to know *how* and *what,* which is to make a distinction between knowing what something is and knowing what it is to experience something.

He noted that knowing that something is red is not the same as seeing red; further, knowing that an object in a painting can be seen as appearing from either above or below is something one cannot actually see until one actually does it or experiences it for oneself. In his view, this is the distinction between knowing what it is to do something and knowing what it is like to do it. Therefore, propositional knowing (i.e., what to think about) is different from knowing what it is to perform properly despite one's effort to do everything one has been taught to do.

Howard's argument clearly demonstrates that knowing something propositionally is fundamentally different from knowing what it is to use that knowledge in practice, which is to realize the distinction between knowing what something is and knowing what it is to experience something. Hence, a knowledge about art is a distinctly different kind of knowing than the kind of knowing associated with the actual making of artistic objects. More important, improvement in what is accomplished in the act of practice suggests an increased knowledge of what one wants to accomplish and a transference of focal to procedural knowledge. What this suggests in a curricular sense is that any effort to construct a curriculum on the basis of artistic practice must address the student's need for both focal and procedural knowledge.

Focal Knowledge

According to Howard, focal knowledge in practice is to know that which is to know:

- What one is doing, and to be able to describe it and to explain that action
- What to think about and what percepts, images and sensations to keep in consciousness in the process of practice.
- What concept is to be practiced.
- What caused a failure to perform.
- What it is you need to be good at.
- What historical, cultural, and philosophical knowledge one needs to know about.

In *The Unschooled Mind,* Gardner (1991) suggested that the focal knowledge taught in schools can be determined by what it is a society wishes to preserve, what societal roles are to be fulfilled, or what cultural values are to be transmitted. Gardner also believed these goals can be met in schools by using three kinds of content: (a) content that assures adult performances, (b) memorizing as much information as possible, or (c) minimizing practice and mastery of facts that emphasize the understanding of concepts and principles. As to choosing which goals to pursue, Gardner noted, "The test of understanding involves neither the repetition of information learned nor performances mastered. Rather, it involves the appropriate application of concepts and principles to questions and problems newly posed" (Gardner, 1991, p. 116).

Gardner also acknowledged that the content to be learned in any domain or discipline is featured in its own forms of understanding. That is, to gain an understanding of physics is different than gaining an understanding of poetry, painting, or politics. Gardner also suggested that what is to be taught in any discipline is determined by how we view the mental processes needed to function in that discipline and how we order the tasks of what students need to know and be able to do. It therefore follows that, in the practice of art, it is necessary to know both what mental processes are needed to make art and what products it is that we want students to be able to produce.

Howard believed metacognitive, conscious, critical, and factual knowledge are all important to artistic practice. How these knowledges impact on what tasks are to be performed in art learning is, however, shaped by what we hope to achieve in artistic conceptual development. However, we must be aware that concepts are not associational nor does their formation suggest an associative chain, which is built up of successive amounts of associational knowledge. Therefore, concepts are not isolated, ossified, and changeless formations, but are rather an active part of the intellectual process used in communicating, understanding, and problem solving. This should remind us that concepts are not developed through associations between verbal symbols and objects nor are they simply a quantitative overgrowth of a lower associative activity. Rather, they represent a qualitatively new type of activity shaped by intellectual processes.

Knowledge About Art. For one to be successful in art, one must acquire a broad range of historical, critical, aesthetic, and technical knowledges of art. In Howard's topology, these knowledges permit the student to know what one is doing, describe and explain it, have images and percepts in memory and consciousness, and know what it means to be good at what one is doing, what concept is being pursued, and why an effort may have failed. One cannot function effectively in art if one does not have such historical, critical, technical, or aesthetic knowledge. Yet these knowledges are only useful in the context of a problem to be solved and in knowing what kind of critical thinking is necessary to solve that problem. Therefore, all forms of knowledge about art are useful, but in art practice only as these knowledges impact on the procedural knowledges necessary for active forming.

Critical Thinking and Problem Solving. Problem solving in any discipline requires: (a) that the student have a goal or a description of what would be accepted as a solution to a problem; (b) the objects, tools, materials and other resources needed to achieve that goal; (c) knowing what operations or actions can be taken; and (d) knowing what constraints or rules to follow in problem solving (Zechmeister & Johnson, 1992). It is also important to know that problem solving in art involves an ill-defined problem, where the goal is either not clearly defined or where there may be more than one possible goal or more than one path to solving a goal. Because such goals are not clearly defined, it is difficult to know to what extent a given solution moves toward achieving a goal and that the tools necessary to solve the problem are not always obvious. In an ill-structured domain, one deals with the particular details of individual cases rather than knowledge in the abstract; this employs a case-by-case interpretation, yet can also use well-constructed knowledge.

To the contrary, well-structured problems have clearly defined goals as well as clear paths to reaching those goals. The objects and tools needed to solve a well-defined problem are usually readily available. Well-structured problems also use well-structured knowledge, which permits a hierarchial or top–down approach to informational processing and uses concepts that are constant from one case to another.

Higher order thinking skills in structured domains generally follow what are described as deductive and inductive thinking strategies. Deductive models start with the idea the teacher wants to impart; the material about it is noted and presented from the general to the specific. This starts with the principle or main idea, which then develops with supporting information that can be broken into parts. A general deductive concept model requires: (a) naming a concept, (b) defining it, (c) enumerating its characteristics, (d) providing exemplars of the concept, and (e) relating it to any superordinate, subordinate, or ordinate concepts. In contrast, the inquiry teaching method is a type of inductive model where the teacher plans outcomes and selects activities that will lead to the desired outcome. This model requires: (a) identification of the problem, (b) generation of a hypothesis, (c) collection of data, (d) interpretation of data, (e) development of conclusions, (f) verification or replication of results, and (g) generalization of results.

Both the inductive and deductive models and/or some combination of the two systems are advocated in the art education literature for use in both historical and critical instruction in art. Of course, these models are useful when the task is defined as a well-structured problem, in which the goals of the problem and the methods for solving the problem can be clearly defined, the pathway to solving the problem is clear, and the concepts are constant from one case to another. However, many psychologists challenge such five- or six-step processes as not really ensuring that students will learn to actually solve problems. These approaches to problem solving, even when used by traditional academic areas, have been challenged because they only have one correct solution and are subject specific. Although problems of this order do exist, most problems have no single right answer and, in some cases, may not even be answerable.

Some psychologists also believe that ill-defined hard cases can teach higher order thinking skills better than those where tried-and-true rules apply. In well-structured domains, the student must perceive the complexity of the material being learned, whereas in ill-structured domains, students must pay attention to particular details of individual cases and develop case-by-case interpretations. Problem solving in such cases are much closer to real-life problems and are certainly more compatible with the problem-finding behaviors associated with creative thinking. It is thought that artistic problem solving may indeed be more true to life than the inductive and deductive models used in most science and humanities programs.

Another approach to problem solving addressed in the literature is the approach associated with heuristics, which are generally described as "rule of thumb" or "seeking to discover" approaches. Although treated in the literature as the least reliable methods, they are also advocated as being better than no method at all. However, such methods do make sense in an ill-structured domain and in life, for that matter, where one deals with individual cases and employs case-by-case interpretations, and where goals are not always apparent, the necessary tools not always known, and the pathways to solving a problem not certain. Some of these strategies, as identified by O'Tuel and Bullard (1993), include:

- Working backward, where you identify the goal state and look for procedures that result in reaching the goal.
- Means–end analysis, where you decide what subprocesses you can do to lead you to a goal.

- Working forward, where you assess where you are and where you want to go, choosing processes that will change where you are and reduce the difference between where you are now and where you want to be.

- Analogies, where you transfer a procedure from one domain that you are familiar with and use it in a new situation.

- Restructuring, where you reword or redescribe the problem by simplifying and dropping details or creating a more generalized problem.

- Pattern recognition, where you look for similarities between a current problem and one you have dealt with in the past. The pattern sought could involve physical similarities or cognitive-procedural similarities.

- Verbal and graphic doodling, where you provide a visual, verbal record of the givens in a particular problem to correct misconceptions or eliminate irrelevant data as a means to juggle one's working memory.

Procedural Knowledge

Howard defined *procedural knowledge* as basically to know how. These knowledges include:

- to know how to create something,
- to have the skills to accomplish tasks,
- to know one's standard of achievement,
- to know what occurs in the creative process, and
- to know what it is to experience something.

Procedural knowledge in artistic conception is the result of creative activity. It is the consequence of and emerges from the activity of creating something, including knowledge of what it is to know how to create, to have command of the skills necessary to do it, to know it has been done effectively, and to know how one got to that point through an experiential process. As a process, it has to do with both correcting errors and establishing a mode of thought, which is to make the creative act a state of expressive consciousness. As Howard suggested, it is also being aware of the circumstances and behaviors needed to create, eliminating propositional awareness in the interests of knowing how to accomplish something, knowing what to think about when doing it, and knowing what precepts, percepts, images, or sensations to keep in consciousness at any stage of the creative act.

Thus, procedural knowledge is also technical knowledge, which means students need to master skills and techniques to make expression possible and create images available to vision. Visual concepts, which require the integration of images and abstract forms, cannot be realized without possessing the skills and techniques necessary for the construction of a visual concept; this allows us to see what we have imagined as well as evaluate its effectiveness.

Without art skills and techniques, students cannot effectively carry out the necessary actions required to develop a visual concept and integrate into that image the focal knowledge, emotion, ideas, and creative inspiration essential to the evolution of expressive form. Although artistic skill only seems irrelevant to those who have not mastered it, it is also true that, as artists, we do not resist using what we know or even to claim such skills are subordinate to expression. Yet at the same time, we know that without them we would lack self-confidence, flexibility in visual problem solving, and the understanding of art itself. As Howard effectively noted, the maker must know how to create, have the skills to do that, know whether a goal has been reached, know what is occurring in the process, and know what it is to experience that process.

THE CURRICULUM PLAN

As already noted, to construct a curriculum in any domain, we are obligated to recognize that it has its own forms of understanding. This suggests that learning in art depends both on knowing what mental processes are needed in that discipline and how we order the tasks of what students need to know and be able to do in that discipline. When we define art learning as coming about through the creation of conceptual images, it requires students to acquire both focal and procedural forms of knowledge and learn how these knowledges are integrated in the act of creative forming.

Because the outcomes of a conceptual curriculum comes through a process where students learn more advanced visual concepts through the mental processes of consciousness, memory, reasoning, and problem solving and the procedural knowledge of how to create something, these behaviors eventually become the curriculum content to be learned and/or developed. Because of this, the conceptually based curriculum to be described here is decidedly different from other more traditional curriculum designs, which can be more logically and sequentially ordered with respect to the subject matter content to be learned, skills to be achieved, and learning experiences (activities) to be undergone to achieve the curriculum goals. However, this does not mean that in a conceptual curriculum there are no knowledges or skills to be learned. Rather, these knowledges and skills are ordered according to the visual concepts students undertake to accomplish and the mental abilities students need to accomplish them.

For the teacher constructing a conceptual art curriculum, this means all the traditional forms of art knowledge and skills that are normally part of the school art program still constitute a repertory for good art learning. However, they need to be reordered according to what students need to know and be able to do to form personally constructed visual concepts that involve the integration or fusion of two or more real or imaginary images into a newer and more expansive or reductive visual concept.

In this curriculum, children make things, study art history, and critically examine their work and the work of others. They do so to build visual concepts where the concepts acquired over time become increasingly more complex forms of personal visual discovery rather than through experiencing a prescribed sequence of activities, skills, and media or acquiring more information about art history or criticism presented in some fixed historical or procedural order. In this process, language also remains an important tool for learning, especially through facilitating the cognitive development necessary to connote concepts, serve as a tool for recognition, and provide a system for cognitive classification and organization to manipulate increasingly larger amounts of data. However, the use of language here is to facilitate thought; it is not thought itself nor is it, in and of itself, evidence of conceptual knowledge.

Thus, to construct a conceptual art curriculum, the teacher is not required to develop new historical, critical, or productive content, but rather to reorder the critical, historical, and productive strategies already available and apply them in a more focused way. The goal is artistic conception rather than acquisition of art knowledge and skills learned in isolation of the creative activity that inspired it.

Therefore, the content of such a curriculum is found in the reordering of visual form through the increased use of memory, consciousness, reasoning, and problem-solving abilities in the interest of visual concept formation. Therefore, the curriculum sequence is determined by the age-specific, innate, and acquired abilities of students to attempt increasingly more sophisticated forms of visual abstraction. Its scope is ordered by the various ways students learn to create visual abstractions prior to, during, and following the creative act.

The suggested curriculum sequence and scope outline that follows is one that orders sequence roughly along the age-specific mental development of the learners as specified in the developmental literature. However, even here we must generalize because children rarely do exactly as they are supposed to do according to even the best predictions. Therefore, this outline is only a framework for determining what art activities may be appropriate at any given age-grade level. Even then it should still be recognized that children are individuals; their rates of growth and needs are individual and cannot be based on any set developmental goal to be achieved according to some arbitrary time line.

These curricular recommendations are intentionally loose or sketchy. For some readers, they may lack the specificity needed to immediately apply them in the classroom. To do otherwise would, as earlier noted, require a list of all the possible projects one might attempt to do over 12 years of schooling, which is unnecessary given the dozens of good "how-to-do-it" art activity books on the market. For the reader not familiar with these books, I have referred to several of these in chapter 4 of *Thinking in Art*. They include but are not limited to these art education texts: *Teaching Drawing from Art* by Wilson and Wilson, *Children and Their Art* by Hurwitz and Day, *The Joyous Vision* by Hurwitz and Madeja, *Preparation for Art* by June McFee, Mary Townly's *Another Look,* the *Art in Action* series by Guy Hubbard, *Learning to Look and Create* by Kay Alexander, *Becoming Human Through Art* by Feldman, and *Approaches to Art Education* by Chapman, just to name a few. Some of the foundation texts also mentioned in chapter 3 of that work are helpful, especially *Vision and Invention* by Harlan, *Design in the Visual Arts* by Behrens, *Drawing* by Bett and Sale, and *Art Synetics* by Roukes. Most of the examples cited in the following curriculum outline can be found in one or more of these works.

Visual Concepts Evidenced in Performance

Because this curriculum depends mostly on the creation and recognition of visual abstractions (concepts), it is necessary to clarify the issue of what a visual concept in practice is before the curriculum is sketched out. However, to define a visual concept in words is not easy because it is something that is apparent to vision and is known to be either present or absent, effective or ineffective. This is measured mainly through our aesthetic response to it, which can be described as the "raised hair on the back of the neck" syndrome, which signals that the viewer knows when it is present, at least to their own personal vision.

One scholarly effort that addressed this phenomenon is contained in the early doctoral work of the late Glenn B. Hamm of Virginia Commonwealth University, who, while pursuing a doctorate at Purdue University in West Lafayette, Indiana, developed a study focusing on the act of what he then called visual *fusion.* Although Hamm (1975) looked at fusion from the viewpoint of his interests in teaching design at the college level, his ideas about it do come close to what we are calling here a visual concept or abstraction.

Hamm defined *fusion* as a subdivision of the illusion of third dimension on a two-dimensional plane, which he believed was essential to the articulation of both abstract form and realistic phenomena, which included the subject matter of people, places and things. He further believed that for fusion to exist it must result in an image composed of what he called *united forms.* He reasoned that fusion drew on many different visual techniques becoming, in effect, a purposeful organizer of these techniques. He noted that fusion results in an identifiable, concrete concept that offers the means for testing the effectiveness of joined form and matter.

Hamm saw the act of fusion as involving at least two forms in a union, which became the ultimate realization of the integration of form and matter. Something that would fall short of fusion he called *reticulation,* which meant to merely deal with the change of one form through such forces as twisting, crumpling, and so on. True fusion, he believed, came only through the realization of pictorial form or Gestalt, where two distinct forms become one, thus losing their boundaries. His criteria to be applied in deciding whether the act of fusion was complete included:

- That the fused forms retain individual and noticeable identities.
- That when an illusion is complete it is not necessary to imagine or infer the forms being fused.
- The fused form is an illusion that provided ambiguity, mystery, and provocativeness to the image.
- That the illusion achieved will inspire emotional reactions and aesthetic responses from the viewer.
- That a concept is not sufficient as an idea alone nor easy to comprehend through verbal or abstract mental means.
- That it is totally visual, is achieved visually, and its meaning generalizable enough to be applied in other visual settings.
- That it unites different kinds of original and separate identities, such as geometric shapes and more complex structures such as those required in the depiction of the human anatomy.

Although Hamm's description of visual concept formation (fusion) is fairly clear, the problem of conveying this idea to others is still not easy. It can escape us because, after all, an illusion has an appearance that presents itself to our consciousness as a visual paradox—being at times one thing and another.

Although it may be possible to further expand on the theory of such constructs, the task here is to provide more useful concept definitions that make the achievement of visual concepts in the art classroom easier to see and evaluate. It might also be helpful for the reader to review Roukes' (1982) work *Art Synectics,* most specifically the section at the conclusion where he talked about the term *synectic,* which in Greek means to bring forth together. Roukes believed that the basic task in the creative process is to bring together, in some useful fashion, some ideas that are remote from each other (i.e., to make the familiar strange or the strange familiar; Fig. 6.8). His "art synector" or artist "think tank," he believed, can be used to evolve cohesive structures and art forms from disparities. Roukes created 100 words for objects, events, emotions, artistic devices, styles, forms, materials, art elements, art principles, symbols, subjects, literary forms, tools, myths, food forms, popular images, body parts, and so on. He asked the reader to create an art form that involves Word 1, Word 2, and Word 3 (Roukes, 1982, p. 126). Although his approach is not totally conceptual, the result would be to move the student toward a fusion of images in some cases and toward various levels of reticulation in others.

There are a number of visual concepts, abstractions, or fusions that can be seen in some well-known contemporary artists' images. These include efforts that fuse two different artists' images, such as is seen in a Frank Stella, which combines a Matisse still life with an Albers "Homage to a Square"; a Hockney, which fuses an Albers line structure and a Japanese woodprint; a Julian Schnable which combines a Motherwell splash litho with a Japanese calligraphy; or a Robert Colescott, which fuses a Van Eycks wedding portrait with a William Johnson auto scene. Other kinds of fusions can be seen in works where an artist merges his or her own signature style with another artist's image, such as occurs in Peter Saul's interpretation of a deKooning (Fig. 4.1) or Robert Colescott's interpretation of Boticelli's "Three Graces" (Fig. 6.9).

Still different kinds of fusions occur when an artist casts his signature image in a different medium, such as one can observe in a Roy Lichtenstein's Ben-day cartoon (Fig. 6.10), Tom Wesselman bathroom nude on a Renaissance style wood panel, or a Robert Rauschenberg lithograph combining intact or altered images from oil painting, photography books, and drawings (Fig. 6.11).

Other kinds of fusion can occur when an artist fuses another artist's two-dimensional image with related or unrelated three dimensional forms, such as occurred in Kelly's use of an actual window frame in his Window, Museum of Modert Art Paris (1949), or as in a Jim Dine Robe interpreted in open weave West African Kente Cloth, a Jeff Koons wood sculpture made from a photograph of puppies, or a Sherrie Levine sculpture made from a Man Ray photo (Fig. 6.12).

These examples illustrate how some artists' visual concepts may have evolved from the fusion of two or more images into a single visual image (concept). Although most of these fusions have actually been acknowledged by the artist and still others are, according to historians and critics, clearly influenced by other work, it should not be assumed in all cases that the final work is simply a matter of fusing these particular images, nor that every such fusion would result in the same image. One advantage in suggesting that art instruction might focus on the creation of such fusions is that the ends sought are not so much about the replication of the borrowed artists' imagery, but rather about how we can arrive at an open concept—where the final image created comes from the student's own conceptual initiative rather than from the teacher. Hence, visual concepts achieved in this manner are not about what facts are to be learned, but are rather about what personal conceptual images can be constructed by a student while still honoring the teacher's choices as to what possible images, media, and strategies are assigned to capitalize on the students' strengths

FIG. 6.8.   Martha McKenzie and Leah MacLellan, grade 4. "Mr. Mayor" after Marisol, art teacher Susan J. Slavik, Livonia, Michigan Public Schools.

FIG. 6.9.   COLESCOTT, Robert. *The Three Graces: Art, Sex and Death.* 1981. Synthetic polymer on canvas, 84" x 71 7/8 " (213.4 x 182.6 cm). Frame: 84 13/16 x 72 3/4" (215.4 x 184.8 cm). Collection of the Whitney Museum of American Art, Gift of Raymond J. Learsy. 91.59.1.

and weaknesses. Thus, in a conceptual art class, the teacher can broaden the units to be fused to demonstrate the students' virtuosity and/or, at a lower level, narrow the choices to strengthen the work of a class or even just one individual in that class (e.g., in using some particular media, skill, or technique that the student[s] is not now effective in using).

FIG. 6.10.   LICHTENSTEIN, Roy. *Drowning Girl* 1963. Oil and synthetic polymer paint on canvas, 67 5/8" x 66 3/4" (171.6 x 169.5 cm). The Museum of Modern Art, New York. Philip Johnson Fund and gift of Mr. and Mrs. Bagley Wright.

The suggested curriculum that follows (see Figs. 6.13, 6.14, 6.15, 6.16, and 6.17) is designed to offer some general suggestions as to what activities one might offer; what kinds of verbal, procedural, and intellectual abilities to develop; and what kinds of media might be appropriate for use at different levels in the school art program. This curriculum outline is ordered into three developmental stages: (a) preconceptual, (b) conceptual/perceptual, and (c) conceptual, which are all age specific according to what might be expected given the general cognitive development of the learner. Here again, it should be noted that concept development, in one form or another will occur at all stages—even where the child only learns that the marks on the paper are by intention and/or when a pictorial form can be used repeatedly as a symbol or pictogram representing a person, object, or event, both of which are evidence of conceptual growth. The

FIG. 6.11.   RAUSCHENBERG, Robert. *Centennial Certificate M.M.A.* 1969. Color lithography, sheet and image: 36" x 24 1/2" (91.4 x 62.2 cm.) Collection of the Whitney Museum of American Art, Gift of Stanley and Renie Helfgott. 70.9. (c) Robert Rauschenberg/ULAE /Licensed by VAGA, New York, NY

distinction in the use of the conceptual stages is to focus on the kind of conceptual learnings that give evidence of the students' ability to fuse two or more images, become conscious of that activity, trace it back to its origin, and describe that process to others. These stages are to be used only as benchmarks. The term *preconceptual* indicates a stage that creates a consciousness of visual forms and their ordering in space; *perceptual/conceptual* indicates concept formation not always being conscious and deliberate; and *conceptual* indicates that visual concept formation is the main focus although not all children or adults may advance to this stage.

What is included in this general curriculum outline are some of the focal and procedural knowledges that could be developed, some of the verbal/speech skills to be encouraged, and some appropriate art activities to be engaged in, as suggested by the Piagetian–Lowenfeldian developmental stages and as arranged into the preconceptual, conceptual/perceptual, and conceptual/growth stages referred to previously. This curriculum is intended only as an example and is not nearly exhaustive of all the possibilities or concerns that could be addressed or required to achieve maximum conceptual growth in art. This sequence is also generalized and assumes a normal and sequential development occurring in the three areas of focal knowledge, language, and art procedural knowledge. For more information on the structure of these activities, the reader should consult the texts already mentioned.

FIG. 6.12.   LEVINE, Sherrie. *"La Fortune" (After Man Ray: 4)*. 1990. Temporary documentation - subject to change. Felt and mahogany, 33" x 110" x 60" (83.8 x 279.4 x 152.4 cm.) Collection of the Whitney Museum of American Art. Purchased with funds from Joanne Leonhardt Cassullo, Beth Rudin DeWoody, Eugene Schwartz and Robert Sosnick. 92.1.

PRECONCEPTUAL STAGE (ages 4–7)   shape object relationships in space

THINKING SKILLS	FOCAL KNOWLEDGE	PROCEDURAL KNOWLEDGE	LINGUISTIC KNOWLEDGE
	Learning:	*Learning:*	*Learning:*
knowledge	the difference between tall and wide	to control random movements	to apply names to shapes
	to observe more than one object at a time	to combine shapes in two and three dimensional forms	words like long, round, square, little
	to perceive shape differences	to use simple tools	to talk about how things work
	to remember shape names	to place objects on the picture plane	to talk about the shapes in your house
comprehension	to notice things which appear sideways, up, or down	to increase pictorial detail	to talk about things which are closer or farther
	the position of things	to paint to the edge of a shape	the names of tools and materials
	to count eyelets in shoes or openings in objects	to draw lines, shapes and textures	the names of colors
	to recognize objects that are alike or different	to make a drawing, painting or sculpture	the names of shapes
seeing	to count the number of windows in your house	to use different sizes and shapes of paper	to describe art works from reproductions
	what things are made of	to use different sizes of brushes	to identify elements in art work
applying	to match object characteristics	to discover thick and thin lines	to talk about lines going up and down
	to differentiate words and images from objects and events	to repeat and vary geometric shapes	to talk about things tall, short, round, pointed
	about distance and direction	to make abstract art	to talk about things which are near and far
		to create big faces and little faces in crowds	to talk about kinds of art, drawing, painting, etc.
		to cut out and place things near and far	
		to show things in environmental space	
		to show what it's like when it snows or rains, etc.	
		to use crayons, chalk and tempera paint	
		to paste, glue, cut, and rub	
		to make contour drawings	
		to make maps	

FIG. 6.13.   A suggested performance based framework for a K–12 Standards–Based Art Curriculum, including Sequence Scope and activities Preconceptual Stage (ages 4–7).

STAGE 2

CONCEPTUAL/PRECONCEPTUAL STAGE EARLY STAGES OF CONCRETE OPERATION
(ages 7–8) recognizing similarities and locations

THINKING SKILLS	FOCAL KNOWLEDGE	PROCEDURAL KNOWLEDGE	LINGUISTIC KNOWLEDGE
	Learning:	Learning:	Learning:
application	to remember objects, shapes and colors seen	to invent shapes and objects	to describe objects
	the differences in natural and man made objects	to put shapes in context through positioning	to give names to parts of objects
	to break down things into smaller units	to use a horizon line	to explain and interpret images
	about art in the community	to draw geometric shapes	to know the language of judging things
	to classify things	to show size relationships	to know the language of preference
classifying	to think about things not present to vision	that color varies in value	to describe the characteristics of objects and art works
	about objects being closer or farther away	to show texture	to talk about problems
	to distinguish between shapes	to use chalks, inks, charcoal, felt tips	to talk about speed and distance
	to order shapes in an environment	to combine shapes and make compositions	to talk about art works, according to shapes and colors
comparing	to understand size and shape constancies	to solve space problems	to talk about shapes, colors, lines, etc.
	about circles and angles	to use overlapping and planned color stages	to talk about planning
	to see proportional size	to see and include detail	the names of art tools
	to see perspective	to draw things from memory	to talk to artists about what they do
	to know the color of things	to represent activities involving friends	
	to understand families and classes of things	to draw people in other places	
	to measure things	to create fantasy events	
	to see details	to represent figures with clothing on	
	what is tall and short	to represent something which happened	
	to classify tools and objects	to make landscapes	
	to see objects from different viewpoints	to make a still life	
arranging	about sequences	to draw the figure	
	about expanding shapes	about gesture and mass	
	about open and closed forms	to draw shadows	
	about unfolding things	about monochromatic color	
	about grouping things	about pattern–negating the edge	
	about gathering things together	about zoom techniques, near–far	
	about piling up things	to recombine shapes	
	forms of support such as legs and hooks		

FIG. 6.14. A suggested performance based framework (continued): Conceptual/Preconceptual Early Stage of Concrete Operation (ages 7–8).

CONCEPTUAL STAGE CONCRETE OPERATIONS *(ages 9–11) altering viewpoints/generalizing form*

THINKING SKILLS	FOCAL KNOWLEDGE	PROCEDURAL KNOWLEDGE	LINGUISTIC KNOWLEDGE
	Learning:	*Learning:*	*Learning:*
analysis	to see perspective to see and remember objects from different viewpoints to consciously create symbols to see equivalent sizes in objects to form generalizations about things observed	how to draw three dimensionally how to draw more imaginatively to increase skill in handling tools to use more varied color to use color emotionally	to describe how viewpoint changes appearances to talk about distance and size of objects in art how to describe the relationships between things to describe similarities and differences in things how to interpret events and objects
noting similarities	to see more subtle relationships between things to apply generalizations in different settings to notice size changes from different viewpoints to think about future events	to draw more individualistically to represent distance through size and horizon to paint a scene or event to draw shadows and receding planes	how to describe fantastical objects to talk about painting historically to talk about modern art to talk about theoretical and social issues
making abstractions	to think about things metaphorically to understand visual point of view about social uses of art to pair things to see complimentary things what it means to scatter things to cover, drape, or wrap things to enclose things to encircle things to hide things to put curled things together in contrast about spreading and circling about rising and falling about drooping and flowing about merging and dappling	to represent emotion in art to invent metaphorical images to use stylistic devices to show unusual vantage points to represent things both real and imaginary to draw things and their parts to use light and dark to express mood to make gesture drawings to use tools to make prints and sculpture to draw groups of objects and people to use various new art materials to represent the third dimension to make abstract art to wrap and bend things to make wearable art/joining shapes to make like and dissimilar structures to make stylized masks to make abstractions (stylized) from nature to make animated objects to make crossover images in boxes to make rhythmic designs	to talk about artistic styles terms like pairing and distributing terms such as to cover, drape, wrap, enclose terms such as rising, falling, drooping, flowing to describe similarities and differences to talk about abstract art

FIG. 6.15. A suggested performance based framework (continued): Conceptual Stage, Early Concrete Operations (ages 9–11).

STAGE 3

CONCEPTUAL STAGE CONCRETE OPERATIONS (ages 11–13)

THINKING SKILLS	FOCAL KNOWLEDGE	PROCEDURAL KNOWLEDGE	LINGUISTIC KNOWLEDGE
	Learning:	Learning:	Learning:
analyzing	to think analytically to think symbolically to construct mental concepts to use observations more effectively to think creatively through problem finding to become more objective	to draw things with social content to make art as a personal identification to draw with more advanced media to make informational drawings to pictorially record an event to create architectural fantasy	to verbally describe, analyze and evaluate works of art to talk about how formal design concepts are used to talk about art representing social issues to talk about art according to artistic style to critique one's own work and the work of others
decision making	to assess what is real and what is imagined to solve problems logically to classify, explain and interpret events to use criteria and concepts for judgments	to create visual puns to appropriate images to juxtapose objects to work neo-expressionistically	
synthesis	new ways to think about color new approaches to subject matter to plan and design functional objects to organize ideas historically about world affairs	to remake discarded objects to make science-fiction art to make surrealistic images to create optical illusions	
problem solving	to think about things being rolled, creased, folded to think about things being twisted, intertwined about severing things, to cut, to tear, to chip	to create a ritual event to design a game to create visual paradoxes to create labyrinths to use interlocking shape compositions to use aerial perspective to use multiple perspectives to make monument drawings to make object sculptures to draw crushed objects to create personal myths to interpret ancient myths to use scientific discoveries as a source	

FIG. 6.16. A suggested performance based curriculum (continued): Later Concrete Operations (ages 11–13).

LATER CONCRETE OPERATIONS (ages 13–16)

THINKING SKILLS	FOCAL KNOWLEDGE	PROCEDURAL KNOWLEDGE	LINGUISTIC KNOWLEDGE
	Learning:	*Learning:*	*Learning:*
evaluation	to think abstractly to develop objective analysis to develop abstract reasoning powers to think realistically to think about the future	to create logical analogies to create visual analogies to create texture through erasing and stippling to use arbitrary value to use contour and tone	to talk about the characteristics of an art work to compare and contrast architectural components to describe the artistic devices and techniques to describe the works of a given period to describe how form and content are integrated
inquiry	to think about social relationships to think inductively and deductively to reason systematically to create complex systems of mental functioning	to make color-field compositions to use stacked perspective to use shaped picture planes to make a drawing series	to describe the devices artists use to explain the effects of color in a given work to talk about art and cultural activity
experimentation	to compare relationships to compare representational systems and models to use meta-systematic reasoning to create new systems	to make a visual narrative to make an art history series to make environmental art to make neo-naive or bad painting	
invention	to create forms of transfigurations how things look when they are agitated about art history and the various epochs to identify important art works to compare art works form different epochs about architectural structures to select the appropriate images	to integrate non alike forms to make a metamorphosis	

FIG. 6.17.   A suggested performance based curriculum (continued): Later Concrete Operations (ages 13–16).

SUMMARY

Chapter 6 addressed objectivist conceptual theories and the visual concept process used by artists in making art as outlined in chapter 5 from the viewpoint of how the conceptional modes of thinking scientifically and artistically could be used to determine the goals, content sequence, scope, and activities offered in an arts education program in Grades K to 12. This has been accomplished through providing a sample curriculum outline dealing with what curricular content sequence, scope, and activities might be offered in a conceptually focused school art curriculum.

Furthermore, this chapter addressed the concept formation process through the acquisition of visual data, through its organization sequentially by age-specific development, and through the tasks of concept formation involving the integration of perceptual data and the role of speech in concept development. These were specifically addressed through providing a curriculum model based on the creative act itself and as ordered by the artistic practice and skills needed for creative conceptual forming in art, including both the focal and procedural knowledges students need to have and be able to do. The curriculum outlined also addressed the issue of artistic conception or fusion sequenced according to both the K to 12 developmental stages addressed by Piaget and by the three stages of concept formation—the preconceptual, perceptual/conceptual, and conceptual. The content and activities outlined were sequenced according to the mental and focal knowledge to be emphasized, the language (speech) abilities needed to support memory, and the procedural knowledge students need to acquire to know what it is to form something creatively.

Chapter 7 focuses on the classroom learning environment and the evaluation process, including the use of portfolio reviews and rubric systems for reporting, the monitoring of perceptual/conceptual development, and the demonstration of the value of artistic activity in terms of the world of work and the opportunities afforded for advanced study and learning.

REFERENCES

Brittain, L. (1979). *Creativity, art and the young child.* New York: Macmillian.

Dorn, C. M. (1994). *Thinking in art: A philosophical approach to art education.* Reston, VA: The National Art Education Association.

Gardner, H. (1991). *The unschooled mind: How children think and how schools should teach.* New York: Basic Books.

Hamm, G. B. (1975). *An aesthetic morphology and comparative functional analysis of visual design, forms and strategies, together with corresponding perceptual predispositions which contribute to the articulation of the illusion of three dimensional mass and space configuration on a two dimentional plane.* Unpublished manuscript, Lafayette and Purdue University.

Howard, V. A. (1977). Artistic practice and skills. In D. Perkins & B. Leondar (Eds.), *The Arts and Cognition* (pp. 208–240). Baltimore: Johns Hopkins University Press.

Lansing, K. (1976). *Art, artists and art education.* Dubuque: Kendall/Hunt Publishing Company.

Lowenfeld, V. (1964). *Creative and mental growth* (6th ed.). New York: Macmillian.

Nicolaides, K. (1941). *The natural way to draw.* Boston: Houghton Mifflin.

O'Tuel, F. S., & Bullard, R. K. (1993). *Developing higher order thinking skills in the content areas K–12.* Pacific Grove: Critical Thinking Press and Software.

Roukes, N. (1982). *Art synectics.* Worchester: Davis Publications.

Silk, A. M., & Thomas, G. V. (1988). The development of size scaling in children's figure drawings. *British Developmental Psychology, 6,* 258–299.

Tyler, R. (1950). *Basic principles of cirriculum and instruction.* Chicago: University of Chicago Press.

Van der Tas, J. M. (1990). *A theory of the art world*. Rotterdam: Erasmus Universiteit Rotterdam.
Vygotsky, L. S. (1978). *Mind in society: The development of higher psychological processes*. Cambridge: Harvard University Press.
Zechmeister, E. B., & Johnson, J. E. (1992). *Critical thinking: A functional approach*. Pacific Grove: Brooks/Cole.

KEY TERMS

Developmental stages	Phenomenology
Class concepts	Propositional knowledge
Memory rehearsal	Procedural knowledge
Metamemory skills	Ill-defined problems
Symbolization	Deductive reasoning
Centering	Inductive reasoning
Reversibility	Heuristic reasoning

STUDY QUESTIONS

1. What are the elements of a formally written art curriculum and how do you think these elements differ when the content of the curriculum is specified in the visual concepts achieved rather than in terms of the subject matter knowledge to be acquired? Compare and contrast a visual concept-oriented curriculum with a discipline-based art education or on Gardner's seven intelligences.

2. Using one of your own art works, explain what perceptual data you used, what visual strategies you employed in its making, what it is you wanted someone viewing your work to pay attention to, and what changes you made in the work during the course of time you worked on it.

3. What range of mental abilities would a Grades 1 to 6 elementary art teacher need to consider in adapting a given lesson for use at different grade levels? Give an example of an activity you might conduct in Grades 2, 4, and 6 on a given day, noting how you would alter each grade's assignment.

4. Obtain a copy of Lowenfeld's *Creative and Mental Growth*. Document how he would conduct a drawing lesson. Compare and contrast Lowenfeld's approach to the approach recommended by Nicolaides in *The Natural Way to Draw*, Betty Edwards in *Drawing from the Right Side of the Brain*, or Robert Henri in *The Art Spirit*. In what ways are these authors alike? In what ways do they differ?

5. How do linguists such as Vygotsky and Chomsky differ from the structuralists' view of language as public speech and as an analogy for sci-

ence? Would their view agree with or be in contrast to art education approaches advocating connoisseurmanship or enlightened cherishing as goals for art instruction?

6. Conduct an experiment to test what it is you had to think about and what it meant to apply that thinking in the making of an art object. Trace your own thinking process in completing the work. Identify what it is you think you wanted to do in the beginning and what forces you came up against when you sought to apply your thoughts in the making of the work. Analyze the focal and procedural knowledges evident to you at the beginning of the work and at its conclusion. What do you think happened?

7. Describe the strategies used in inductive, deductive, and heuristic thinking. Which process comes closest to the way you work in art? Would you need to use the same or different thinking processes in making art, studying art history, or criticizing art? Which of these problem-solving approaches best matches your cognitive style? Why does that particular one serve you best? Do you also think different art problems need different ways of thinking? If so, why?

8. What is the difference conceptually in a work that Hamm called *reticulative* and one that he noted achieves a fusion in visual form? What are the characteristics of a fused visual form? Can you cite some examples of fused forms evident in the works of some contemporary artists not mentioned? Which style—abstract, realist, or pop art—provides the best evidence of fused form? Why do you think this is so?

9. Develop a lesson plan from the performance-based framework in this chapter by selecting one of the stages of development and using one or more of the focal, procedural, and linguistic knowledges supplied. Describe what you think the student will reveal about thinking skills and knowledge in the finished work. What kinds of evidence of the student's achievement will you look for in the work? What will that evidence tell you about the student's mental and artistic behavior?

7

Art Learning and Its Assessment

What this work has attempted to do thus far is acquaint the reader with the learner's basic mental functions, the current conceptions of cognitive development, the nature of concept formation, how children learn in art, and what developmental concerns shape the sequence and scope of a conceptually based art program. What this chapter specifically addresses are the connections between what it is art teachers want learners to know and what it is they actually learn, which links what teachers do in the art classroom with whom they teach, what it is they teach, and how effective they are in teaching it. Answers to some of these questions have been addressed in more detail in *Thinking in Art*. These do not require revisiting except to note that there are several equally useful conceptions of art teaching driven by the varied goals of the teacher, learner, and school.

The choice to begin with looking at what teachers do in teaching art and how this connects with what it is that students learn is based on the assumption that effective instruction depends mostly on teachers knowing what it is they want their students to know and be able to do and whether they have been successful in doing that. Therefore, this chapter is not so much about what formally needs to be taught or how to evaluate it, but rather about teachers needing to become more aware of what they are teaching and how they and others can come to know that they have been successful.

Such a beginning runs counter to the ideas of both those who claim that "art is caught and not taught" and those who believe that instruction can only be validated through performance-based behavioral objectives as measured by paper-and-pencil tests. Hopefully it is not necessary to repeat the earlier argument that thinking about and making art is an intelligent activity and, when focused on conceptual art learning, will result in products that give evidence that effective learning has taken place.

To pursue these connections, however, it is necessary to first consider a number of important factors about art instruction as practiced in American schools, including the following notions: (a) there is diversity in the kind of goals sought, (b) making and performing activities remain the dominant mode of instruction, (c) student achievement reflects divergent learning styles, (d) varied approaches to problem finding and solving are desired, and (e) evidence of achievement occurs mainly in products that meld both focal and procedural knowledge.

Given the difficulties posed by such conditions, some art teachers all too frequently resort to offering either a random array of novel activities for students to undergo or assign reductive exercises in using the elements and principles; memorizing artists' names, dates, and titles of works; or the steps for analyzing and criticizing works of art. This is not to suggest that to do such things lacks value. Rather, when done in isolation with little or no clear conception of what it is that students should achieve, it becomes a shotgun approach to learning—where the most one can hope for is that at least some of what is being taught will hit the target.

THE NEED TO ASSESS

Although most art teachers know they need to assess instruction, they also have trouble deciding what it is they need to teach and in what order they need to teach. This is due, in part, to both the range and variety of content material they are expected to cover and the kinds of learning environments in which many art teachers work. For example, art teachers who are expected to teach studio production and the understanding of art and culture, relate these understandings to other key forms of knowledge, critically assess and evaluate works of art, and make connections between all of this and the real world have far too much to do. This is especially so if they have to teach nine 25-minute periods a day to over 1,300 children a week. Of course, not all art teachers face such odds. However, many, especially at the elementary level, do. Even if they could accomplish all this, they still have to meet the additional responsibility of helping students improve in their other academic subjects, stay in school, graduate, remain drug free, and so on.

There is no satisfactory way to solve all the difficulties that art teachers face in our most demanding art teaching situations. Even in the most challenging ones, some approaches can prove to be more educationally defensible than the shotgun approaches previously identified. For example, one approach is to adopt a philosophically based curriculum that integrates expressive, historical, and critical thought into a coherent system for thinking and making, which at least avoids separating art teaching into the separate domains of art production, art history, criticism, and aesthetics. In *Thinking in Art* (Fig. 7.1), I suggested that these could be integrated under the paradigms, schema and correction, form-Gestalt, and linguistic-metaphor, which would, I believe, help students to philosophically integrate knowledge across the disciplines. I have also argued elsewhere that too much knowledge can actually inhibit creativity and that thinking skills do not necessarily transfer unless students use and practice these skills (Dorn, 1993). This suggests that we need to focus first on what it is we most want students to be able to do and second on the kinds of student performances that provide the richest content and greatest utility in a given classroom environment.

Few professionals would be surprised to learn that not all art teachers can teach everything a student needs to know. If school leaders are to be truly realistic as to what can be accomplished in schooling, we also need to take into account teachers' strengths and weaknesses. Realistically, most art teachers know how to teach some things really well, but few teach everything equally well. This is due, in part, to teachers' training, interests, and abilities and to the classroom environment in which they work.

Curriculum reformers have always viewed the varying abilities of teachers as one of the major problems to be faced in school reform. Unfortunately, too many of the solutions they come up with are handed down to the schools in the form of automated instructional devices, schemes designed to make learning "teacher proof," or in the guise of new curriculum standards and regulations to be implemented. The latter approach occurred in some Goals 2000 state efforts, which have framed state instructional standards in law and mandated that teachers implement these invectives through testing. This most recent top–down approach to school reform, like other past reforms (i.e., nobly inspired), may also, in the long run, prove ineffective. Such efforts usually fail not because the goals sought were unworthy, but rather because the standards were too vague or the teachers did not know how to implement them in the classroom.

What all this really suggests is that reform mandates coming down from on high, despite good intentions, rarely change how teachers teach. More often teachers are in a better position to know what they do best and what they need to do to improve what they are doing. Moreover, what seems to be the teachers' intractability to change may really be more an effort to rely on approaches that seem to work best for them, the students, and

PARADIGMS	ART PRODUCTION	ART HISTORY	CRITICISM/AESTHETICS
SCHEMA/ CORRECTION	Producing individually expressive products in a variety of art media, influenced by both contemporary and traditional art exemplars and the study of the techniques of professional artists.	The chronological study of significant art works from pre-historic to modern with emphasis on the study of art style, pictorial schema and thematic interpretation.	Recognizes that art is a concept which is a thought or idea that can be analyzed only through identifying the process the artist underwent in expressing it. Value is found in the uncensored expression of thought.
FORM/GESTALT	Producing individually expressive products through study of the elements and principles of organization. Experiments in surface encounters, perspective, light and shade, foreshortening, viewpoint, proximity, pattern, direction and closure.	Can include chronological study of art works both from the viewpoint of design, organization, illusion and its effect on viewer emotions and in the time period in which it was created.	Art works are individual expressive forms which excite similar, but not the same expressive responses in viewers. They have a state of "otherness" which inhibit criticism because the work refers only to itself and not to things outside of it. Criticism is limited to the affects on our emotions.
LINGUISTIC/ METAPHORICAL	Solving human problems through discovery and exploration including: personal imagery, study of man made communities, practical objects and city planning. Students study problems, develop visual hypotheses, and test solutions through constructing art objects or events. Students create visual metaphors through binocular disparity, bi-association humor and unit making.	Art history is a logical progression toward a higher truth in which works of art change in their meaning over time and are only what we can observe about them. From the viewpoint of contemporary life. A conception of the work is the most important feature and can include conceptions driven by feminism, Marxism, social history, popular arts, and the arts of institutions.	Criticism rejects surface qualities or study of original artistic intents and calls for the deconstructive reinterpretations of surface, space, time and materials in order to construct a language of criticism. Art and criticism can be essentially the same thing through converting art to language about art which can be discussed, manipulated and resolved through discourse.

FIG. 7.1.   Integrative paradigms from *Thinking in Art*.

the school. The fact that things work, however, does not ensure the best teaching, but it is a starting place from which one can begin the process of true school reform.

Assessing What Teachers Do Best

When we anchor instructional outcomes to what it is that teachers do best, we achieve two advantages over top–down reform approaches driven by administrative fiat. First, we provide the teacher with ownership of both the learning and evaluation process. Second, we make the teacher responsible for making his or her goals clear to both the student and school. Third, we can provide an assessment process that is fair to both the student and parent.

Also, when we link assessment directly to what it is that teachers teach, teachers feel they are no longer required to perform according to someone else's rules, but rather according to their own conscious effort to make evident what it is they want their students to be able to do. In doing this, the responsibility is placed squarely on the teacher to ensure that the instruction offered is consistent with the goals the teacher seeks and that the results clearly reflect those goals. To do this in what we previously referred to as an *ill-defined domain* requires that student learning in art production, art history, and art criticism be evident in the written, spoken, and visual products of instruction in both the expressive and cognitive domains.

When a teacher claims that art learning cannot be evaluated, he or she admits that the instruction being offered may have no ultimate effect on what the student is learning, and hence is not worthy of being included in the curriculum. By making such a claim, the teacher is also admitting that what was learned had no relation to the rest of the environment, would not affect or be affected by anything else, and would enact no causes nor bear consequences—or, for that matter, as noted in chapter 5, really exist.

When assessment is linked to what teachers teach, it becomes the responsibility of the art teacher—who really has the greatest stake in what it is he or she wants the student to learn—to provide the reasons why others should concur that significant learning has taken place. Who is better qualified than the art teacher to do that?

Providing an Effective Learning Environment

Although it is true that *what* teachers do in their teaching is critical to school reform, it is not the only factor to be considered in effecting quality art instruction. As teachers cannot teach everything a student needs to know and be able to do, students also cannot always learn everything they need to know in every classroom. This means that connections also need to be made between what it is teachers want students to learn and what students are capable of learning. This requires us to also look at how the learning environment needs to be structured so that classroom learning conditions are optimized for all students.

According to Fraenkel (1980), there are several principles that should be observed on the structure of learning. Those that are particularly germain to art teaching include these concerns:

1. Learning is a product of an active process of change in the ways that learners attribute meaning to the environment.
2. Individual perceptions and values are considerably influenced by the cultural environment.
3. Behavioral modification is largely dependent on the ability to perceive abstract relationships.
4. Meaningful tasks and materials are more readily learned than nonmeaningful content.
5. Active participation of learners is preferable to passive reception.
6. Practice reinforces many types of school learning.
7. Inserting dissonant objects or content into a learning sequence often increases curiosity, attention, and interest.
8. Transfer of learning is facilitated when individuals are made aware of underlying principles guiding the content and are afforded adequate and varied practice.

In analyzing Fraenkel's list of principles, Slavik (1995) noted two overriding principles that Fraenkel stressed: (a) content alone supplies only the basic knowledge necessary for the construction of meaning, and (b) learning activities are experiences designed to involve thinking about and using subject matter. Slavik also highlighted Fraenkel's so-called seven activity design factors, which include:

Justifiability, which requires that a purposeful learning activity be directed toward clearly demonstrated outcomes.

Multiple focus, which requires the learning process to address two or more objectives concurrently.

Open-endedness, which affords opportunities for varied and multiple approaches and responses.

Inquiry potential, which allows students to take ownership of their own learning.

Sequential structure, which requires some learning activities to serve as prerequisites for others and gradually increase foundational knowledge.

Transferability, which requires the application of knowledge learned in one situation to future and different contexts.

Variety, which occurs in four categories: *Intake*, or perception; *organization*, or technical practice; *demonstration*, or mastery; and *creative expression*, or the production of an original product.

Fortunately, given the art program's acceptance of diverse goals, making and performing, divergent learning styles, and products involving the integration of focal and procedural knowledge, most art teachers already operate in what Fraenkel called a well-structured learning environment. Although he may not have intended it to be so, his seven activity design factors fit the general structure of the typical school art program as closely as it does any subject in the school.

Justifiability, Fraenkel's first design factor, is evident in most school art programs because most school art learning focuses on the practical activity of making expressive objects. Effective art teachers use visual exemplars, teach about the principles of design and plastic elements, provide critical and historical information and insights, and ensure that these knowledges are evident in the expressive products that students form in the art room.

Art teachers who stress concept formation in art, which is the conversion, transformation, and integration of ideas and images taken from a number of different sources, also use Fraenkel's multiple focus design factor, which utilizes two or more differing conceptions to arrive at a new artistic concept. The altering and morphing of aesthetic schema is, for most art teachers, the heart of the creative process.

The open-endedness factor is almost always evident in the way art teachers approach problem solving in creative forming. Students are neither expected to replicate someone else's images or ideas per se, nor are their products viewed as models for replication by others. Art as an expressive activity encourages students to use multiple approaches to visual problem solving and to respond to their own visual work and the work of others in highly personal and unique ways.

In an ill-defined domain such as art, a student also finds the opportunity to become engaged in forms of visual inquiry, especially in visual forming. Artistic problem-solving and problem-finding activities require Fraenkel's inquiry potential factor by including solutions using the inductive, deductive, and heuristic. In planning, executing, and evaluating art thought and production, many points of view are also examined. In expressive forming, individual approaches to judging encourage students to be owners of their own feelings as well as their own efforts to learn.

Although not all art activity requires logical or sequentially organized approaches to problem solving, nearly all forms of expressive activity require the use of Fraenkel's sequential structures for finding and solving problems. As noted earlier, this may even involve deliberatively creating barriers to be overcome as a means of finding out just what the expressive goal of the work might be. In addition to deciding strategies for accomplishing a work, new skills, understandings, and goals must be considered; they must be sequentially ordered according to what expressive end is required. For example, although the sequences an artist uses in making a traditional watercolor differ from those used in a scumbling search to cover or uncover form in an oil painting, the final product of both efforts involves deciding on a strategy, developing new techniques, ordering a sequence of steps, and determining when that activity is ended.

When the disciplines of art education (i.e., art production, art criticism, art history, and aesthetics) are integrated in the act of conceptual forming, the knowledge gained in each discipline is transferred into a single, focused activity. When an art paradigm such as occurs in a schema and motif approach is used to integrate the disciplines, all outcomes—whether evidenced in a creative product, essay, or oral discussion—become equal in their instructional value. This is mostly due to the design factor of transferability, which occurs between disciplines when the creation of a new concept rather than knowledge of a concept is the goal of the activity.

Art instruction also has Fraenkel's notion of variety, which involves intake in the form of visual perceptions, organization through the act of doing, demonstration through mastery, and creative expression through the production of original products. Without these four factors, variety as learning in art cannot occur.

THE ART PROGRAM STANDARDS

Although effective art teachers know, through training and experience, what it is that students should know and be able to do and that they are more likely to do that in an environment that respects students' interests and abilities, they also do not make such judgments totally divorced from the concerns of the society, the profession, and the school. This is because most art teachers spend at least 4 years in a teacher education program determined by the state and profession that licenses them. In addition, they are also employed by school districts regulated by states, which require that at least some minimum standards be met with regard to the curriculum they teach and level of achievement their students are expected to achieve. In reality, teachers are civil servants of the state in which they teach. For the most part, they operate according to standards specified by the state and the school with regard to what it is that students should know and be able to do in art and the levels of achievement they are expected to reach.

Having said all this, many art teachers still provide art instruction guided informally by only a few scribbled directions and sketches of their own choosing as written in a daily lesson plan book. This is despite school districts may have detailed curriculum guides, classrooms furnished with graded art texts, and even a school-specified curriculum framework to follow. However, many teachers may not even be aware of the existence of the system's guides, rarely use the texts provided in the classroom, and only casually follow the school's general guide to instruction. Why this occurs has to do with the teacher's experience with the curriculum, the amount of freedom teachers are given to choose content, their ability to translate the specified standards into the activities that students learn by, and what valid and reliable ways exist to assess student achievement.

Given the freedom that most art teachers have, it may seem to those outside the art teaching profession to be a pretty loose way to run a business. If we are honest, given such conditions, it is probably amazing that we do as well as we do. Despite such latitude, however, most American school art programs are effective because teachers operate as trained professionals within the paradigm structure of a profession that shapes its practitioners according to certain rules of conduct and specified standards, including accepting the responsibility for credibly representing the profession, the school, the state, and the nation.

Many educational and civic leaders today are beginning to question whether we can afford this kind of 20th-century flexibility in a 21st century that now requires that we effectively educate *all* the children and not just those who come to schools adequately prepared and interested in receiving such an education. This suggests there will be a new kind of 21st-century schooling—one that is more responsive to the political, social, and economic problems, to an increasingly more pluralistic society, and one that demands more accountability from students, teachers, administrators, and governments. Although it may seem to seasoned practitioners that such current reform efforts are, in effect, "the same old same old," both veteran and inexperienced teachers will be facing increasingly more pressure to be accountable to the school and government. In fact, teachers will have little other choice than to be increasingly more regulated. Fortunately, they can also play a part in deciding what kind of regulations are most useful and consistent with the creative ends they seek.

Because of the increased demand for accountability, it is necessary that art teachers today become familiar with the various art teaching standards advocated by their professional associations, their state, and the schools that are charged with the responsibility of assessing the quality of instruction in American schools. What follows are the national instructional standards in art as published by a consortium of national arts education associations, which are not necessarily the same as the standards adopted by some state departments of public instruction or those developed by National Assessment of Educational Progress (NAEP) governing board.

Knowing about the national standards is important to both the beginning teacher, who lacks the experience to know everything that they are expected to do, and the veteran teacher, who knows that children and schools change over time and that, to remain effective, their teaching must also reflect that change. Under the Goals 2000 mandate, art teachers are expected to match what it is they want students to learn with the national and state standards, specify what performances students are expected to achieve, and measure them accurately.

The National Content and Achievement Standards

The national standards that follow are a result of the Goals 2000 Educate America Act written into federal law and adopted into state law by participating Goals 2000 states. They have been developed by the professional associations in arts education first at the national level and later at the state level. These standards cohere from the top (national) down (state-local); they were written in such a way that individual states and later the school districts could write standards that, in effect, take into account all these jurisdictions. The federal standards are intended as guidelines because the U.S. constitution does not provide for a federal system of schools, but rather leaves that responsibility to the states, which can then regulate schools respecting also the tradition of local or "common schools" determining the actual school's curriculum. In effect, teachers following their state standards in the development of local school standards could expect them to also reflect the standards set at the national level.

The federal standards were originally developed to aid educational reform in American schools. In general, they reflect national educational concerns for knowledge transferability among disciplines, cultural diversity, and appropriate technologies and to provide a foundation for student assessment. By definition, the content standards are statements of what students should know and be able to do. The achievement standards underneath them specify the understandings and levels of achievement that students are expected to attain in a given competency. Student performances, rubrics, and anchors for evaluation, which are discussed later, are determined by these content and achievement standards, although not explicitly evident in the standard. Herein lies the rub: Although a standard may specify a goal, it does not explain how to reach that goal or describe what evidence is needed or from what educational products an evaluation is derived. Put in the jargon of the standard writer, the standards describe the cumulative skills and knowledge of all students on exiting a specific grade level, but does not specify the curriculum or activities to be used in achieving the standard, which is supposedly the responsibility of the states, local school districts, and individual teachers. This is another reason that this chapter begins with what it is teachers normally do, which the standards never specify nor, for that matter, necessarily ensure can be achieved or evaluated.

Despite weaknesses, the standards carry the weight of law in many states and offer some excellent goals developed by some of the most knowledgeable art professionals in the United States. In the last analysis, of course, what instructional performances we choose to assign students to do and how we evaluate them in schools is the bottom line in providing the evidence we need to show that the system is working.

Two sets of national standards for arts education were developed by the profession in 1994: *The Opportunity to Learn Standards for Arts Education, Dance, Music, Theatre, Visual Arts* (CNAEA, 1995) and *Dance, Music, Theatre, Visual Arts: What Every Young American Should Know and Be Able To Do In The Arts* (CNAEA, 1994). Both were developed by the consortium of National Arts Education Associations; the *Opportunity to Learn...* publication was developed under the direction of the National Dance Association (NDA), and *What Every Young American Should Know...* under the Music Educators National Conference (MENC, 1994). The *Opportunity to Learn...* standards are intended to specify the physical and educational conditions necessary in the schools to enable every student to meet the national voluntary content and achievement standards. The actual achievement standards adopted by the National Committee for Standards on the Arts are contained in the *What Every American Should Know...* document, which is considered the final standards to be achieved, with the *Opportunity to Learn...* standards being used mainly to determine when the standards are not met and the reasons behind that failure.

Although the Opportunity to Learn standards are useful and do specify the curriculum to be offered in general terms, the What Every American Should Know national standards are primarily focused on the national achievement standard and therefore is the only one described here. The descriptions reported, according to its authors, define *art* in two ways: (a) as creative works and the process that produces them, and (b) the body of work that makes up the entire human intellectual and cultural heritage. The standards are couched in terms of what students should know and be able to do in the arts; they are presented in each discipline as the specific competencies that the arts education community nationwide believes are essential for every student. The competencies are not considered to be equally weighted; they are interrelated with the mixture and balance to vary by grade level, course, instructional unit, and from school to school.

Two different types of standards are used to guide student assessment in each of the competence areas. These are the content standards, which specify what students should know and be able to do in the arts disciplines, and the achievement standards, which specify the understandings and levels of achievement that students are expected to attain in each of the arts at the completion of Grades 4, 8, and 12. The standards also specify two levels of achievement: proficient and advanced. The advanced level is used for students who have elected specialized courses in a discipline. Essentially, the standards ask, as noted next, what students should know and be able to do by the time they have completed secondary school (MENC, 1994).

- They should be able to communicate at a basic level in the four arts disciplines—dance, music, theatre, and the visual arts. This includes knowledge and skills in the use of the basic vocabularies, materials, tools, techniques, and intellectual methods of each arts discipline.
- They should be able to communicate proficiently in at least one art form, including the ability to define and solve artistic problems with insight, reason, and technical proficiency.
- They should be able to develop and present basic analyses of works of art from structural, historical, and cultural perspectives and from combinations of those perspectives. This includes the ability to understand and evaluate work in the various arts disciplines.
- They should have an informed acquaintance with exemplary works of art from a variety of cultures and historical periods and a basic understanding of historical development in the arts disciplines, across the arts as a whole, and within cultures.
- They should be able to relate various types of art knowledge and skills within and across the arts disciplines. This includes mixing and matching competencies and understandings in art-making, history, and culture and analysis in any arts-related project. (p. 19)

The following is according to the National Art Education Association (NAEA[1]):

Grades K–4
To meet the standards, students must learn vocabularies and concepts associated with various types of work in the visual arts and must exhibit their competence at various levels in visual, oral, and written form.

---

[1]From *The National Visual Arts Standards* by the National Art Education Association. Copyright © 1994 by the National Art Education Association, 1916 Association Drive, Reston, VA 20191. Reprinted with permission.

In Kindergarten—Grade 4, young children experiment enthusiastically with *art materials and investigate the ideas presented to them through visual arts instruction. They exhibit a sense of joy and excitement as they make and share their artwork with others. Creation is at the heart of this instruction. Students learn to work with various tools, processes and *media. They learn to coordinate their hands and minds in explorations of the visual world. They learn to make choices that enhance communication of their ideas. Their natural inquisitiveness is promoted, and they learn the value of perseverance. As they move from kindergarten through the early grades, students develop skills of observation, and they learn to examine the objects and events of their lives. At the same time, they grow in their ability to describe, interpret, evaluate, and respond to work in the visual arts. Through examination of their own work and that of other people, times, and places, students learn to unravel the essence of artwork and to appraise its purpose and value. Through these efforts, students begin to understand the meaning and impact of the visual world in which they live. (NAEA, 1994, p. 15)

1. **Content Standard:** Understanding and applying media, technique, and processes
   Achievement Standard:
   Students
   a. know the differences between materials, techniques, and processes
   b. describe how different materials, techniques, and processes cause different responses
   c. use different media, techniques, and processes to communicate ideas, experiences, and stories
   d. use art materials and tools in a safe and responsible manner

2. **Content standard:** Using knowledge of *structures and functions
   Achievement Standard:
   Students
   a. know the differences among visual characteristics and purposes of art in order to convey ideas
   b. describe how different *expressive features and *organizational principles cause different responses
   c. use visual structures and functions of art to communicate ideas

3. **Content Standard:** Choosing and evaluating a range of subject matter, symbols, and ideas
   Achievement Standard:
   Students
   a. explore and understand prospective content for works of art
   b. select and use subject matter, symbols, and ideas to communicate meaning

4. **Content Standard:** Understanding the visual arts in relation to history and cultures
   Achievement Standard:
   Students
   a. know that the visual arts have both a history and specific relationships to various cultures
   b. identify specific works of art as belonging to particular cultures, times, and places
   c. demonstrate how history, culture, and the visual arts can influence each other in making and studying works of art

5. **Content Standard:** Reflecting upon and *assessing the characteristics and merits of their work and the work of others.

Achievement Standard:

Students

   a. understand there are various purposes for creating works of visual art
   b. describe how people's experiences influence the development of specific artworks
   c. understand there are different responses to specific artworks

6. **Content Standard:** Making connections between visual arts and other disciplines

Achievement Standard:

Students

   a. understand and use similarities and differences between characteristics of the visual arts and other arts disciplines
   b. identify connections between the visual arts and other disciplines in the curriculum. (NAEA, 1994, p. 17)

Grades 5–8

In grades 5–8, students' visual expressions become more individualistic and imaginative. The problem-solving activities inherent in art making help them develop cognitive, affective, and psychomotor skills. They select and transform ideas, discriminate, synthesize and appraise, and they apply these skills to their expanding knowledge of the visual arts and to their own *creative work. Students understand that making and responding to works of visual art are inextricably interwoven and that *perception, *analysis, and critical judgment are inherent to both.

Their own art making becomes infused with a variety of images and approaches. They learn that preferences of others may differ from their own. Students refine the questions that they ask in response to artworks. This leads them to an appreciation of multiple artistic solutions and interpretations. Study of historical and cultural *contexts give students insights into the role played by the visual arts in human achievement. As they consider examples of visual art works within historical contexts, students gain a deeper appreciation of their own values, of the values of other people, and the connection of the visual arts to universal human needs, values, and beliefs. They understand that the art of a culture is influenced by *aesthetic ideas as well as by social, political, economic, and other factors. Through these efforts, students develop an understanding of the meaning and import of the visual world in which they live. (NAEA, 1994, p. 18)

1. **Content Standard:** Understanding and applying media, techniques, and processes

Achievement Standard:

Students

   a. select media, techniques, and processes; analyze what makes them effective or not effective in communicating ideas; and reflect upon the effectiveness of their choices
   b. intentionally take advantage of the qualities and characteristics of *art media, techniques, and processes to enhance communication of their experiences and ideas

2. **Content Standard:** Using knowledge of *structures and functions
   Achievement Standard:
   Students
   a. generalize about the effects of visual structures and functions and reflect upon these effects in their own work
   b. employ organizational structures and analyze what makes them effective or not effective in the communication of ideas
   c. select and use the qualities of structures and functions of art to improve communication of their ideas.

3. **Content Standard:** Choosing and evaluating a range of subject matter, symbols, and ideas
   Achievement Standard:
   Students
   a. integrate visual, spatial, and temporal concepts with content to communicate intended meaning in their artworks
   b. use subjects, themes, and symbols that demonstrate knowledge of contexts, values, and aesthetics that communicate intended meaning in artworks

4. **Content Standard:** Understanding the visual arts in relation to history and cultures
   Achievement Standard:
   Students
   a. know and compare the characteristics of artworks in various eras and cultures
   b. describe and place a variety of art objects in historical and cultural contexts
   c. analyze, describe and demonstrate how factors of time and place (such as climate, resources, ideas, and technology) influence visual characteristics that give meaning and value to a work of art

5. **Content Standard:** Reflecting upon and *assessing the characteristics and merits of their work and the work of others
   Achievement Standard:
   Students
   a. compare multiple purposes for creating works of art
   b. analyze contemporary and historic meanings in specific artworks through cultural and aesthetic inquiry
   c. describe and compare a variety of individual responses to their own artworks and to artworks from various eras and cultures

6. **Content Standard:** Making connections between visual arts and other disciplines
   Achievement Standard:
   Students
   a. compare the characteristics of works in two or more art forms that share similar subject matter, historical periods, or cultural context
   b. describe ways in which the principles and subject matter of other disciplines taught in the school are interrelated with the visual arts. (NAEA, 1994, p. 20)

Grades 9–12

To meet the standards, students must learn vocabularies and concepts associated with various types of work in the visual arts. As they develop greater fluency in communicating in visual, oral, and written form, they must exhibit greater artistic competence through all of these avenues.

In grades 9–12, students develop deeper and more profound works of visual art that reflect the maturation of their creative and problem-solving skills. Students understand the multifaceted interplay of different *media, styles, forms, techniques, and processes in the creation of their work.

Students develop increasing abilities to pose insightful questions about *contexts, processes, and criteria for evaluation. They use these questions to examine works in light of various analytical methods and to express sophisticated ideas about visual relationships using precise terminology. They can evaluate artistic character and *aesthetic qualities in works of art, nature, and human-made environments. They can reflect on the nature of human involvement in art as a viewer, creator, and participant.

Students understand the relationships among art forms and between their own work and that of others. They are able to relate understandings about the historical and cultural contexts of art to situations in contemporary life. They have a broad and in-depth understanding of the meaning and import of the visual world in which they live. (NAEA, 1994, p. 21)

1. **Content Standard:** Understanding and applying media, techniques, and processes
   Achievement Standard, Proficient:
   Students
   - **a.** apply media, techniques, and processes with sufficient skill, confidence, and sensitivity that their intentions are carried out in their artworks
   - **b.** conceive and *create works of visual art that demonstrate an understanding of how the communication of their ideas relates to the media, techniques, and processes they use

   Achievement Standard, Advanced:
   Students
   - **c.** communicate ideas regularly at a high level of effectiveness in at least one visual arts medium
   - **d.** initiate, define, and solve challenging *visual arts problems independently using intellectual skills such as analysis, synthesis, and evaluation

2. **Content Standard:** Using knowledge of *structures and functions
   Achievement Standard, Proficient:
   Students
   - **a.** demonstrate the ability to form and defend judgments about the characteristics and structures to accomplish commercial, personal, communal, or other purposes of art
   - **b.** evaluate the effectiveness of artworks in terms of organizational structures and functions
   - **c.** create artworks that use *organizational principles and functions to solve specific visual arts problems

Achievement Standard, Advanced:

Students

    d. demonstrate the ability to compare two or more perspectives about the use of organizational principles and functions in artwork and to defend personal evaluations of these perspectives

    e. create multiple solutions to specific visual arts problems that demonstrate competence in producing effective relationships between structural choices and artistic functions

3. **Content Standard:** Choosing and evaluating a range of subject matter, symbols, and ideas

Achievement Standard, Proficient:

Students

    a. reflect on how artworks differ visually, spatially, temporally, and functionally, and describe how these are related to history and culture

    b. apply subjects, symbols, and ideas in their artworks and use the skills gained to solve problems in daily life (NAEA, 1994, p. 22)

Achievement Standard, Advanced:

Students

    c. describe the origins of specific images and ideas and explain why they are of value in their artwork and in the work of others

    d. evaluate and defend the validity of sources for content and the manner in which subject matter, symbols, and images are used in the students' works and in significant works by others

4. **Content Standard:** Understanding the visual arts in relation to history and culture

Achievement Standard, Proficient:

Students

    a. differentiate among a variety of historical and cultural contexts in terms of characteristics and purposes of works of art

    b. describe the function and explore the meaning of specific art objects within varied cultures, times, and places

    c. analyze relationships of works of art to one another in terms of history, aesthetics, and culture, justifying conclusions made in the analysis and using such conclusions to inform their own art making

Achievement Standard, Advanced:

Students

    d. analyze and interpret artworks for relationships among form, context, purposes, and critical models, showing understanding of the work of critics, historians, aestheticians, and artists

    e. analyze common characteristics of visual arts evident across time and among cultural/ethnic groups to formulate analyses, evaluations, and interpretations of meaning

5. **Content Standard:** Reflecting upon and assessing the characteristics and merits of their work and the work of others

Achievement Standard, Proficient:

Students

    a. Identify intentions of those creating artworks, explore the implications of various purposes, and justify their analyses of purposes in particular works

    b. describe meanings of artworks by analyzing how specific works are created and how they relate to historical and cultural contexts

    c. reflect analytically on various interpretations as a means for understanding and evaluating works of visual art

Achievement Standard, Advanced:

    Students

    d. correlate responses to works of visual art with various techniques for communicating meanings, ideas, attitudes, views, and intentions

6. **Content Standard:** Making connections between visual arts and other disciplines

Achievement Standard, Proficient:

Students

    a. compare the materials, *technologies, media, and processes of the visual arts with those of other arts disciplines as they are used in creation and types of analysis

    b. compare characteristics of visual arts within a particular historical period or style with ideas, issues, or themes in the humanities or sciences

Achievement Standard, Advanced:

Students

    c. synthesize the creative and analytical principles and techniques of the visual arts and selected other arts disciplines, the humanities, or the sciences. (NAEA, 1994, p. 23)

Interpreting the National Art Standards

As previously noted, the national content standards are an important curriculum tool. Incidentally, they also tell us what the arts disciplines agree on and what they do not. On the positive side, they provide us with a generic language that enables us to talk about a curricular content fitting for all the disciplines. On the negative side, they do so in a language unconnected to the creative act and, consequently, to what it is that art teachers are trying to teach and what art learners are actually learning in school arts classrooms.

To those experienced in the art of creating multidisciplinary curriculum standards, especially where the task is to unite several disciplinary perspectives into one unified statement, it is clear that whatever language one decides on that is not objectionable to any one discipline ends up not having much relevance to any of the disciplines involved. One needs only to analyze the national content standard in the various disciplines to see that, although these standards may differ in the number and kinds of tasks performed, each can ultimately be reduced to five domain content performances: (a) performing and making, (b) organizing and structuring, (c) criticism, (d) historical–cultural, and (e) relation to other disciplines.

Such a unified approach to describing arts content first appeared in the college boards' Project Equality (CEEB, 1983) effort in 1983, which claimed:

Students going to college will profit from the following preparation in the arts:
- The ability to understand and appreciate the unique qualities of each of the arts.
- The ability to appreciate how people of various cultures have used the arts to express themselves.
- The ability to understand and appreciate different artistic styles and works from representative historical periods and cultures.
- Some knowledge of the social and intellectual influences affecting artistic form.
- The ability to use the skills, media, tools, and processes required to express themselves in one or more of the arts. (p. 17)

The Board's Ad Hoc Committee on the Arts, which prepared this statement, was, at the time, clearly influenced by psychologist Jerome Bruner's notion that to educate a student in physics (art) it was necessary to educate him or her as a physicist (artist; Bruner, 1960) and by Manuel Barkan's notion that to be fully educated in art one should study art production, art history, and art criticism (Barkan, 1962). The Getty trust, in its so-called discipline-based art instruction (DBAE), also followed this approach, which was only recently expanded to include all of the arts.

Barkan, along with Eliot Eisner and a number of their contemporaries in art education in the 1960s and 1970s, adopted the discipline-centered approach, choosing to describe school art content in terms of the art world occupations of the artist, critic, historian, collector, and so on. The art critic's methods of describing, analyzing, interpreting, and evaluating thus became the critical behaviors students were expected to learn in school. The functional behaviors of: (a) skill in perceiving qualitative relationships, (b) skill in management of materials, (c) skill in inventing form, and (d) skill in creating spatial order became the skills to be learned in art production and art structure (Eisner, 1972). Although it still remains questionable as to whether any critic or visual artist actually uses these behaviors, this reductive approach to defining art content nevertheless remains a part of the lexicon used by those in the arts standards movement.

As can be noted in Fig. 7.2, what power struggles those in the business of art face in the arts world may have little, if any, relevance to the creative performances students pursue in art classrooms. To say the least, curriculum planners need to carefully consider such disparities when they attempt to convert national content standards into what it is we want students to learn and be able to do in schools.

What art content teachers finally decide to use and how they use it involves solving a broad range of issues, as can be noted in Fig. 7.3. The relationship of the art content to the teaching of art, as shown in this diagram by the National Board for Professional Teaching Standards, finally comes down to the teacher knowing what students need to know and *how* to help students learn to create expressive objects of meaning. Neither is more important; rather, both are equally important as they become apparent in the unification of form and matter in the expressive object.

THE SOCIOLOGY OF THE ART WORLD	THE INDIVIDUAL AND THE EXPRESSIVE OBJECT
POWER OF ART WORLD FIGURES	STUDENTS AS LEARNERS
• ARTISTS MAKE AND SELL OBJECTS TO DEALERS AND THE PUBLIC	• TAKE RESPONSIBILITY FOR WHAT THEY CHOOSE TO DO
• ART DEALERS MARKET OBJECTS TO MUSEUMS AND COLLECTORS	• CREATE EXPRESSIVE OBJECTS OF MEANING
• ART CRITICS DECIDE THE VALUE OF OBJECTS IN THE MARKETPLACE	• MAKE ABSTRACTIONS AND INTERPRETATIONS OF THEIR WORLD
• ART HISTORIANS WRITE SCHOLARLY PAPERS FOR PUBLICATION	• USE THEIR FEELINGS, EMOTIONS, AND INTELLECT IN RESPONDING TO AESTHETIC OBJECTS
• ART COLLECTORS BUY, COLLECT, AND CURATE OBJECTS FOR PRESTIGE	• THINK ABOUT THE FEELINGS AND EMOTIONS THEY EXPRESS AND ATTEND TO
• MUSEUM DIRECTORS BUY, CURATE, AND DISPLAY OBJECTS FOR PUBLIC SERVICE	• FIND VALUE IN DOING SOMETHING FOR ITS OWN SAKE

FIG. 7.2. Art world and art learner outcomes compared.

State Art Content Standards.   The content standards set by the individual states have even greater utility for the art teacher than do the national standards. However, the state standards vary in number and kind among the states, including some states that have decided not to construct them. However, consulting one's state standards is the most efficient starting place for establishing the school content standards and may even help simplify that process. For example, some states have reduced the number of standards to be achieved by compressing several different national standards into one. In the state of Vermont, the number of national art content standards has been reduced from six to four: (a) skill development, (b) reflection and critique, (c) making connections, and (d) approach to work (VAAP, 1995). In Florida's Sunshine State Standards, the number has been reduced from six to five: (a) skills and techniques, (b) creation and communication, (c) aesthetic and critical analysis, (d) applications to life, and (e) cultural and historical connections (FDEP, 1996). In these states as well as others, the state standards normally encompass the national standards, although they may differ in their number and phraseology.

The Local School (District) Art Content Standards.   In some cases, the local school art standards, which include both the district and individual school content standards, will duplicate the state's art content standard. In other cases, they will reduce or expand them to meet the district's policy on student assessment. Most states require that the local content standards reflect the state standards, define what art performances students are expected to engage in at different levels, and how these performances are to be evaluated. The validity and reliability of these evaluations is based on their being authentic, which is to meet the criterion of fairness. This requires students to know, as a part of the assigned performance task, what it is they are to be evaluated on. School and district assessments are also expected to yield numerical data to provide empirical evidence that the student has achieved the content standard at a given level. Although it is questionable whether all expressive outcomes are necessarily quantifiable (i.e., one's feelings, emotions, beliefs, etc.), there are still many effi-

THE RELATIONSHIP OF THE CONTENT OF ART TO THE TEACHING OF ART

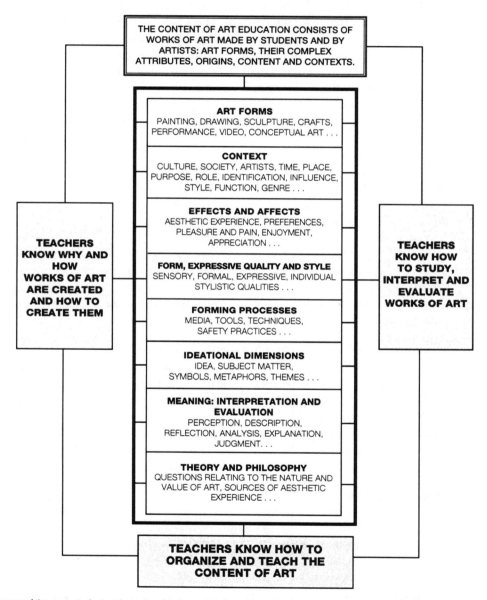

THE CONTENT OF ART EDUCATION CONSISTS OF WORKS OF ART MADE BY STUDENTS AND BY ARTISTS: ART FORMS, THEIR COMPLEX ATTRIBUTES, ORIGINS, CONTENT AND CONTEXTS.

ART FORMS
PAINTING, DRAWING, SCULPTURE, CRAFTS, PERFORMANCE, VIDEO, CONCEPTUAL ART . . .

CONTEXT
CULTURE, SOCIETY, ARTISTS, TIME, PLACE, PURPOSE, ROLE, IDENTIFICATION, INFLUENCE, STYLE, FUNCTION, GENRE . . .

EFFECTS AND AFFECTS
AESTHETIC EXPERIENCE, PREFERENCES, PLEASURE AND PAIN, ENJOYMENT, APPRECIATION . . .

FORM, EXPRESSIVE QUALITY AND STYLE
SENSORY, FORMAL, EXPRESSIVE, INDIVIDUAL STYLISTIC QUALITIES . . .

FORMING PROCESSES
MEDIA, TOOLS, TECHNIQUES, SAFETY PRACTICES . . .

IDEATIONAL DIMENSIONS
IDEA, SUBJECT MATTER, SYMBOLS, METAPHORS, THEMES . . .

MEANING: INTERPRETATION AND EVALUATION
PERCEPTION, DESCRIPTION, REFLECTION, ANALYSIS, EXPLANATION, JUDGMENT. . .

THEORY AND PHILOSOPHY
QUESTIONS RELATING TO THE NATURE AND VALUE OF ART, SOURCES OF AESTHETIC EXPERIENCE . . .

TEACHERS KNOW WHY AND HOW WORKS OF ART ARE CREATED AND HOW TO CREATE THEM

TEACHERS KNOW HOW TO STUDY, INTERPRET AND EVALUATE WORKS OF ART

TEACHERS KNOW HOW TO ORGANIZE AND TEACH THE CONTENT OF ART

This diagram of the content of art and art education is meant to be neither exhaustive nor prescriptive. Nor does it imply a hierarchy. In the creation or study of art any aspect may come first, last or serve as an entry point.

FIG. 7.3. The relationship of the content of art to the teaching of art. Reprinted by permission of the National Board for Professional Teaching Standards, from the *Early Adolescence Through Young Adulthood/Art Standards*, 1996, all rights reserved.

cient ways one can accurately estimate student growth in the acquisition of both focal and procedural knowledge and in the power of their expressive work.

When using the national, state, and local art content standards to decide what performances students are expected to master, the two most important concerns are that (a) the artistic process be held first and foremost in the decision process, and (b) the standards serve as a means for deciding what is possible and not merely used as a checklist of items to be measured. In setting their own standards, teachers can also begin by thinking about the lessons or activities currently being used to decide what content and achievement standards are likely to be met in the pursuit of that particular lesson or activity. Where a school district has no formal curriculum and operates on the basis of teacher lesson plans alone, this may be the only way the teacher can begin to construct a classroom standard. Using such an approach at least offers the advantage of the classroom standards and assessment tools being linked to instructional practice, rather than to some ideal level of performance handed down from above.

To begin the process of finding out what students need to know and be able to do in the art classroom, one could construct a personal framework or checklist of the kinds of understandings and behaviors a student needs to master in practice to meet the lesson requirements. Figure 7.4 reveals how Vernon Howard's Topology can be used as a framework for artistic practice, where the art focal and procedural knowledge acquired can be structured so as to cohere with the national and state art content standards (Howard, 1977). What this figure effectively demonstrates is that a coherence among the local, state, and national standards and what teachers actually do in art production will occur when the teachers' lessons are constructed as a framework for practice. Such a coherence is further ensured by using a concept-centered approach to the lesson, where two or more existing images are converted into a new image or concept.

Developing Classroom Art Content Standards. Thus, to build a set of classroom art content standards (i.e., to decide what students need to know and do with a commitment to making the artistic process first and using the national standards mainly as possibilities) requires the process to begin with a topology of practice rather than with a set of behaviors connected to selected art world figures and their power struggles. Unless the state and district's standards reflect a topology of practice, one either has to invent one's own or use one that exists. For purposes of illustrating how one can use such a topology as a starting place, we can use the Vernon Howard's Topology discussed in chapter 5.

Developing Art Achievement Standards. It is necessary to decide on the achievement standards that specify the students' understandings and levels of achievement. Here one can directly refer to the achievement standards specified in either the national or state standards. However, it should be recognized that, at the national level, these are more or less ideal standards of achievement to be met at specified 4-year intervals (e.g., Grades 4, 8, and 12). They are generally based on the assumption that conceptual thinking is sequentially acquired and in accordance with the hierarchy set by Bloom's taxonomy, where students move up from descriptive to analytical behaviors (i.e., at Grades K–4, to know, describe, and use; at Grades 5–8, to generalize, employ, select, analyze, compare, etc.; and at Grades 9–12, to conceive, evaluate, demonstrate, reflect, apply, correlate, etc.; Bloom, 1956).

Although such descriptors can be useful in setting classroom achievement standards, they also assume the student should achieve the higher order thinking skills most associated with inductive and deductive modes of thinking. As a consequence, they do not mention such behaviors as seeing, noticing, and performing identified in chapter 6, where at various levels students are expected to note shape differences, positions, distance, and direction; control arm movement; paint; draw; cut and tear; measure; unfold; recombine; think; metaphorically represent; exaggerate; think symbolically; reason metastematically, and so on. Another advantage of using the chapter 6 framework in addition to the state or national standards is that all the focal and procedural knowledges and language abilities listed are linked to both artistic practice and developmentally appropriate levels of performance. As previously noted, not all children are able to do all the things specified at every developmental stage, nor, for that matter, are they all necessarily interested in learning the same things in the same way, which has much more to do with their cognitive style than with their achievement.

Converting Art Content and Achievement Standards to Practice. Figure 7.4 reveals how the National Content Standards Grades 5 to 8 can be met: through using (a) Howard's Topology of Practice to determine classroom content and achievement standards, and (b) the chapter 6 developmental framework of practice to determine what classroom performances can be used to evaluate the standards. Howard's typology becomes the content standard listed in Column 2, his explanations of the mental processes involved from the achievement standards are listed in Column 3, and the developmentally prescribed visual performances for ages 11 to 13 from chapter 5 and the appropriate activities or performances listed in column 4. It should be noted, however, that only some of the ages 11 to 13 activities are used in Column 4; those selected are most likely to include all or most of the national content objectives. What should become apparent in such choosing is that one needs to use several different behaviors in the topology and not just concentrate on a single one (i.e., if one hopes to make the classroom standards essentially encompass all of the national and the state art content standards).

What should also become evident from viewing this figure is that the studio lessons already described in the art education literature, when carefully selected, can meet most of the content and achievement requirements set by the state and national standards. This is possible because the making of expressive objects requires many different cognitive and affective ways of knowing and many different kinds of art content. The primary difference between this model and the one constructed from art world behaviors is that the former focuses on the creative act and on the doing and undergoing process, which is experienced when students are engaged in creating expressive objects of meaning.

Constructing Conceptually Based Performances. As suggested earlier, teachers offering conceptually based classroom activities actually increase the chances that student performances will closely relate to the state and national standards. One obvious advantage in using conceptually based performance tasks is that they can be expanded or contracted to meet one or more different standards and at many different developmental levels. Conceptual performance activities also simplify the processes of standard setting and performance evaluations. Indeed, it would be quite possible, using only a few basic concept performances, to form a framework of activities useful for nearly all the different grade levels, thus eliminating the need to construct dozens of different performances for each grade level and commit to memory all the different kinds of performances and measures needed to assess them. An example of a concept-based performance that requires the integration of two or more different visual concepts and specifies nearly all the art content standards required in the national standards might look like the following:

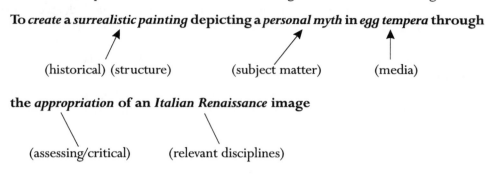

This particular performance would be, in truth, a kind of *monster* performance, requiring the student to use an inordinately large number of higher order thinking skills and procedural behaviors at a very advanced level. Although few teachers would actually want to invent such a complex assignment, it can be used here mainly to show how a single written performance requirement could meet all six of the national content standards. This performance, although a 13th- or 14th-grade-level assignment, can also be reduced or expanded in scope to achieve even more or less complex behaviors.

To achieve all of what is stated in this performance would require the student to have sufficient focal and procedural knowledge to: (a) understand the historical style and content of surrealist imagery; (b) know the basic structure of painting as an art form; (c) understand the concept and visual character of a myth, fetish, and totem; (d) be skilled in the complicated process of egg tempera painting; (e) be able to critically analyze a Renaissance work to appropriate it; and (f) understand the social forces shaping the conventions used in Renaissance painting.

In carrying out this performance, the student would also need to examine, analyze, compare, contrast, reorder, adapt, simulate, convert, test, create, and synthesize the various ideas, values, images, historical styles, and art processes needed to construct such a work. In that process, various kinds of perceptual data and visual concepts would be integrated into wider or narrower categories, move toward more extensive and intensive knowledge and wider integrations, provide more precise perceptual differentiations, use increasingly more knowledge and perceptual evidence, and involve three fundamental methods of cognition: inductive, deductive, and heuristic. With regard to human consciousness, the student would also be expected to perceive, evaluate, think, reminisce, feel, and imagine. All of these can be either expanded on or simplified by altering the performances, the extensiveness of scope, and the intensity of the psychological processes used. In addition, the intensity of the student's observations, reasoning, and skills used in reaching the objective can also be reduced or expanded through altering the range of the factual material involved, the length of the conceptual process used, and the complexity of the skills needed. In the lower grades, this could be limited to simply assigning students to make paintings and become familiar with Renaissance religious art. In the middle grades,

CONCEPT STANDARDS GRADES 5–8

NATIONAL STANDARDS	CONCEPTUAL CONTENT STANDARDS	CONCEPTUAL ACHIEVEMENT STANDARDS	CONCEPTUAL PERFORMANCES (5–8)
Understanding and applying media		To develop a skill To routinize a process To use a skill consciously To use a process to achieve an effect	Draw using an advanced media Make a scribbled gesture drawing Draw crushed objects Make an interlocking shape composition Create a labyrinth
Using knowledge of structures and functions	Understanding what it means to make an expressive object (Procedural knowledge)	To improve in the use of a process To know the results of trials To know how a process changes a work To explain the behaviors used in the construction of a work	Make an informational drawing Use aerial perspective Juxtapose objects Remake discarded objects
Choosing and evaluating a range of subject matter		To know what historical knowledge is needed To know how to compare images To know the effects of a process To be aware of what process is used	Design a game Create a personal myth Appropriate an image Use multiple perspective
Understanding history and culture	Using knowledge of the artistic process, skills, percepts, images, etc. (focal knowledge)	To know what design knowledges are required in a work To know what cultural knowledges are needed in a work	Draw something as a social commentary Interpret an ancient myth
Assessing works of art		To know historical schemas To reflect on a skill used To have a standard of achievement	Make a surrealistic image Work neo-expressionistically Create an optical illusion
Connecting with other disciplines			Create a visual pun Make a science fiction art Use a science discovery as a source Create a visual paradox

FIG. 7.4.   Concept standards for grades 5–8.

students could be instructed to study myths and totems used by primitive soieties and learn some newer and more advanced art processes. In the senior high years, students could use an expanded knowledge of art history, more sophisticated modes of analysis, more advanced kinds of art structures, and different kinds of pictorial content, which the teacher can alter through reordering the various elements in the assignment.

Another reason for encouraging the use of conceptual performance activities over the more conventional approach of students simply acquiring more art knowledge and more complex performance skills is that neither the student nor the teacher is required to deal with all the possible knowledges, skills, and processes that can be advanced. Thus, the need to "pile on" could be avoided in a conceptual approach mainly because meeting the standards conceptually is not so much about how many things a student can remember or how many skills can be performed, but rather about how the student's visual and mental abilities are integrated in the act of meaningful, expressive forming.

ASSESSING STUDENT PERFORMANCES

When art teachers and art students think about assessment objectives, they most often think about paper-and-pencil tests and grading, both of which are deemed inappropriate in the assessment of creative and expressive products. Looking at the problem of educational evaluation, Eisner (1985) chose to use the term *outcome* rather than *objective* because he believed objectives are intended goals and ones that "do not always lead to the destination one intends" (p. 204). The three outcomes he identified are what he termed: student specific, teacher specific, and subject specific. *Subject specific* refers to the content being taught, *student specific* refers to what the student actually learns, and *teacher specific* is what the teacher learns about him or herself.

Both arguments—that it is really impossible to measure a feeling and that we cannot always expect what it is we want students to know and be able to do to be what the students actually learn—are based on the belief that art learning is mostly concerned with the transference of specific units of subject matter knowledge from the teacher to the students. Moreover, the success of that transfer depends on the suitability of the content, the teacher's ability to transmit it, and the students' readiness to absorb it, none of which, incidentally, is directly concerned with students' expressive development. This belief exists despite that no educator really believes that all the tasks we assign students to do are really all that useful, that all the ways we structure a learning environment are equally effective, or that we can always know what every individual student will ultimately know and be able to do in creating expressive objects whose meaning perhaps is not likely to be known in advance of its making. Art teaching conceived of as the delivery of artistic *goods* to students in need of receiving artistic welfare is not likely to succeed at connecting what it is we want students to know with what it is we need to do to instruct them. Such connections can occur when our evaluation efforts are authentic (i.e., when they aim to assess the students' conceptual development). Therefore, the only way we can truly know whether our teaching efforts are successful is to discover what it is that students mentally do in the process of creating expressive objects, which is also what makes students' art performances the primary focus in the school or program assessment process.

Designing an Authentic Assessment

According to Armstrong (1994), authentic assessment requires the construction of alternative assessment items. Alternative assessment is what she called an alternative to what is traditional (objective tests and essays). It is also focused on student performance, which is observable evidence of what students know and can do. Also according to Armstrong, such an assessment calls for authentic performances, which include

> real life decisions including the behaviors of aesthetitions, architects, art historians and critics, artists working in all forms including folk artists, persons who confront art in their daily lives and persons whose avocational activities relate to art. (Armstrong, 1994, p. 11)

Authentic learning in art implies purposeful, meaningful application of relevant information, as opposed to acquiring factual knowledge for itself. It also inspires changes in curricular practices in the assessment process.

Those seriously considering developing an authentic or traditional art assessment in their school should consult Armstrong's book, *Designing Assessment in Art*. Her work provides an extremely detailed and informative discussion of the art assessment process, with sample test instruments and advice on their administration, scoring, and reporting of results. Like others in the testing field, she also has reservations about authentic assessment, especially in an art production-oriented general education program. She stated that such an approach is inherently inconsistent, although she also admitted it is better than other approaches in responding to the nature of the student and the school, "as one would do in real life" (Armstrong, 1994, p. 110).

Most criticism of alternative assessments is based on the desires of empirical scholars to have a stable population to acquire hard data that can be treated statistically and reported as predictive (i.e., as norm-referenced scores). This requires that the student and subject matter content to be measured also be stable and predictable. The problem with any effort to assess performances in real-life situations is that they are usually unstable because, as in real life, both the student and school undergo change. In art, where instructional outcomes are evident in performances designed to encourage both originally and innovative responses, it is hard to imagine outcomes as ever being either predictable or generalizable.

The point to be made here is twofold. First, an ill-defined field such as art, where the outcomes of instruction do not require all the students to learn the same thing in the same way, there may not really be any other choice than to use alternative modes of assessment. Second, in the construction and use of these alternative assessments, we should also be extra careful to construct the most valid and reliable performance assessments we can make to ensure that what it is we want students to know and do is at the center of every instructional assessment.

What Makes an Assessment Process Authentic?   An assessment is authentic when it involves students in tasks that are worthwhile, significant, and meaningful. Such assessments appear as learning activities, involve conceptual and higher order thinking skills, and interrelate several different forms of knowledge. They make explicit what students' work is judged on and, in effect, are standard setting rather than standard testing in their character. Thus, authentic assessment makes the development of students' content and achievement standards the ultimate goal to be reached in the instructional program.

Designing an Authentic Assessment.   The philosophy of every authentic assessment process should reflect three important conditions:

1. All statements about assessment should look back to the purpose or artistic intent of the activity.
2. Assessment is not the pursuit of a perfect scoring guide or perfect documentation.
3. The assessment plan should center on the student's development of the artistic intent, expression, and skill that makes creative vision possible.

Setting Objectives

The objective of a school-based authentic art assessment program should include assessments that:

*   can be used to evaluate student arts performances at every level of the school art program.
*   recognize that students have diverse backgrounds, varying abilities, and learning styles and make explicit the standards by which the work is judged.
*   use grading processes that reflect performance goals and reveal student and program strengths rather than weaknesses and that can be scored according to clearly stated performance objectives.

Developing Authentic Performance Tasks

The authentic performance tasks used in the assessment process should be ones that grow out of the curriculum, are feasible in terms of available time and resources, and can be scored and reported in ways that satisfy teachers, parents, and administrators. Furthermore, these performance assessments should be designed in such a way that they include:

*   both the procedural and focal knowledge that students need for them to know how and be able to do various learning activities in the arts.
*   the core performance roles or situations that all students in Grades K–12 should encounter and be expected to master.
*   the most salient and insightful discriminators that can be used in judging artistic performance.
*   sufficient depth and breadth to allow valid generalizations about student competence.
*   the training necessary for those evaluating artistic performances to arrive at a valid and reliable assessment.
*   a description of audiences that should be targeted for assessment information and how that assessment should be designed, conducted, and reported to these audiences.

Writing Performances

In writing the art performances to be evaluated, a number of concerns must be addressed: How much time will it require to complete them? How many layers of investigation and content are included? What new knowledge will be constructed? What standards are to be met? What focal and procedural knowledges are needed and what reasoning (conceptual) process needs to be evident? As noted in chapter 5, these factors increase in complexity and range as the student matures (i.e., the layers of investigation, the time, the knowledge, and the reasoning process will be severely limited for children ages 4–7, where students only need to count, notice, match, and recognize; the layers will be rather complex for students ages 13–16, where they are expected to think abstractly, reason systematically, create new systems, etc.).

For the performances to have validity, they should be written and rewritten to identify: (a) the content standard included, and (b) the conceptual (reasoning) process to be employed (i.e., whether the concept is simply to recognize visual similarities or transfigure whole forms through simplifying, changing, or disarranging them). Also, one needs to take into account what focal and procedural knowledges are needed to make the standard explicit and in what kind of product it will be assessed (i.e., as in training exercise, a painting, or a series of paintings, essays, or critical reviews). It should be remembered, however, that proficiencies from no more than three or four categories of standards should be included in any one task (Marzano, Pickering, & McTighe, 1993).

The most important concern in the physical design of the performance assessment is that it reflects the nature of the exercises already embedded in the art curriculum and that it encourages students to study their own train of thinking as perhaps revealed in notes, sketches, or practice efforts. Not every behavior one wants to assess is evident in a single work, which may also require that the performance description specify the steps to be followed prior to and during the execution of a work or made evident in a succession of works. Efforts to assess such things as content quality, prior knowledge, content coverage, and cognitive complexity are not always clearly evident in every finished work. Procedural skills such as practice toward improvement, doing something smoothly and quickly, understanding the direction practice should take, controlled improvement, or getting the *feel* of something are equally difficult to discover in a single product.

Despite such difficulties, performance assessment, because it is involved in what we normally do in instructing art, is authentic and therefore less of an intrusion on the existing curriculum. Although performance-based assessment alone may not always offer the same assessment results as paper-and-pencil tests do, they are generally more relevant to the art instructional task and, as a result, are more likely to change the teacher, the student, and the curriculum for the better, as research results suggest.

Howard (1977) suggested we look for these changes in mental behaviors in art products:

changes in rhythm, dynamic, or expression

fluency, contrast, balance

attention to task

accepting the possibility of failure

awareness and routinization

controlled improvement

care in execution

intelligent, strategic choices

mastery

taking risks

developing pattern

letting the tool do the job

the pattern of decision making

the ways things are built up

what student goals are revealed

visual resemblances and parallels

showing how something might look

what pictorial units and subunits were changed in the making

Of course, there are other things we may want to know about students' progress that may not be evidenced in an art product, including students' ability to monitor the details of their own performance, their visual memory, the reordering of forms, changes in cognitive strategies, and shifts of awareness. With reference to the assessment of such behaviors, teachers may need to use other formal or informal means for assessment (i.e., sketch books, reports, journals, etc.). However, such efforts should also take into account Howard's concern that the primary aim of heuristic principles of performance is not to explain, justify, confirm, or disconfirm performance results, but rather to achieve them. As he also noted, there is a major difference between the critical skills used in art performance and art evaluation, which are detachable in the arts, because they tend, on the whole, to be different skills, differently trained, and with different aims. This suggests that students' criticism of their own work requires other attributes, skills, and knowledges than are used in the criticism and evaluation of art per se. Parenthetically, these differences also suggest that the assessment of students' skills in art criticism may not be attained solely through the criticism and evaluation of their own studio production.

Language use is another skill that is not always evident in viewing art products. To be able to name things; talk about how they work; describe them; talk about such things as distance, size, social issues, style, and so on; and use terms like *pairing* and *distributing* while noting similarities and differences is essential in the development of visual memory and student-to-teacher interaction. Language development is usually best evidenced in students' journals, class discussions, essay writing, and through paper-and-pencil tests. Although such measures can be useful in assessing some art learning, current research does not support that these multiple forms of assessment are necessarily interchangeable, with note taking and direct observation being the only ones found to be fairly compatible (CRESST, 1993). Nevertheless, teacher-constructed paper-and-pencil tests may still be considered a useful evaluative tool even when their validity and overall generalizability in assessing art outcomes may be suspect.

Using Rubrics in Assessment

Performance assessment in the arts involves doing what we generally do in the process of teaching art in schools, which is to make things and evaluate them in the process. Although performance assessment is not something really new to us, the development of scoring procedures that focus on defining tasks and providing a range of points for scoring each task is. The scoring process most frequently used in performance assessment is contained in what is known as a *rubric*.

Rubrics provide a process for making a scoring decision using a cardinal or Likert type scale that rank orders the performance being evaluated. The scale used is normally criterion referenced, which means to reach a level of performance commensurate with what the student generally should be able to do at a particular grade level rather than measure up to some vague or absolute standard of artistic excellence. Therefore, scores derived from rubrics are more likely to indicate whether the student's achievement is on, above, or below the standard set for what a student of a particular age and at a specific grade level should be able to achieve.

Rubrics can be used successfully in assessing art performances. This is evident in the example provided by the Advanced Placement (AP) Examination in Studio Art Exam administered by the College Entrance Examination Board and Educational Testing Service (ETS). In the AP exam, qualified art judges assess portfolios of high school student work using various rubrics to produce scores as evidence that a high school student is capable of performing various tasks at a Grade 13 level. The AP exam is not designed as a college entrance exam, but rather as a way to recognize students in high school who are already performing at a college freshman level. Institutions of higher education that accept an AP examination score of 3 or higher offer either college credit for a beginning drawing or design course or advanced placement in the student's program.

What this program effectively demonstrates is that agreement can be reached among teams of art judges independently assessing student portfolios when they are given appropriate training and effective scoring rubrics. These assessments have been used successfully over the past 25 years to verify that secondary art students are capable of performing at the college freshman level. As testimony of the program's success, more than 500 colleges and art schools now accept the AP studio exam score for either credit or advanced placement. One way ETS ensures the comparability of the AP judges scoring is to blindly insert freshman college level work into the high school work being judged. More important, it was through the process of college art faculty reviews of AP-scored portfolios that most colleges decided to enter the program and accept AP scores for advanced placement or credit.

Holistic Rubrics.   The holistic rubrics used to score art portfolios vary in form and complexity according to which aspects of the art performance is to be evaluated. A holistic rubric can only exist as a mental construct, as was evident in the early years of the AP studio exam, where judges were trained to use a selected sample of portfolios grouped according to four scoring levels. This training process was used to provide the judges with an advanced mental Gestalt of what a sample portfolio might look like at a given scoring level. Such a system works well when only a few judges and a limited number of portfolios are involved. Holistic scoring in AP was introduced early on in the program at the urging of artists Paul Brach and Allan Kaprow, who insisted on looking for the Gestalt or "wow" factor as central in judging the students' work. What the holistic assessment process challenges is the use of reductive measures, such as checklists, to assess individual characteristics of the work, such as the quality of line, color, balance, unity, and so on, thus separating form from matter and divorcing what the work expresses from the means used to express it. The concern was that, although some students might achieve high scores on each of these points, the work as a whole might still lack expressive quality and aesthetic impact. Although ETS today provides its AP studio judges with a written 6-point scoring rubric, with more than 38 descriptors for scoring, the method remains holistic in that the descriptions are less than exhaustive, sometimes contradictory, and not in every case needed to award a given score. Although most test developers agree that such holistic rubrics may be less discriminating than those that specify all the behaviors to be evaluated, given use of effectively trained and qualified judges, it still makes a holistic approach the most truly authentic.

Analytic Rubrics.   Analytic rubrics are those designed to examine only certain dimensions of learning as is seen in the rubric illustrated in Fig. 7.8, which provides an analysis of forming behaviors and the use of media in assessing a student work.

Classroom Rubrics.   Classroom rubrics are used to assess student learning in a specific lesson or on a specific skill. They are usually constructed by the teacher and address the specific goals of a given assignment in a manner appropriate for the student and the teacher's learning goals.

Designing Scoring Rubrics

A scoring rubric uses a set of established criteria for scoring students test portfolios or performances. It describes the levels of performance students might be expected to attain relative to a desired standard of achievement (Figs. 7.5, 7.6, 7.7, 7.8, 7.9). It also provides descriptors or performance descriptions, which tell the evaluator what characteristics or signs to look for in a student's work and how to place that work on a predetermined scale. This occurs somewhat differently in holistic and analytical rubrics.

Holistic Rubrics.   A holistic rubric has two virtues: It communicates generally how the work appears in the context of other works and provides a scoring system that is easy to learn and use.

Rubrics used to assess performance in Grades 1 to 12 also use maturation benchmarks that suggest higher and higher levels of performance based on both the maturity level of the student and the expectation that, as students progress, they will receive the benefits of more advanced instruction in art. Higher level rubrics contain descriptors that reflect increasingly higher levels of thinking and visual abstraction. By using the maturation charts presented in chapter 7, it is possible to develop holistic rubrics for Grades 1 to 12 with increasingly higher levels of difficulty as can be noted by comparing Figs. 7.5, 7.6, 7.7, 7.8, and 7.9.

By comparing the different performance descriptors used in Fig. 7.5 with those used in Fig. 7.6, it is fairly easy to see that the performance expectations used in Fig. 7.6 are developmentally and artistically more advanced than those used in Fig. 7.5. It is also reasonable to assume that these expectations for advancement would continue to increase as students move up through the grades, as can be noted in Figs. 7.7, 7.8, and 7.9.

Analytic Rubrics.   Analytic rubrics differ from holistic rubrics because they tend to be more specific in communicating what standard of achievement is desired and what abilities or knowledges are evaluated (Fig. 7.8). Analytic rubrics usually provide more specific and observable performance descriptions, which reduce the likelihood of inaccurate scoring and help students assess where they are on the achievement scale. They also can be

PERFORMANCE BASED HOLISTIC RUBRICS FOR STANDARDS BASED ASSESSMENT IN ARTS
GRADES K-2
(noticing and applying shapes pictorially)

Exemplary Response Level A	Makes shapes which vary in height and width Includes multiple objects Places shapes/objects higher and lower on the picture plane Adds details which show the ability to count Provides details which show what objects are made of Represents distance and direction pictorially
Excellent Response Level B	Uses different size shapes Shows more than one identifiable object Shows some arrangement of objects on the picture plane Provides some recognizable details Show some evidence of thought in placing shapes
Satisfactory Response Level C	Makes some variable shapes Shows some recognizable objects Places objects on the picture plane Makes objects vary in their position
Inadequate Response Level D	Makes shapes which generally lack structure Makes forms which lack recognition Provides little or no detail Objects or shapes appear isolated

FIG. 7.5.   Performance based holistic rubrics for standards based assessment in art for grades K–2 (noticing and applying shapes pictorially).

PERFORMANCE BASED HOLISTIC RUBRIC FOR STANDARDS BASED ASSESSMENT IN ART
GRADES 2-4
(recognizing shape differences and placement)

Exemplary Response Level A	Uses recombined shapes Makes invented shapes and objects Places shapes in environments Uses geometric shapes Makes color vary in value Uses texture Shows awareness of spacial problems Shows overlapping forms Makes objects from memory Produces fantasy pictures
Excellent Response Level B	Uses a variety of shapes Places objects of meaning appropriately Uses some geometric lines Shows variety in surfaces Places forms above or below each other Organizes objects pictorially
Satisfactory Response Level C	Makes some different shapes Positions objects unrelated to their environments Makes randomly placed curved and straight lines Objects show some arrangement in space Objects are not always recognizable
Inadequate Response Level D	Makes shapes which are undifferentiated Makes objects which seem to float in space Objects and forms which are unrecognizable Organizes space randomly

FIG. 7.6.   Performance based holistic rubric for standards based assessment in art for grades 2–4. (recognizing shape differences and placement).

PERFORMANCE BASED HOLISTIC RUBRIC FOR STANDARDS BASED ASSESSMENT IN ART GRADES 4-6
(noting shape similarities, patterns and postions)

Exemplary Response Level A	Shows objects from different viewpoints Consciously creates symbols Generalizes things observed Notes subtle relationships between objects Shows interest in future events Pairs and distributes similar forms Recognizes patterns
Excellent Response Level B	Shows objects in different environments Reveals actual or past events Orders similar shapes Represents events in a literal way Varies positions of objects Sees and arranges similar shapes
Satisfactory Response Level C	Places objects in relation to where work began Makes shapes correspond with appearances Makes shapes in isolation Shows evidence of order
Inadequate Response Level D	Places objects randomly Makes objects from one point of view Uses stereotypes rather than seeking likenesses Places shapes or objects in unrelated spaces

FIG. 7.7.   Performance based holistic rubric for standards based assessment in art for grades 4–6. (noting shape similarities, patterns and positions).

PERFORMANCE BASED ANALYTIC RUBRIC FOR
STANDARD BASED ASSESSMENT IN ART GRADES 7-9

Name: Objects: _____		drawing skills	invention	design elements and composition	informational content	handling of media	art historical content	problem finding and critical skills
Exemplary Response Level A	Shows knowledge and control Applies elements conceptuality Integrates forms graphically Relates form and content Integrates elements expressively Applies elements experimentally Reflects visual observations							
Excellent Response Level B	Shows knowledge Applies images logically Effects form relationships Integrates pictorial units Applies elements literally Show observed qualities							
Satisfactory Response Level C	Shows some knowledge Applies images randomly Integrates some form and matter Integrates units infrequently Lacks visual observations							
Inadequate Response Level D	Lacks knowlege Lacks application pictorially Does not integrate form and matter Units relate infrequently if at all Lacks interest in observing							

FIG. 7.8.   Performance based analytic rubric for standard-based assessment in art for grades 7–9.

**Advanced Placement Studio Art
Scoring Rubric--Section III, BREADTH, General Portfolio
DRAWING**

6   EXCELLENT BREADTH

- Work addresses a broad range of drawing issues and/or techniques, and is of generally excellent technical quality.
- Shows line and tone; three dimensional space, volume, depth

5   STRONG BREADTH

- Not as successful as work that merits a score of 6; more successful than work than merits a score of 4.

4   GOOD BREADTH

- Work is of variable technical quality (must include some strong pieces) and demonstrate some breadth.
- Work demonstrates good breadth, but shows less convincing technical quality.

3   MODERATE BREADTH

- Not as successful as work that merits a score of 4; more successful than work that merits a score of 2.

2   POOR BREADTH

- Work is technically poor.
- Work shows a very limited range of breadth.

1   VERY POOR BREADTH

- Not as successful as work that merits a score of 2.
- Slides are virtually impossible to see.
- Very little work is presented.
- Work presented is only tenuously connected to the task.

FIG. 7.9.   Advanced Placement Studio Art Scoring Rubric—Section III, BREADTH, General Portfolio. *DRAWING.* Reprinted by permission of Educational Testing Service and the College Entrance Examination Board, the copyright owners. Permission to reprint AP test materials does not constitute review or endorsement by Educational Testing Service or the College Board of this publication as a whole or of any other testing information it may contain.

used to assess the effectiveness of the art program in providing the focal knowledge necessary for effective expression. As can be noted in Fig. 7.8, an analytic rubric is more complex to score, contains more features to be evaluated, and has greater specificity. Many analytic rubrics actually combine holistic and checklist approaches in one instrument.

Holistic Scoring.   When using scoring rubrics, evaluators generally assess student work in one of two ways. The first method is holistic scoring, which gives a general impression of a single work or group of works viewed as a whole. Holistic scoring produces a single number that is typically based on a 4- to 6-point scale. An example of a 6-point holistic scoring rubric with benchmarks used in the AP exam evaluating breadth defines a range of performances, as can be noted in Fig. 7.9.

Analytic Scoring.   The second method used is analytic scoring, which involves awarding separate scores for different traits or dimensions of a student's work. Analytic scoring is more time-consuming, but it also yields more detailed information. For that reason, it may be more useful for diagnostic purposes or when students need specific feedback on their strengths and weaknesses. This type of scoring may also be useful in evaluating curriculum and instruction and to pinpoint areas that need improvement. Figure 7.10 (see also Armstrong, 1994) provides a sample analytic scoring rubric recommended for evaluating student portfolios.

In designing a scoring rubric:

- There should be a tight match between the demands of the performance and what criteria are used in scoring.
- It should, as much as possible, specify observable aspects of the performance or product to be looked for and scored.
- It should be written in ordinary language so that assessment results can be understood.

Choosing Among Rubrics

Whether one should use a holistic or analytic rubric or a combination is both a philosophical and practical issue. Holistic rubrics tend to assess expressive qualities, whereas analytic rubrics inductively analyze several different dimensions of a given learning situation. Not all teachers in a school or school system will agree that holistic rubrics should be the only ones used. For example, some teachers and administrators would like to address specific dimensions of the program, including the effectiveness of instruction in art production, art history, and criticism. If one's goal is to evaluate the effectiveness of various aspects of a program, the use of analytic rubrics and other forms of assessment also needs to be considered. These include student interviews, conferencing, student self-assessment, and peer assessment. Such assessments also frequently use rubric checklist scales, which indicate only the presence or absence of a given behavior.

Interview Rubric.   Interviews require the student to verbally respond to specific questions and the teacher to interpret answers and record the student's response. This form of assessment, although time-consuming, encourages the student's metacognitive development and metacritical skills, which also encourage the student's verbal development. These interviews also enhance the teacher's effectiveness in conducting class discussions and provide an interactive way for teachers to relate to the student's values and learning difficulties. An example of an interview checklist on art criticism provided by Armstrong, which could be used for recording the responses of one or more students, appears in Fig. 7.11.

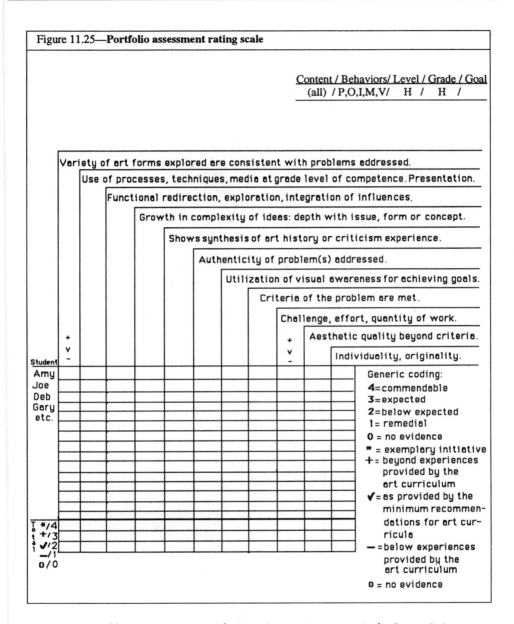

Figure 11.25—Portfolio assessment rating scale

FIG. 7.10.   Portfolio assessment rating scale. From *Designing Assessment in Art*, by Carmen L. Armstrong, © by the National Art Education Association, 1916 Association Drive, Reston, VA 20191. Reprinted with permission.

Conferencing Rubric.   Conferencing involves a two-way dialogue between a teacher and a student or among several students for the purpose of evaluating progress on a specific standard, benchmark, or product. This usually takes the form of an individual or group critique. Armstrong developed a conferencing rating scale to be used in a dialogue or group discussion about the nature and value of art or other philosophical issues; it appears in Fig. 7.12. Such discussions encourage students to think and reflect on their judgments in art, as in this case where students are asked to draw comparisons between art works of different genres.

Self-Assessment Rubrics.   Self-assessment rubrics enable students to examine and evaluate their work according to their own personal goals, accomplishments, progress, and development. The teacher may supply students with assessment criteria or assist students in developing their own. This form of assessment assists students in developing critical thinking and evaluating skills and can be used when students complete a given assignment or at the culmination of a long-term project.

Student self-assessments can also be used to assess the effectiveness of a given exercise or limited assignment. An exercise asking the student to construct a value scale could be submitted with an accompanying self-critique of the work. A student self-evaluation on a tonal exercise appears in Fig. 7.13.

Peer Assessment.   A peer assessment involves students evaluating each other's work, including art products, essays, and verbal critiques. It requires students to reflect on the accomplishments of their classmates, which helps them see alternative reasoning patterns and develop and appreciate diverse ways to approach and solve problems. In a peer critique, students can orally discuss the art work they have produced. Figure 7.14 is an example of a critique sheet used by students to critique fellow students by marking a yes or no under each criterion to report to that student.

Content/ Behaviors/ Level / Grade / Goal

AC /   O, I /   H /   P /   _____

Criteria : Observed	Gave reasons	Offered a meaning
objects that shape the meaning	for artist's decisions about organization	of the work and supported it with reasons

Student

1 Jaclyn _____   _____   _____

2 Jack _____   _____   _____

FIG. 7.11.   Art criticism rating scale. From *Designing Assessment in Art* by Carmen L. Armstrong, (p. 123). © 1994 by the National Art Education Association, 1916 Association Drive, Reston VA 20191. Reprinted with permission.

Content/Behaviors/Level/Grade /Goal

AES , O,I , H , J ,

CRITERIA

Thoughtfully considered reasons for judging something to be "art"	Expressed relevant, life-oriented big ideas based on art learning in the encounter	Synthesized contributions of others	Used information from diverse sources, periods of art or cultures

Student

1. Sze-Oi

2. Brian

etc.

FIG. 7.12.   Aesthetics dialogue about the value of art from different eras. From *Designing Assessment in Art* by Carmen L. Armstrong, (p. 122). © 1994 by the National Art Education Association, 1916 Association Drive, Reston VA 20191. Reprinted with permission.

Project to Make a Value Scale

	YES	NO
Look at your value scale from a distance of about 3 feet.		
• Is there an even transition from light to dark?	___	___
• Is the middle-grey tone in the center of the bar?	___	___
• Did you eliminate most of the light and dark spots?	___	___
• Did you build up the tones slowly and patiently using both the side and point of your pencil?	___	___

FIG. 7.13.   A student self-evaluation on a tonal exercise.

PLANNING PROGRAM ASSESSMENT

Planning an individual classroom, school, or district assessment requires deciding what aspects of the program are to be assessed, who will do that assessment, where it will be done, and to whom it will be reported. Detailed answers to these questions are not possible here, but they can be found through seeking out the references used in this chapter.

		Content/ Behaviors/ Level / Grade / Goal
		AC / O,I / H / J /
	CRITERIA	

	Reflective, analytical thinking approach	Discusses with appropriate objectivity	Supports interpretation or judgment with observations	Points to role of concepts taught in the project
Student:				
1. Erica	_____	_____	_____	_____
2. Michael	_____	_____	_____	_____
etc.	_____	_____	_____	_____

FIG. 7.14.   Peer critique assessment. From *Designing Assessment in Art* by Carmen L. Armstrong, (p. 129). © 1994 by the National Art Education Association, 1916 Association Drive, Reston VA 20191. Reprinted with permission.

What can be discussed here are some of the concerns individual teachers should be mindful of in assessing their own classroom efforts, with the main concern being to make the evaluation process both authentic and manageable.

Making the Assessment Authentic

To make the assessment authentic, our efforts need to be focused on helping students learn; we also need to be clear about what it is we want students to be able to know and do; whatever measures we use, the results should accurately reflect what it is that the students really know and are able to do. In authentic assessment, we also need to recognize what our goals are to improve the quality of student learning and capitalize on the students' strengths rather than their weaknesses. The bottom line in authentic assessment is really about helping students set their own high standards of achievement.

It is in knowing what we want students to know and be able to do that we are then able to decide what skills and knowledges are critical to their expressive development and what measures are most likely to assess them at a given level. In general, what we need to assess are: (a) the aesthetic, artistic quality of the student's expression, (b) the knowledge base from which their aesthetic judgments are formed, and (c) how they have advanced in their conceptual development. These concerns suggest the need to develop at least three kinds of instruments: some directed toward assessing student expression, others directed toward assessing student knowledge, and still others to assess student conceptual growth.

Assessing Expression.   To assess students' expressive development, some holistic assessments of students' creative work should be developed to answer the question of whether the instructional program and the students' learning is philosophically consistent with the means and ends of art and whether it has sufficient subject validity to provide representation that the curriculum provides for accurate and significant representation of the products of artistic inquiry as well as the means for that inquiry. The need for this form of assessment will increase as students' expressive efforts increase in purposefulness and intensity. As students advance from K to 12, the number and variety of these assessments should increase in both the amount of the focal and procedural knowledges assessed and the degree of integration achieved between the ends and means of expression.

Assessing Knowledge and Skills.   Because student products may not always reveal all the knowledges and skills needed in production and, because, for instructional purposes, we need to know how successful we are in providing such knowledge and how valuable that knowledge is in achieving expressive kinds of knowing, some analytic forms of assessment are needed in the art program. Also, because students learn in different ways and require different kinds of knowledge to be successful in their studies, these instruments need to have sufficient scope and variety that they can assess a broad range of instructional circumstances at different grade levels.

The need for checklists indicating the presence or absence of a given knowledge, skill, or ability is especially vital in the early years of schooling, where teachers face larger numbers of students and lower order cognitive ability. As students mature expressively and cognitively, the use of analytic rubrics to assess students' creative work should be increased in both number and range of focal and procedural knowledge to be assessed.

The results of such assessments can be used to estimate the psychological validity of the curriculum, which accounts for human growth and development, learning, individual differences, and the like. For diagnostic purposes, analytic assessments answer the questions of what can be taught, when and how it can be taught, and to whom. This kind of assessment is also more likely to reveal how effective the art program is in achieving general education goals and the individual knowledges and skills associated with study in art history, art structure, and art criticism.

Assessing Conceptual Development.   Because concept formation in art is also not solely a matter of development nor always evidenced in a student's individual creative works, some efforts should also be given to reviewing and analyzing a selected body of student work over time. This should be done to discover what changes are occurring in the student's thinking over time and whether the student's visual concepts are becoming more complex and better integrated, and involve more extensive and intensive knowledge, wider integrations, more precise perceptual differentiations, and increasingly more knowledge and perceptual evidence. We also want to be able to know about the student's use of inductive, deductive, and heuristic logic and how the student progresses in his or her ability to analyze, compare, construct, reorder, adapt, simulate, test, and synthesize various ideas, values, and images.

Evidence of these integrations is most likely to be found in a student portfolio, which includes samples of easily stored student work collected by the teacher over a semester or a year's time. The work should be analyzed by the teacher according to the sequence in which it was created. Student self-evaluations addressing certain particular forms of integration could be attached to the work, which would then be looked at as a record of the student's cognitive growth over time. This could be looked at as a Gestalt. The teacher could record his or her observations in a teacher log book, which could then be used to support a particular observation or observe trends or consistencies.

During the beginning years of schooling, these observations would be quite simple and anecdotal. Later on, they could become more detailed as the student moves up in the grades. At the high school level, they could even take the form of a directed, month-long investigation of a visual idea in progress—similar to the concentration section of the AP student art exam. A *concentration* is defined in the AP examination as a body of work unified by an underlying idea that has visual coherence. In that examination, judges look for four things: (a) Is the work presented a concentration? (b) Is there evidence of thinking and focus? (c) Is the degree of investigation evident in the work? and (d) What is the quality of the work?

Making the Assessment Manageable

No single art teacher in any one school is capable of doing everything that needs to be done to assess all students' art achievement. For the elementary art specialist with 1,300 children and nine classes a day, all one can expect is that some effort at a checklist documentation and a Gestalt look at children's development as they progress in that teacher's art room over the years. For those teaching in middle school, some effort to conduct analytic assessments of student products is quite feasible. For those at the high school level with more advanced portfolio classes, a more intensive look at students' progress over time is not only possible but critical.

Given the range of instructional tasks assigned, the number of students involved, and preparation time most art teachers have, it is highly unlikely that we can assess everything we want to assess in the school art program with as great an accuracy as we really want. What assessments we can conduct and the validity of the data we derive from these assessments depend mostly on what one can reasonably expect an art teacher to be able to do in addition to what he or she already does in meeting regular classroom responsibilities.

If a school district is truly concerned with doing an authentic assessment, some effort will have to be made to release teachers from some of their regular classroom responsibilities to meet various assessment tasks, provide for some division of labor with respect to the development and use of the assessment tools, and, in general, facilitate a cooperative effort among the art teachers in a school or within the district. The Vermont Assessment Project suggests four ways for doing this: (a) spreading the assessment among grade levels, (b) spreading the assessment across teachers, (c) spreading the assessment across expertise, and (d) targeting certain grade levels for assessment.

Spreading the Assessment Among Grade Levels. To spread the assessment among grade levels, the school might assess Grades 1, 3, and 5 one year and Grades 2, 4, and 6 the next year. The school could also decide to look at different dimensions each year, adding and pairing results for a view of the program over time.

Spreading the Assessment Among Teachers. Every teacher does not always have to assess or contribute the same things to an assessment. Different art teachers in a school or district can develop and assess different dimensions of the program (i.e., skills and techniques, historical knowledge, critical abilities, etc.). Different art teachers can also be used to blind score student work, become involved in group grading, and train others in the scoring process.

Some key teachers can also be used to verify the results of individual teacher assessments using selected sample portfolios from each class and comparing them to in-school results to determine the reliability of the scoring. The portfolio samples can also be scored by these teachers to ensure that common standards are being applied within a school or among the schools in a given district.

Spreading the Assessment Across Areas of Expertise.   Using a variety of people from various areas of expertise can also help spread the load in the assessment process. Art teachers might best be used to assess skill development, reflection, and critique; area artists to assess skill development in a particular media or technique; museum personnel to assess reflections, critiques, and making connections; and students to assess reflection, critique, and approach to work.

Targeting Grade Levels for Formal Assessment.   This is accomplished in the Vermont project by establishing learning environments that foster all dimensions but concentrate formal assessment on certain grade levels. It further suggests asking professional organizations to give inputs into teaching practice for grade levels not being assessed. Alternating the frequency of assessment by assessing approaches to work on a quarterly basis and periodic assessment of skills in Grades 3 and 6 are recommended. Embedded assessment, which assesses reflection and critique and interim feedback using skill development rubrics, can be used in the years when no formal assessments occur.

SUMMARY

This chapter began with a discussion of what it is that art teachers do in the process of teaching art and with making connections with what it is that teachers do and what it is that their students come to know and are able to do. Despite the concern that not all students and not all teachers are able to do everything that needs to be done, teachers must assess their instructional efforts to ensure that quality instruction and learning is taking place. It was further suggested that art teachers need to structure the learning environment, help establish the appropriate content to be learned and standards to be achieved, and structure an authentic assessment of what it is students ultimately know and are able to do. The chapter further identified the primary attributes of authentic assessment, what kind of instruments needed to be developed, and how such an assessment process might function at a school or district level.

REFERENCES

Armstrong, C. L. (1994). *Designing assessment in art.* Reston, VA: National Art Education Association.

Barkan, M. (1962). Transition in art education: Changing conceptions of curriculum and Teaching. *Art Education, 15*(7), 12–18.

Bloom, B. (1956). In J. Englehart, E. Furst, W. Hill, & D. Krathwohl, (Eds.), *Taxonomy of educational objectives: Handbook. Cognitive domain.* New York: David McKay.

Bruner, J. (1960). *The process of education.* Cambridge, MA: Howard University Press.

CEEB. (1983). *Academic preparation for college: What students need to know and be able to do.* New York: College Entrance Examination Board.

CNAEA. (1994). *Dance, music, theatre, visual arts: What every young American should know and be able to do in the arts.* Reston, VA: Music Educators National Conference.

CNAEA. (1995). *The opportunity to learn standards for arts education: Dance, music, theatre, visual arts.* Reston, VA: National Dance Association.

CRESST. (1993, Spring). *What works in performance assessment: Proceedings from the 1992 CRESST Conference, evaluation comment, Los Angeles, CA.*

Dorn, C. (1993). Art as intelligent activity. *Arts Education Policy Review, 95*(2), 2–9.

Eisner, E. W. (1972). *Educating artistic vision.* New York: Macmillan.

Eisner, E. W. (1985). *The educational imagination: On the design and evaluation of school programs.* New York: MacMillan.

FDEP. (1996). *The sunshine standards.* Tallahassee, FL: Florida Department of Education.

Fraenkel, J. R. (1980). *Helping students think and value: Strategies for teaching the social studies* (2nd ed). Englewood Cliffs, NJ: Prentice-Hall.

Howard, V. A. (1977). Artistic practice and skills. In D. Perkins & B. Leondar (Eds.), *The arts and cognition* (pp. 208–240). Baltimore: The John Hopkins University Press.

Marzano, R. J., Pickering, D., & McTighe, R. Jr. (1993). *Assessing student outcomes.* Menlo Park, CA: Addison-Wesley.

MENC. (1994). *National standards for arts education.* Reston, VA: Author.

NAEA. (1994). *The national visual arts standards.* Reston, VA: Author.

NAGB. (1994). *Arts education assessment framework.* Washington, DC: National Assessment Governing Board.

NBPTA. (1994). *Early adolescence through young adulthood: Art.* Detroit: National Board for Professional Teaching Standards.

Slavik, S. V. (1995). *An examination of the effects of selected disciplinary art teaching strategies on the cognitive development of selected sixth grade students.* Doctoral dissertation, Florida State University, Tallahassee, FL.

VAAP. (1995). *Vermont Assessent Project: Focusing on the nature of artistic practice in learning.* Montpelier, VT: Vermont Assessment Project.

KEY TERMS

Content Standards	Holistic
Achievement Standards	Analytic
Authentic Assessment	Conferencing Rubrics
Validity	Self Assessment Rubric
Rubrics	Peer Assessment
Ordinal Scale	Imbedded Assessment
Criterion Reference	

STUDY QUESTIONS

1. Why do art teachers need to assess what it is they teach and what it is that students learn in the art classroom? Does the assessment process need always to interfere with the student's creative growth or are there effective ways to go about finding out what individual students need to know in creating expressive objects? How, for example, do you go about assessing your own work and how do you keep the process you use from hindering your own creative effort?

2. Citing Fraenkel's principles, describe how you would conduct an art class in a manner that would provide an effective learning environment. In what

ways do you think your art class would support his eight principles? Write a sample letter to parents explaining what students will learn in your art class and how it will help them to learn how to learn and apply that learning in other contexts.

3. Describe the differences between a content and an achievement standard and why you think it was important for those who develop the national standards to provide both. Why do you think it is important to have national standards in art and why it is you would or would not use them in developing the standards you would use in teaching?

4. Does the State Department of Education in your state have state standards? If not, why not? How do the standards in your state differ from the national art standards and local school district standards where you reside? Which of these standards make the most sense to you, and explain why.

5. Why do you think it is important for the art teacher to convert the various standards into the performances students actually do in the art classroom? Do you think everything a student should know and be able to do can be assessed through the student's art work? If so, explain how both focal and procedural knowledges can be assessed in art objects, if not, what other kinds of assessments are really needed and why?

6. Describe the characteristics of an authentic or alternative assessment. How does it differ from more traditional forms of assessment such as those used in true–false and multiple choice tests. Why is authentic assessment more consistent with what it is students learn in the art class? How important is it that the students actually know what it is you want them to learn? Have you ever had a class with a teacher where you did not know what it was you were to learn? Explain.

7. Design a holistic rubric you could use to assess a drawing assignment required of a sixth grade class. Using the developmental charts presented in chapter 7, specify what forms of focal, procedural, and linguistic knowledge you would assess in your rubric and what the score would reveal about the student's artistic and cognitive development. Assuming you had one student who achieved the top score and another the lowest, what specifically would you write on the student's report card to justify the grade you gave them?

8

Summary
and Conclusions

INFLUENCES OF
THE COGNITIVE SCIENCES
    Authentic Assessment

AN AGENDA FOR RESEARCH
    Research Today
    Descriptive Research
    Applied Research

INSTITUTIONAL POLICY
    Influencing State and National Organizations
    Working With State Departments of Education
    Working With School Districts

No author attempting an effort as broad as this one can be totally objective in every way. Certainly those readers who have hung in with me since the beginning know of my Gombrichian bias—"that making comes before matching"—and my belief that only through understanding the phenomenology of the creative act is it possible to know what causes art to exist. However, I hope my readers also agree that I have at least tried to be objective in discussing the pros and cons of a number of important issues raised by the aesthetic and scientific communities. Yet perhaps in doing so I have left readers wondering what all of this really means. Given the choice of using either a Book I and Book II approach, as R. G. Collingwood did when he changed his mind in writing *Principles of Art,* or writing yet a third work to explain the second, I have elected to write this brief concluding chapter to identify at least some of the things discovered in the course of pursuing this effort.

I still believe that writers, like painters, only discover the true meaning of what they write about at the end of their writing, which is to admit that what I am about to reveal here was not altogether evident to me when I began and that, only in ending it, do I find it possible to finally reveal what I meant to say in the first place. Of course, the only rightful conclusion one can have after reading any text is in the mind of the one who reads it. I do not wish to usurp that right by challenging the reader's own feelings about these matters. Therefore, it is my hope that the reader will simply assume that I am pointing out only a few of the many possible understandings one might come to after reading this work.

To merely summarize the chapter summaries would contribute little to this effort. Thus, I attempt to focus on my initial premise—that making art is an intelligent activity. I do that from the perspective of what impact the artistic and scientific communities should have on art education today and in the new millennium. More specifically, I attempt to answer these questions: What should the future role of the cognitive sciences be in shaping art education theory and practice? What agenda needs to be set for the conduct of new research in the field? What policies need to be developed in the pursuit of newer and more authentic forms of assessment in art education?

INFLUENCES OF THE COGNITIVE SCIENCES

Although it is true that the cognitive sciences will never tell us what art is for, its methods can provide the much needed hard evidence those who provide the funding for school programs need to have to know what art educators believe art learning can contribute to the overall intellectual, cultural, and aesthetic development of the children we teach. Of course, such evidence does not offer proof of art, but rather what art learning can do to positively affect intelligent learning in the nation's classrooms.

Authentic Assessment

To acquire this hard evidence, we in the art education profession need to (a) be clear about what students in art need to know and be able to do, (b) identify the kinds of visual evidence needed to assess what students learn, and (c) provide the kind of authentic assessment tools that can yield valid and reliable estimates and can be manipulated statistically to provide sound evidence that the arts offer important and intelligent forms of knowing in American education. It is the primary responsibility of the art teaching profession to specify what kinds of evidence most needed, how that evidence to be obtained, and how it should be interpreted.

To provide the evidence needed for the authentic assessment of art learning, art teachers need to be much more aware of the phenomena of art forming, the iconographic character of the art image, and the teaching strategies needed for effective growth in students' perceptual awareness and aesthetic expressiveness. To do this, art teachers need to abandon teaching strategies that stress mere novelty in expression and adopt those that focus on the conceptual character of creative forming and reveal important evidence of intellectual and aesthetic growth. To merely provide a random array of novel activities without carefully thought out aesthetic and cognitive ends will not suffice if our goal is to be clear to others what it is we think art can contribute to the expressive and intellectual development of our students.

Even more important, the necessity to obtain this needed evidence also requires art teachers to accept full responsibility for the authentic assessment of the outcomes of their teaching and use that evidence to assess the effectiveness of their own instructional efforts and the efforts of their students. In acquiring such data, it is also incumbent on the art teacher to modify and/or supplement those teaching strategies that prove generally ineffective. When too many students fail to reach their goals, the art teacher must also consider and choose from a broad range of possibilities those actions that are the most likely to improve the learning environment. However, it is not possible to know which actions need to be taken when the teacher does not know what he or she wants to achieve.

The art teacher also needs to adopt appropriate ways for identifying student progress—both to the student and the school. In doing this, it is essential to make the appropriate connections between the assignments teachers make and what it is they evaluate. When teachers, at the beginning of an assignment, have only a vague idea of what it is they want students to achieve, change their minds about those goals while a project progresses, or are unclear in communicating to students what they will be evaluated on, they are rarely capable of showing students, parents, or administrators what it is that activity contributes to the students' knowing. Finally, the teacher must adopt methods of reporting that make clear what it is that the student is expected to learn and the visual evidence that supports that the student has indeed learned it.

AN AGENDA FOR RESEARCH

Research in art education has evolved in a number of different directions and has had a number of different emphases over the years, as can be noted in the chronology of the research studies reported in chapter 4. It is particularly noteworthy that interest in doing descriptive or empirical research has declined in recent years. The largest number of such studies was done prior to the 1970s and the lowest number attempted in the 1990s, when research interests in art education turned more to so-called qualitative or ethnographic research.

There are a variety of reasons why this has happened, including changes in the administrative organization of university art education departments, some notable excesses in the past statistical reporting of empirical research in our journals, and, of course, the perceived need for more research in areas dealing with the disadvantaged, gender, and ethnicity. On the positive side, these new qualitative approaches have broadened the scope of the research undertaken. On the negative side, they have focused mainly on the more immediate social issues to the detriment of achieving the hard data needed on what children should know and be able to do in art classrooms.

Research Today

It is now readily apparent that the decline in the number of hard data studies is, in part, linked to the acceptance of stand-alone art education departments in our research universities. By looking chronologically at the research studies reported, it is fairly easy to note that the output of empirical studies was at its highest when the researchers came from either out of field or were working in art education departments linked to colleges of education, which required representation of university research interests on art education doctoral committees. Once art education departments became respectable in research universities, more professors with art education doctorates were hired and more stand-alone programs authorized, art education researchers seemed less inclined to consider the generalizability of their research findings for K to 12 school art programs.

In the 1960s and early 1970s, empirical research in art education did, for a time, become quite fashionable, with art education researchers achieving respectability and many graduate schools receiving financial support for the conduct of empirical studies from the federal government through the Department of Health, Education, and Welfare in support of scientific approaches to art study. As a result, the NAEA began a series of annual research publications that finally resulted in a new quarterly journal on research and issues called *Studies in Art Education.* Because of the availability of these outside funds for support of research and these new venues for its publication, an elite group of researchers in art education began to develop. Perhaps as a result, their research seemed to turn more and more to producing research for other researchers. As a consequence, many of these research studies appeared to focus more on proving the value of the research and justifying the methods used for the edification of other researchers. Unfortunately, what most practitioners in the field found in reading these studies were scads of tables and copious amounts of statistical calculations that, to them, seemed wholly unrelated to the teaching of art in schools.

What is now clear to the profession is that we need a national research agenda: one that is not subject to the selfish self-interests of researchers or those who fund that research. This agenda requires our profession to come up with an outline of what kinds of research are most urgently needed for art education to make a positive contribution to the intelligent education of children and youth in American schools. To do that, the research agenda pursued needs to prioritize these forms of research: define the most relevant to the kinds of art instruction we pursue in schools, offer valid and reliable assessments of what children know and are able to do in art, and address the ways in which art learning impacts on overall intellectual and aesthetic development.

This agenda also requires research to be relevant, generalizable, and focused on what school practitioners need to know and be able to do for them to become more effective in communicating the values of art learning in the overall aesthetic and intellectual development of students. To do this, we need to pursue at least two parallel research goals: one to provide the descriptive research needed to understand the phenomena of art making and the other the applied research required to adequately assess student progress in learning art.

Descriptive Research

The kinds of descriptive research most needed are the kinds of research studies that identify the various visual strategies needed for effective creative forming, which is essential to our knowing what it is we can evaluate. Without identifying what processes are used in creative forming, we cannot possibly know what kinds of focal and procedural knowledges are needed to ensure student growth in expressive thinking and making. In the conduct of such research, it will also be necessary to investigate the entire morphology of the creative act, including what students need to know prior to making, what knowledges need to be considered in the act of forming, and the effect of those knowledges on future creative actions. Efforts to research such areas as cognitive style, instructional strategies, and program interactions, although still useful, more often than not will lead to entanglements that stereotype the behaviors of both students and teachers sidestepping the more important issue of what it is students need to know and be able to do.

Applied Research

As previously noted, applied research in art education lacks a sustained focus especially when its goals are determined by the research fashions of doctoral programs and the vagaries of public funding. This will not change unless art education researchers begin to match their research goals with the needs of K to 12 schooling. Fortunately, the Goals 2000 effort, which requires many schools to come up with program assessments for K to 12, does offer a spring board for such future school and university partnerships. What is needed now is a plan of action to help develop the kinds of partnerships that benefit both groups (i.e., affording university researchers access to the populations they most need to research and practitioners in schools the opportunity to apply their first-hand experience in ways that make their jobs more effective and rewarding).

That we are at least starting out to pursue such a research agenda and that its direction is toward more concern for practice is evident in the NAEA's continuing effort to pursue such an agenda over the past several years. A recent report issued by the task force on student learning suggests that it focus on "how art teachers recognize or 'read' children's artistic endeavors and how they interpret and respond to what they read" (Burton, 1997). This was further explained in the report by noting:

> Specifically, the Task Force group was concerned to have more insight into what features or aspects of a student work in progress—or on completion—become salient to teachers and why, and then how teachers respond to nurture artistic learning. The rationale for this particular tack on the problem derived from the observation that there was little research in this arena of classroom behavior, yet, insights into teacher–student interaction in the body of a lesson are of paramount importance to an understanding of how artistic learning occurs. (p. 1)

Although the statement contains the vagaries of a committee-authored collective softness and lacks precisely what features and aspects need to be read, it certainly suggests that this is one of the priorities the task force intends to pursue.

INSTITUTIONAL POLICY

My third point, which addresses the need to change arts institutional policies to encourage newer and more authentic forms of assessment in schools, is not an easy one to resolve. It is difficult because there are no mechanisms for creating a national policy in American schools; even when such policies are developed at the state and local levels, they are resolved mostly by boards of education rather than by teachers.

Without the help of national educational policies and without direct ways for teachers to change school policy, the only way practitioners can influence decision making is to act as a unified voice for change within the institutions they are positioned to influence. Teachers can become a powerful voice for change in these institutions, especially when they are informed on the issues and when they offer positive ways to make schools a better place for students to learn. They become even more effective when they know what it is they want to achieve and when they focus on getting across their concerns to their state and national professional associations, their state departments of education, and the schools in which they serve.

Influencing State and National Organizations

Kindergarten to grade 12 art teachers represent a clear majority in their state and national professional organizations. Therefore, they have the power to influence changes in policy matters, but only if they are willing to exercise that power in an intelligent manner, which is to set an agenda for change and use their organizations as a forum for a dialogue between the various constituencies making up its membership. For example, university art education professors are not likely to undertake the kind of research needed in schools if there are no opportunities for K to 12 teachers and researchers to engage in a dialogue or when an organization's program is weak or unfocused. Research in art education is too precious to leave to the researchers alone, yet practitioners will not have an impact until they are clear as to what changes in assessment policies are needed and how, through cooperative efforts, they can help these changes to become a reality in schools.

The Goals 2000 initiative in art, as noted earlier, was developed by representatives chosen by our national associations. If these organizations are capable of helping set the standards for what children in American schools should know and be able to do in art, they are certainly capable of specifying the conditions under which these standards will be implemented in schools. Because the standards will be implemented in the schools by teachers, it is the teachers who will, in the last analysis, make that transition authentic.

All voluntary professional associations are in business to serve their members through: representing them to the private and public agencies that do business with the schools, conducting conferences, issuing publications, and forming task forces and study groups. What associations offer is an even more powerful voice for changing the way governments, schools, colleges, and other arts institutions respond to the needs of teachers. However, art teachers can help frame that voice only if they join and take an active part in influencing all these association professional areas of service. Therefore, it should be obvious that our professional associations are only as strong as the teachers make them.

As already noted, our national art teachers association, the NAEA, is already engaged in the development of an arts research agenda. What that agenda will include is up to its members to decide; how it functions will depend on how its members implement it. Nothing of any real importance will happen without the involvement of K to 12 art teachers caring about how that agenda is carried out and what policies guide it. Associations are shaped by the interests of their members, but without those interests being made clear to those who govern them, less relevant and more frivolous interests will prevail.

Working With State Departments of Education

State departments of education vary among the states as to how much they influence the shaping of school policy. The influence of any given state department varies according to how the schools in that state are financed, with the strongest state departments being located in states where most school funding comes from the state rather than the local level. Teachers in service can influence state department policies through serving on state department of education committees, commissions, and task forces and by working through their school districts and professional associations. Although the effect of this influence will vary from state to state, what is certain is that most state departments do not make the assessment of the arts their top priority.

Although most state departments will be sympathetic and interested in arts assessment, they will generally react as even some art teachers do by claiming that assessment in the arts is too difficult, if not impossible, to achieve because there are no tests or agreed on ways to assess student art performances. After all, as some skeptics note, "How can you assess a child's feelings?" Such an attitude does, however, also serve other interests, including those of some school districts and state departments where they do not have either the expertise or financial resources to develop or implement arts assessments. What such policies also encourage is for the goals of the art program to become more trivialized and, as a result, even more vulnerable in a world where what cannot be assessed in schools cannot be said to exist—a concept that only further erodes the place of the arts in the school curriculum.

Faced with the realities of some state departments being at a loss as to what to do in arts assessment and with no empirically verified test instruments with which to work, art assessment at the state level is not likely to occur unless the art teachers in that state offer a plan as to how art learning should be assessed. Without such a plan, the arts will not be valued or assessed; if assessed, they will be done so in inappropriate ways (e.g., using true–false or multiple-choice tests). Unless the art teachers of the state are satisfied with such measures, the only other real choice they have is to work through their state organizations to offer a plan that a state department can use to validly assess art instruction on a statewide basis.

Working With School Districts

The art assessment circumstances in most school districts are pretty much like those found at the state level, except that many state departments of education will mandate that the district has to come up with an accountable assessment plan. If that district plan is developed without a strong positive influence from the districts' art teachers, the art curriculum of the school program may lack credibility. The task of providing the district with that plan rests either on each individual art teacher or their collective efforts to work through their local art organization.

Although no art teacher needs anymore work to do in the school, they are the professionals most qualified to undertake that effort. Because we lack standardized tests in our field, we may even be in a better position than our colleagues in other fields to develop our own assessment instruments and our own evaluation plan. Also, because most school districts do not have baseline data on school art achievement, almost any valid data gathered on student art achievement are valuable even if they only reveal that students in the upper grades know and are able to do more than children in the lower grades.

Lastly, such a plan could be developed by teachers using the instruments and strategies outlined in the previous chapter—using them intact, modifying them, or inventing still other measures to assess student progress. This plan could begin as an individual school effort piloting a common set of instruments in individual schools and then modifying those instruments after use to make them more generalizable for the district as a whole. The only commonality that should be required is that the instruments reflect commonly held beliefs about the child's intellectual, aesthetic, and developmental growth.

CONCLUSION

In ending this work, I am again reminded that, whatever conclusions are reached on, these matters ultimately exist in the mind of the reader. However, if readers conclude that they have even more questions now than they had in the beginning, this ending is yet another beginning. After all, new beginnings are what sustain our commitment to the profession, our students, and to art. The never-ending quest for even greater understandings of what it means to imagine, create, and be conscious is really the only thing that lasts beyond the memory of the last class we taught or the last picture hung in the exhibit. For those art teachers who plan to devote most of their working life to this profession, it is absolutely essential that they nurture the life of the mind, especially if they want their professional careers to matter both to themselves and their students.

Most of the nation's art teachers who serve as specialists in schools experience a rather solitary professional life, especially when they are the only art teacher in a school, school district, or community. For them to grow, be continually enriched, and find professional satisfaction in their work, a dialogue with others in their profession is both necessary and professionally responsible. For this dialogue to happen, they must take an active part in the professional affairs of their national, state, and local art education associations. To be an active contributor, however, also requires an active and engaged professional mind especially if one wants to make a difference in those things that really matter.

Of course, the arts will neither hold their rightful place in the school curriculum nor reach their potential for engaging the hearts and minds of the nation's children until we, as professionals, learn how to more effectively articulate and vigorously demonstrate to others that the arts do make a difference in the lives of our students and the communities in which they live. This is not, however, a simple task, especially in a culture that all too frequently views the arts as being just another kind of entertainment or social frill. We cannot hope to change such perceptions for the better unless we learn to act professionally responsible.

Finally, the only thing that keeps our profession from creating a school, district, state, or national evaluation school art assessment plan is our collective indifference and failure to act. The alternatives of having no plan or no curriculum to assess or, even worse, a plan that seeks inappropriate means for assessing art is not acceptable to an enlightened art teaching profession. What I hope is that this work has inspired the beginning of a dialogue among art professionals working at all levels with those preparing for such service to work together so that art learning achieves its rightful place in the curriculum of American schools.

Of course, more needs to be learned and said about how we can make art instruction in schools a stronger force for intelligent learning. This effort is, after all, only one of many such possible beginnings to achieve that goal. After all is said and done, our school art programs are only as professional as the art teachers who staff them. My fervent hope is that this effort has at least inspired some teachers to take that important first step.

REFERENCE

Burton, J. (1997, September). *NAEA Task Force on Student Learning Research Update.* Unpublished report, Center for Arts Education Research, Columbia Teachers College, New York.

KEY TERMS

Validity	Qualitative Research
Reliability	Applied Research
Empirical Research	

STUDY QUESTIONS

1. Why is it important to explain to others outside of the field of art education why you think art education is important? How would you go about telling someone who didn't know much about art what art teachers teach children to do?

2. Why is research on student learning in art important to the success of school art programs? What kind of research do you think is the most important to do and why do you think this kind of research is most needed?

3. Call or write the National Art Education Association in Reston, Virginia, for information about the organization. Write a brief explanation of the association's missions, goals, governance, and programs, and explain why an art teacher should join the NAEA.

4. Write for information on your state art education association and find out when and where its next state meeting will be held and what the agenda of

that meeting will be. Attend one of their meetings, if possible, and/or talk to some art teachers who have attended to see what they thought of the meetings.

5. Find out where the State Department of Education is located in your state, whether it has an art director or supervisor, a state framework, and Goals 2000 Art Standards. Also find out how your state is supporting art assessment efforts in the various school districts.

Author Index

A

Albert, J., 71, *78*
Alschuler, R., 110, *118*
Amabile, T., 45, *48*
Anaheim, R., 59, *78*
Anheim, R., 105, *118*
Armstrong, C. L., 230, 231, 242, *249*
Arnheim, R., 105, *118*
Ashberry, J., 146, 148, *160*
Ashton, D., 133, 135, *160*
Austin, G. A., 64, *78*

B

Barkan, M., 223, *249*
Benswanger, H., 123, *161*
Bernstein, D., 18, 35, *48*
Bertalanffy, L., 93, *118*
Bloom, B., 229, *249*
Bloom, B. S., 12, *15*
Boring, E. G., 43, *48*
Brittain, L., 178, *202*
Brittain, L. W., 113, *118*
Bruner, J. S., 5, *15*, 64, *80, 223, 251*
Buhler, C., 110, *118*
Bullard, R. K., 188, *205*
Burnham, J., 93, *118*
Burt, C., 110, *118*
Burton, J., 256, *261*

C

Caldwell, H., 114, *118*
Carington, P., 35, *48*
Chomsky, N., 39, *48*, 62, *78*
Clare, S. M., 113, 114, *118*
Colbert, C. B., 113, 114, *118*
Collingwood, R. G., 84, 97, *118*
Conant, H., 4, *15*
Coplans, J., 140, 143, *160*
Cunningham, J. L., 116, *118*

D

Day, D., 71, *78*
Dorn, C., 8, *15*, 209, *250*
Dorn, C. M., 161, *204*
Dowell, M. L., 115, *118*
Dyk, R. B., 70, *78*

E

Eisner, E. W., 11, *15,* 223, 230, *250*
Elizabeth, H. T., 144, *160*
Emler, N. E., 10, *15*
Englehart, M. D., 12, *15*

F

Flack, A., 156, 157, *160*
Flam, J. D., 133, 135, *160*
Flannery, M. E., 114, *118*
Fraenkel, J. K., 211, *250*
Furst, E. V. M. H., 12, *15*
Furth, H., 39, *48*

G

Gardner, H., 6, 11, *15*, 43, *48*, 53, 54, *78*, 114,
    119, 186, *204*
Garver, T. H., 150, *160*
Gibson, J., 26, 29, *48*
Gilber, D., 35, *49*
Globerson, T., 71, *78*
Goldman, J., 154, 156, *160*
Golomb, C., 116, *118*
Gombrich, E., 10, *15*, 47, 100, 102, *118*
Gombrich, E. H., 132, *160*
Goodenough, D. R., 69, *78*
Goodenough, E. H., 110, *118*
Goodenough, O. R., 70, *78*
Goodman, N., 5, *15*
Goodnow, J. J., 64, *78*
Griffin, M. E., 116, *118*
Guilford, J. P., 45, *48*

Subject Index